USING OPEN SOURCE WEB SOFTWARE WITH WINDOWS

USING OPEN SOURCE WEB SOFTWARE WITH WINDOWS

ERIC HUNLEY

CHARLES RIVER MEDIA, INC.
Hingham, Massachusetts

Cover Design: Tyler Creative

Charles River Media, Inc.
10 Downer Avenue
Hingham, Massachusetts 02043
781-740-0400
781-740-8816 (FAX)
info@charlesriver.com
www.charlesriver.com

This book is printed on acid-free paper.

Eric Hunley. *Using Open Source Web Software with Windows.*
ISBN: 1-58450-430-7

Library of Congress Cataloging-in-Publication Data
Hunley, Eric.
  Using Open Source Web software with Windows / Eric Hunley.
      p. cm.
  Includes index.
  ISBN 1-58450-430-7 (alk. paper)
 1. Open source software. 2. Computer software--Development. I.
Title.
  QA76.76.S46H86 2005
  005.3--dc22
                                                    2005031783

Printed in the United States of America
05 7 6 5 4 3 2 First Edition

Contents

Introduction

As more and more businesses find their way online, Web designers' and technicians' workloads are increasing. They need to perform their respective roles, face the challenge of building and maintaining Web servers, and do some basic Web programming.

Not all businesses are large in scale and need server farms and other expensive hardware. Often, they can get by with one machine dedicated as a Web server, or with a shared Web hosting solution. This is where some choices come into play. What do they use?

Currently, the most commonly used client operating system is Microsoft® Windows®. Most users are used to Windows and will likely be most comfortable with a Web server that runs on it.

Microsoft markets Internet Information Services (IIS) for this purpose. It is free on Windows NT/2000/2003 Server, but "free" is misleading; while the Web server is free, the operating system is not. A standard copy of Windows 2003 Server with a five-client license is nearly $1000—a business can buy a fully loaded PC for less. Microsoft also bundles a version of IIS in Windows NT/2000/XP Professional. While this may seem to be a good compromise because the professional versions are much less expensive, it is not. The version of IIS bundled in these editions is limited in its scope. Most notably, it will only allow 10 simultaneous connections. Keep in mind that 10 connections do not equate to 10 users. Many Web services use more than one connection—and this is where open source Web software can be useful.

WHAT IS OPEN SOURCE?

Open source software is created by developers who depend on the entire programming community for improvements in the software. The open source philosophy is that software should be freely distributed, and so should the source code that makes it work. By making the source code available, engineers can both use and add to the software. When a developer revises or adds to the software he is supposed to release it back into the community. More information about open source software can be found at *http://www.opensource.org/*.

Companies that believe software is intellectual property and proprietary support the other side of the argument. Those following this philosophy believe that because they have invested sizeable capital and time to create the software, consumers should be charged for licenses to use it.

Both sides have their points and benefits. While companies may charge for software, they also have dedicated teams of engineers improving on it in addition to clearer support possibilities.

Open source software is often completely free, which allows more developers worldwide to both use and improve upon it. With all of these engineers working with the software, it can gain new features rapidly and new uses can be found. On the flipside, since these engineers are often doing this on their own time, bug fixes can sometimes lag. In addition, documentation can often be confusing and support difficult to find.

THE SCOPE AND PURPOSE OF THIS BOOK

It is likely that you have a computer available that can be used for creating a Web server. It is also very likely that this computer is running Windows. This book gives step-by-step instructions for installing four of the most popular open source programs: Apache HTTP Server, MySQL, PHP, and Perl. When they are installed, you will have a WAMPP (Windows, Apache, MySQL, PHP, and Perl) server.

In addition to providing copies of the software and concise installation directions, this book explores some of the features of the programs, which will help you to see the power of your new Web server and get you on your way to creating dynamic Web sites. After reading this book, you should have a general concept of what each program can do for you. You can then take this knowledge further by studying each of the applications through other books.

A computer with these installed programs can be a fully functional Web server for a small business, or a development machine. The latter is the preferred use of open source software as a Web server on the Windows operating system. There are numerous Web shared hosting solutions available that provide these products at an affordable price. This is often a good cost savings solution because you do not have to worry about the Internet connectivity or backing up your site. The hosting provider is also responsible for controlling security updates on the software.

By creating a development machine, you have the ability to create Web applications locally and fully test them before uploading. This enables you to troubleshoot any issues that may arise without crashing the actual Web server or having visitors experience errors. It also enables you to turn on different error detection and notification parameters that are not secure when run on a production machine, which greatly helps in narrowing down issues in scripts.

AUDIENCE FOR THIS BOOK

This book is written for those individuals who wish to create a Web server on a Windows computer. It is written for beginners. A basic knowledge of HTML would be helpful, but is not required. Appendix A, "An HTML Primer," is an HTML primer that can be used as a refresher on the subject. JavaScript is also mentioned in the book. It is not a requirement; it is just being used at points to demonstrate qualities of the server-side languages covered.

SUBJECTS COVERED

In keeping with general perceptions of the marketplace, different amounts of coverage are given to each product. Apache is the overall Web server that ties all of the products with the end user. That being said, the primary focus on Apache is to install and configure the program to serve general needs.

PHP and Perl are covered next. Of the two, PHP has more coverage, because of the popularity and availability of the language. While Perl is more robust, PHP is generally considered easier to learn. This has made it very popular with Web developers, as can be shown by the number of installed Apache modules.

NOTE

ON THE CD

This book provides numerous code examples of PHP and Perl. Those that have a filename can be found on the companion CD-ROM in an examples/chapter# *folder.*

The last subject discussed in this book is MySQL, and focuses on installation, creating databases, and manipulating the data within. Then, we turn to communication with Perl and PHP for Web database manipulation.

SUMMARY

As stated previously, this book focuses on the installation and configuration of Apache HTTP Server, Perl, PHP, and MySQL. It also introduces features in each program to get you using these products. It is not an advanced treatment of the products, rather a primer to get you up and running.

1   The Web Server Process

In This Chapter

- Server-Side Processes
- Client-Side Processes
- The Overall Process
- Web Protocols
- What Happens to the Request?
- Summary

Getting information off the Internet involves two basic components: the client and the server. The term *client* can be applied to the computer the end user is operating or to the actual user. The most basic example of this is shown in Figure 1.1.

As shown in Figure 1.1, the most basic structure is a Web server serving documents to an end user. At this level, a Web server is simply a file server that shares files over the Web. By itself, it only understands HTML and expects documents to be formatted in that manner. If a file is not HTML, it will either send the file to a program that understands it or force clients to download it to their local machines for use in an installed program. Zipped or compressed files are a great example of this; since they are not actually Web documents, the browser prompts the user to download the document for storage locally.

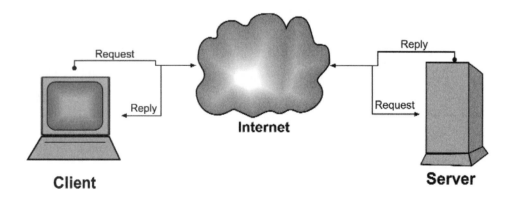

FIGURE 1.1 A Web server and client.

SERVER-SIDE PROCESSES

The first popular servers were file and print servers, which allowed users to share files and limited the number of printers needed for a workgroup. This was very important, because storage and printers were valuable resources and could be quite costly. At one time, the price of a quality printer was sometimes greater than the cost of the entire network. Even today, a color laser printer is extremely costly and worth sharing.

In addition to file and print servers, other types of servers are available: Web servers for HTML pages and images, database servers managing multiple databases, and application servers processing information for users everywhere. This book covers installing and configuring versions of each.

The first of these is a Web server, the definition of which may prove surprising. A Web server is simply any device (not just computers) on a network, running a program in the background. This program is constantly monitoring for any HTTP (HyperText Transfer Protocol) requests for services coming into the device. If it receives a request, it sends the information requested.

Next are application servers, which enable communication and interaction with users for the purpose of data collection and manipulation. Whenever information is read off a form and collected by a Web site, an application server is responsible. Both Perl and PHP can provide this functionality.

Lastly is the exploration of a database server, which controls one or more databases used for storing and organizing information. MySQL is used here for this purpose.

All of this server-side information is back-end technology that the users never see. These processes must take place on the server, or anyone could potentially view sensitive information. Most users don't want their credit card or other personal information broadcast over the Internet.

CLIENT-SIDE PROCESSES

Client is a term that can represent the end user or his computer. The actual end user is whom Web sites are trying to reach, while client-side technology includes everything that is processed on the end-user's machine—the HTML on Web pages, images, Cascading Style Sheets (CSS) for formatting, and some scripting like JavaScript to enhance the user experience. The client's Web browser is responsible for handling these technologies. The server simply sends the requested files and information. It is the responsibility of the client computer to display the Web page and any supporting content. This is very important because it offloads work from the Web server and enhances the user experience.

The server may be processing thousands of requests a second, and any extra work will bog it down. The end user winds up having to wait for the page to load and may quickly decide to click the Back button, whereas results of any processing done on the client side will be nearly instantaneous and make the experience more complete.

For example, sometimes a user may fill out a form and wait for it to process. When it seems that it is finished, the user is alerted that it is only sending back an error because a field was not filled in. If there had been a client-side script on the page to validate the form, the user would have been informed instantly. This saves the server from eating up valuable processor clock cycles while checking for errors. Since the focus of this book is on server-side technologies, there is not much coverage on client-side technologies.

THE OVERALL PROCESS

The overall process is simply a constant communication between client and server. First, the client issues a request to the Web server. In this request, the client is sending out its own information, such as the client Internet Protocol (IP) Address, the browser the client is using, the computer operating system, plug-ins available, and many other pieces of information.

This information must be sent for the Web server to do its job. While it may seem like an invasion of privacy, it simply facilitates basic communication. Where is the return IP Address? If someone sends a letter, a return address must be included if a reply is expected. What browser is being used? Should the computer be sent to another page that is more compatible? What platform is the computer? Should the fonts be changed to fit the capacity of the system? What plug-ins can the computer handle? Should the user be prompted to download any programs?

This is extremely important information, because it enables developers to program applications to know where and how to send the data. By using this information, Web designers and developers can enhance an end-user's experience during the visit.

WEB PROTOCOLS

All communication over the Internet is achieved using protocols. Most important of these is IP, which resides in the TCP/IP (Transmission Control Protocol/Internet Protocol) suite. Protocols are agreed upon modes of communication between devices—they are like languages. The Internet was built on TCP/IP. All devices on the Internet, or any network using TCP/IP, have what is known as an IP Address. The IP Address is broken into two portions, the network and the host. This is what devices use to communicate with one another.

There are four parts of the address, seen by humans as 0–255 and separated by periods. These are known as 8-bit parts or *octets*. On the surface, this makes little sense to the human eye, but computers see all numbers as binary. Binary only uses bits. A bit is either 1 or 0. This works well in an electronic environment because it translates to "on" or "off." The IP Address seen by the computer also has four parts, but with 8 bits in each. For example, while an administrator may refer to an IP Address as 209.15.176.206, the computer sees it as 11010001.00001111.10110000.11001110.

The first part of each IP Address is the network address, which is similar to an area code for a telephone number. The second part identifies the specific device. There are five classes of IP Addresses—A–E. Of these, only A, B, and C are in general use. These dictate how many hosts (devices) can exist on a given network. Classes are easily identified by the first octet of an IP Address. Class A addresses are numbered 0–127, and allow for 16,777,214 hosts. Class B addresses are numbered 128–191, and allow for 65,532 hosts. Class C addresses are numbered 192–223 and allow for 254 hosts. The extreme difference between the numbers of hosts available in each class is due to the portion size of network address. Class A addresses take up only the first octet of an IP address, leaving three octets available for numbering hosts. Class B addresses take up two, and Class C addresses take up three full octets.

Fortunately, users don't have to type in the IP Address or the binary equivalent to pull up a Web site; they just type in the domain name. This is due to a service in the TCP/IP stack called DNS (Domain Name System).

DNS is a hierarchal structure of databases that maps domain names to IP Addresses. For example, the IP Address of the URL (uniform resource locator) for *http://www.erichunley.com/* is 65.110.79.110.

It all starts with "root"; that's the "dot" as in "erichunley dot-com." Then, there are first-level domain names, including .com, .net, .org, .edu, .gov, .mil, and multiple two-letter country codes like .us for the United States, .de for Germany, or .ca for Canada.

Each of the available extensions was originally created for a type of organization. It is a good idea to note this when purchasing a domain name. Domain names originally needed to be purchased through Network Solutions, but now, several companies sell domain names. Most Web hosting companies will offer this service as part of their service package.

The following is a partial top-level domain name list:

.com: Commercial business—sells products.

.net: Originally created for Internet service providers (ISPs), but that practice stopped as fewer .coms were available for purchase.

.org: Nonprofit organization—churches, libraries, and charities use this extension.

.edu: Educational institution—most universities and colleges have this.

.gov: United States government entity—Federal or State governments.

.mil: United States military.

.xx: Two-letter country codes—most countries have one.

New extensions: .tv, .biz, .info, .pro, etc.

The .extension part of the address, or everything to the left of the slash (/) in a URL, is the physical address of the server. Everything to the right of the slash is the file system. This is where things get critical. When the user types to the left of the slash, case doesn't matter—*WWW.CHARLESRIVER.COM* will work just as well as *www.charlesriver.com*. However, to the right of the slash, case can matter and frequently does. Many Web servers on the Internet are either Unix or Linux (actually the majority) and the operating systems are *case sensitive*. If the user types in the wrong case, he will get a *file not found* (404) error. Web designers and administrators need to consider this and, as a standard, save all Web pages as *lowercase* with no spaces.

Since the Web server in this book will be installed on Windows, case does not matter. However, it is a good idea to always treat Web sites in a case sensitive manner —they can always be moved later.

Using *http://www.erichunley.com/* as an example, the first part of the address is *http://www*. The *www* means this is a site on the World Wide Web. Most browsers assume this and it is not always required to type. Left of that is *http://*. This literally means it is a Web request using the HTTP in the TCP/IP stack. Other options may include *ftp://* for File Transfer Protocol (FTP), *news:* for newsgroups, or *mailto:* for sending e-mail.

After the *www*, the domain name will usually follow; in this case, it is *erichunley.com*. However, that does not always hold true. There may be a *subdomain* like *sales.erichunley.com* or *support.erichunley.com*. The only way to specifically determine the second-level domain name is to look immediately to the left of the top-level name (in this case, *.com*).

WHAT HAPPENS TO THE REQUEST?

Now that we have a basic understanding of Web servers and how to find them, it's time to look at what happens in the process.

The Web server sits on the network constantly listening to all traffic. If it hears a request come in on port 80 (the port for HTTP), it will start to process the file requested. Web servers are good at doing one thing well: they generate HTML code and send it to the clients for browsers to display Web pages. As previously stated, the actual processing of the viewable Web page happens on the user's computer.

If the server looks at a requested page and sees that it's straight HTML, it will generate the markup code and send the information down to the client. However, if there is more involved with the page, like a CGI script, the Web server cannot process the code immediately, because it doesn't understand it. Fortunately, it can be configured to know which program is capable of handling the data. It also will be configured to find the program (i.e., Perl or PHP) and send the data.

The external program will in turn process the script, move the data according to the request, and then send back HTML code with the results. This can be thought of as pre-processing. The Web server now passes the modified code down to the client without the browser knowing anything of how it came to be.

Here's how it works:

1. The client computer sends up a request for a file to the Web server, usually through port 80 (HTTP).
2. The Web server looks at the file. If it is pure HTML, it will generate the code and send it to the user for display.
3. If the document has Server Side Includes (SSI) statements within, it will seek out the necessary files to complete the document, merge them, and send the data as one.
4. If the file is a server-side script or external access, the Web server will pass the file to the appropriate program for processing.
5. This application will then parse the information required and pass raw HTML back to the Web server.

6. The Web server generates the new HTML document and sends it down to the client.

7. The client browser receives the HTML and downloads any extra files (e.g., images) needed for display.

SUMMARY

This chapter briefly covered the overall Web process to give the reader a basic overview. Many of the topics covered fill entire books on their own (e.g., TCP/IP and DNS), and here we only provided a general description of each. Having a general understanding of the Internet and how it communicates with clients will assist in adding clarity later.

It is very important to have a general understanding of what is going on with these processes, because building a Web server is a form of network administration. Later chapters cover configuring the Apache HTTP server to accept multiple domain names, handle Server-side Includes (SSI), and to work in tandem with PHP and Perl for server-side scripting.

The rest of this book focuses on programming a Windows computer to function as a Web server, an application server, and a database server. We begin with Chapter 2, "Installing Apache HTTP Server."

2

Installing Apache HTTP Server

In This Chapter

- History of Apache HTTP Server
- Stopping Any IIS Sites
- Obtaining Apache
- Installing Apache
- Running Apache
- Checking the Server
- Summary

In 1995, a new Web server was launched, the Apache HTTP Server Project, and within 10 years grew to dominate the market. According to the March 2005 Web server survey on Netcraft (*news.netcraft.com*), Apache had 68.8 percent of the market. Microsoft IIS (Internet Information Server) came in a distant second with 20.9 percent.

In this chapter, we'll install the Apache Web server, which acts as center point for all Web operations on the WAMPP (Windows, Apache, MySQL, PHP, and Perl) server built in this book.

HISTORY OF APACHE HTTP SERVER

Apache was originally based on the NCSA (National Center for Supercomputing Applications) HTTPd server 1.3 developed by Rob McCool. After he left the NCSA in 1994, development on the HTTPd server was slow, so eight people got together and began the Apache project—Brian Behlendorf, Roy T. Fielding, Rob Hartill, David Robinson, Cliff Skolnick, Randy Terbush, Robert S. Thau, and Andrew Wilson. They released Apache 0.6.2 in April 1995.

NSCA started its own development again and the two groups worked together, allowing interoperability between the applications. This was very helpful because the NCSA HTTPd server is no longer a supported project.

Apache HTTP Server is an open-source application that can be used for free. The developers explain their intentions for the software on their Web site at *http://httpd.apache.org/ABOUT_APACHE.html*.

With the price being free, compatibility with multiple operating systems, and years of stability and support, there is little wonder why it is the number-one Web server on the market. Apache has grown over the years to support more features, and the Apache Software Foundation now supports many different projects.

STOPPING ANY IIS SITES

Windows will only allow one program running to handle requests for port 80, which means that any other Web server must be disabled or removed before Apache will work.

FIGURE 2.1   Selecting the Internet Information Services icon.

The most common Web browser developers will have to contend with is a component of IIS. IIS is available in NT 4, Windows 2000 Professional, Windows 2000 Server (all types), Windows XP Professional, and Windows 2003 Server. Therefore, before installing Apache on any of these operating systems, we must do the following:

1. Open the Services Microsoft Management Console (MMC), which can be found in the Control Panel under Administrative Tools. If XP Professional is the operating system, choose the category Performance and Maintenance and click Administrative Tools.
2. Within the Services MMC, look for IIS Admin. If it is listed and shows the status Started, continue to step 3. If Internet Services Manager is not listed, Apache HTTP Server can be installed without following the rest of these steps.
3. Go back into the Administrative Tools folder in the Control Panel.
4. Double-click the Internet Information Services (Internet Services Manager in Windows 2000) icon shown in Figure 2.1.
5. The Internet Information Services MMC will open. Within this window, find the Default Web site, highlight it, and click the Stop button as shown in Figure 2.2. Repeat this for any other Web sites that may be listed.

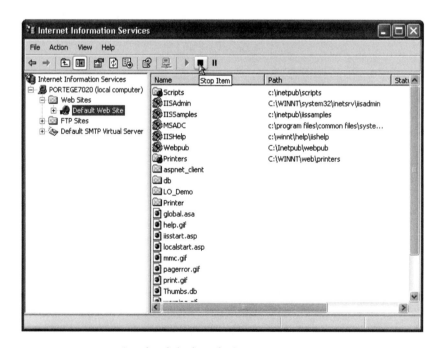

FIGURE 2.2   Stopping the default Web site.

OBTAINING APACHE

There are multiple ways to obtain a copy of Apache HTTP Server. It is included on the CD-ROM accompanying this book under Software/Apache, or it can be downloaded from a link provided on *http://httpd.apache.org/download.cgi.* Here, users have the option of downloading from different mirror sites, which are people or organizations donating Web space and bandwidth to help distribute the load. Each of these sites has downloads organized in the same manner.

The Web page will display which randomly selected mirror will be used for the download and allows users to change to another mirror if they choose as shown in Figure 2.3.

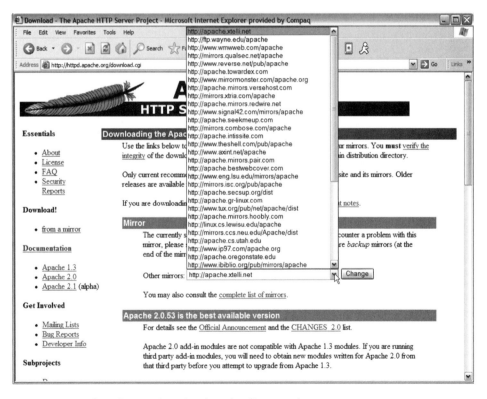

FIGURE 2.3   Choosing a mirror for downloading Apache.

Once the mirror is selected, the program itself needs to be downloaded. Links for this can be found by scrolling further down the page. There are four options immediately available—Unix Source: httpd-2.n.nn.tar.gz [PGP] [MD5], Unix Source: httpd-2.n.nn.tar.bz2 [PGP] [MD5], Win32 Source: httpd-2.n.nn-win32-x86-src.zip [PGP] [MD5], and Win32 Binary (MSI Installer): apache_2.n.nn-win32-x86-no_ssl.msi [PGP] [MD5] (see Figure 2.4).

Apache 2.x is designed to run on NT-based Windows systems. These include NT/2000/XP and Server 2003. Support for Windows 9X/Me is incomplete.

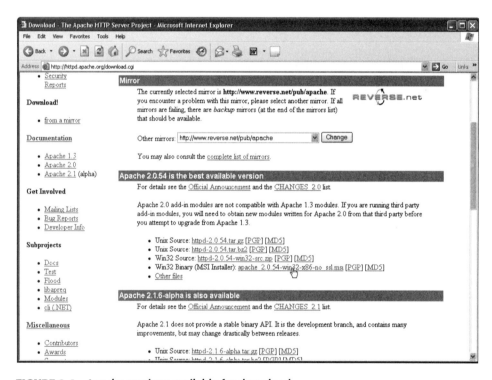

FIGURE 2.4   Apache versions available for download.

The first two of these are versions for Unix/Linux and are not used in this book. The third option is the Win32 Source, used by programmers who wish to get into the source code and compile the program themselves. Both Unix options are source code because, when running Unix/Linux, it is often a good idea to compile the program on the actual machine that will be running it. This helps make the program more stable since there are so many different types of hardware available.

The last option, Win32 Binary, is used in this book. A binary file in Windows means that the program has already been compiled and only needs installation.

Upon clicking on the Win32 Binary link, a prompt will appear offering to open (Run if using XP with Service Pack 2) or download the file to the local system. These options are shown in Figures 2.5 and 2.6.

At this point, it is up to the user which option to choose. Open will copy the file to a temporary folder and immediately start the install. Save allows the user to download the program to the hard disk for later installation. There are arguments for both. If a computer has a solid high-speed connection, Open may be a better choice. This allows the user to get everything taken care of in one step, and doesn't leave any lingering downloads. In the case of Apache, or any open source software, this is often a good idea because the programs are updated frequently. There is no reason to keep copies that will potentially be outdated.

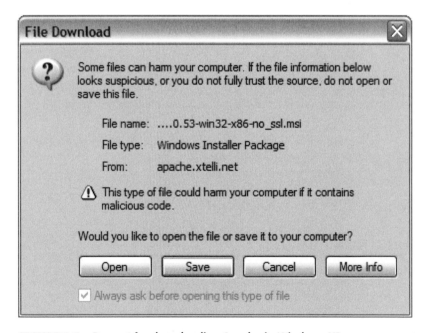

FIGURE 2.5 Prompt for downloading Apache in Windows XP.

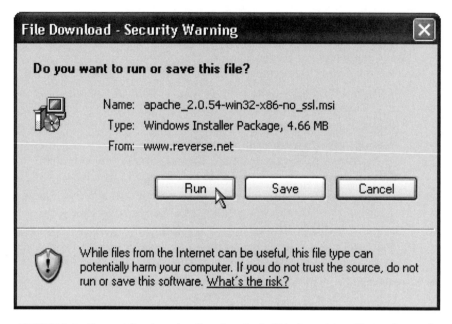

FIGURE 2.6   Prompt for downloading Apache in Windows XP with Service Pack 2.

If a user has a slow Internet connection, the Save option is probably best. This allows for potential interruptions in the process, and can be accomplished at any time; the user only needs to be around for the install.

Again, make sure Microsoft's Internet Information Server is not running when attempting to install and use Apache HTTP Server. Windows will only allow one program to respond to port 80.

INSTALLING APACHE

Whether you download the program or use the copy on the companion CD-ROM, the install procedure is simple:

1. An Installation Wizard will open as shown in Figure 2.7. Press Next to continue.

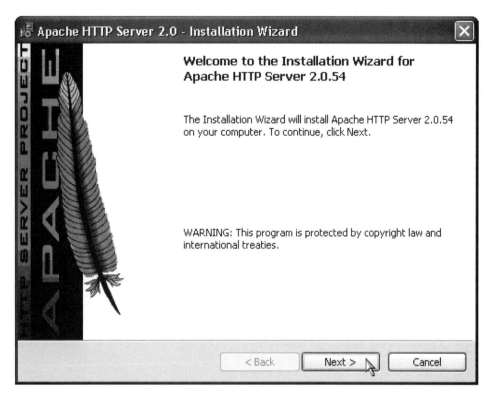

FIGURE 2.7   The Apache 2 Installation Wizard.

2. The License screen appears as shown in Figure 2.8. The license has to be accepted, or the installation will abort. Again, click Next.

3. A brief Read Me file appears explaining what the program is, information about the latest version, where documentation can be found, acknowledgments, and other facts. Click Next to continue as shown in Figure 2.9.

4. The next screen is important. This is where domain information is placed. If the site is an actual domain, it will be placed here. For the purposes of this book, *firstname.com* should suffice. Server name appears next. This determines what the actual server will be. Usually, it is the domain name with a www. placed in front. The last item is the Administrator's E-mail Address. That is for alerting the users whom to contact when error pages are received. With Windows 2000 and newer, the option of Install Apache

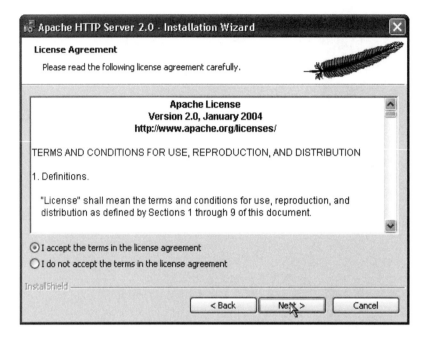

FIGURE 2.8   License Agreement screen.

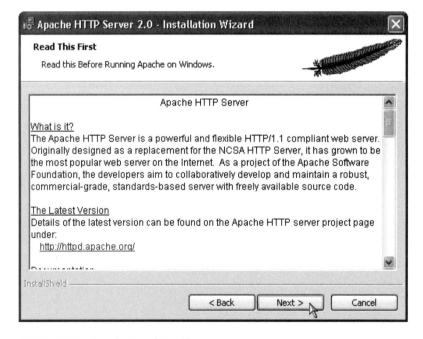

FIGURE 2.9   Apache Read Me file.

HTTP Server 2.0 programs and shortcuts for: appears. This is to determine whether it should be available only to the current user or available no matter who is logged in (see Figure 2.10).

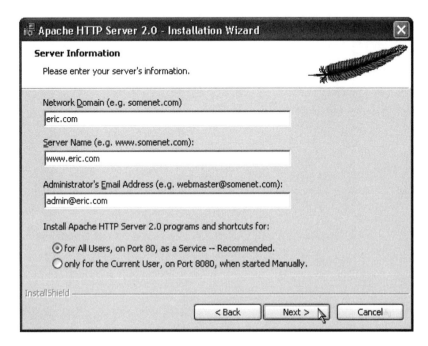

FIGURE 2.10   Server Information screen.

5. Figure 2.11 shows the two installation options, Typical or Custom. A custom installation allows for portions of the program to not be installed. For the purposes of this book, Typical should be selected. Click Next to continue.
6. The next screen to appear is Destination Folder shown in Figure 2.12.
7. The default path is C:\Program Files\Apache Group\. It is a good idea to consider changing it; otherwise, it will need to be typed whenever the program's path needs to be entered. The long path can be aggravating. Click Change to open the Change Current Destination Folder screen shown in Figure 2.13.

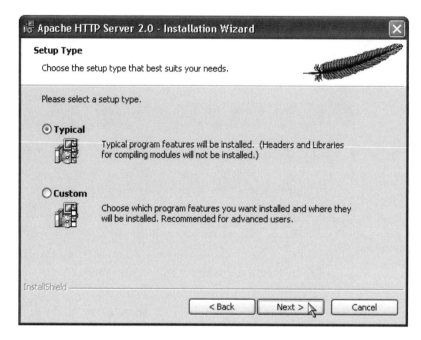

FIGURE 2.11   Setup type.

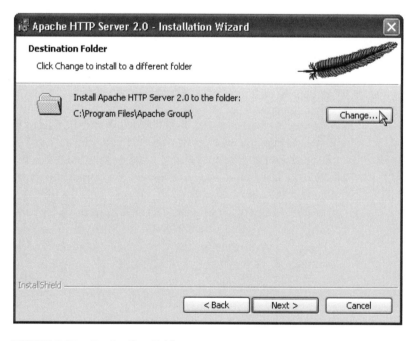

FIGURE 2.12   Destination Folder.

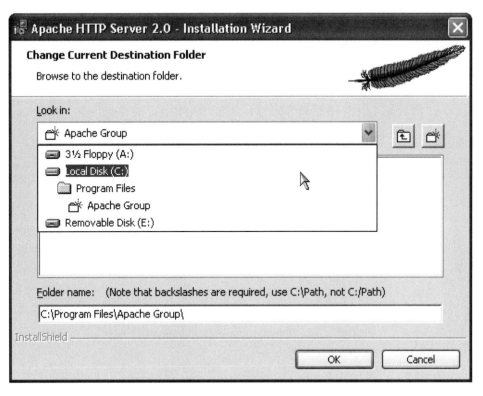

FIGURE 2.13   Change Current Destination Folder.

8. For the purposes of this book, select Local Disk (C:). The screen should appear as shown in Figure 2.14. If C: is not the name of the local hard disk, or another disk is preferred, simply choose the appropriate letter. Click OK to return to the Destination Folder screen.
9. Click Next to continue on the Destination Folder screen.
10. Ready to Install the Program will appear as shown in Figure 2.15. Click Install.
11. After a few moments, the Installation Wizard Completed screen will appear as shown in Figure 2.16. Click Finish to exit.
12. If XP with Service Pack 2 is being used, click Unblock on the Windows Security Alert dialog box shown in Figure 2.17.

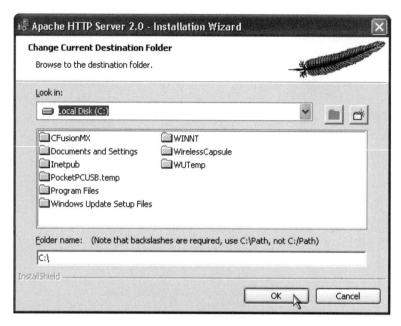

FIGURE 2.14 Change Current Destination Folder screen with the destination location changed to C:\.

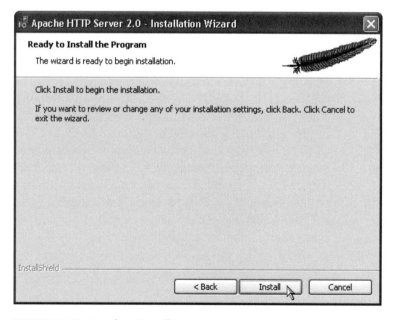

FIGURE 2.15 Ready to Install.

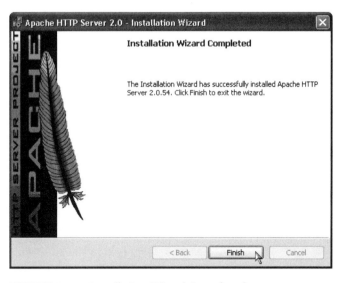

FIGURE 2.16   Installation Wizard Completed.

FIGURE 2.17   Windows Security Alert.

RUNNING APACHE

After installation, the Apache Service Taskbar icon will appear in the System tray. It resembles a wheel with a feather as shown in Figure 2.18. Within the wheel will be a green play triangle if Apache was successfully started and all services are running. This is shown in the first pane of Figure 2.18. If Apache is not running, a small red square will be visible in the center shown in the second pane of Figure 2.18. In addition to showing the status of the Web server, users can click and release their mouse on the icon, which will open a selection menu as shown in the third pane of Figure 2.18. These options are Start, Stop, and Restart with the current status being grayed out.

FIGURE 2.18   The Apache Service Taskbar icon states and options.

Another option available with the Apache Service Taskbar icon is double-clicking. This will open the Apache Service Monitor as shown in Figure 2.19.

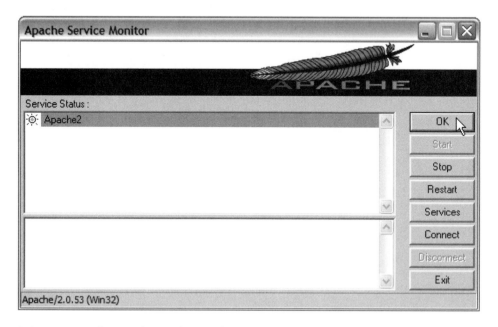

FIGURE 2.19   The Apache Service Monitor.

CHECKING THE SERVER

Once the server is installed, and the Apache Service Taskbar icon shows that it is currently running, the Web site can be checked with a browser. Open a Web browser and type *localhost* or *127.0.0.1* in the address bar. This will open the Apache Start page as shown in Figure 2.20.

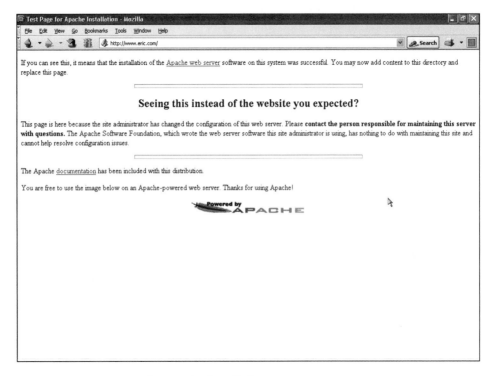

FIGURE 2.20   Test page for Apache installation.

On this page are two links; one leads to the Apache Web site and the other to the documentation, if a typical installation was used. Figure 2.21 shows the documentation page.

While using *http://localhost* will work well for serving up pages, earlier a domain name was entered during installation. At this point, it will not work in the browser, but with a minor configuration trick, it can be made available.

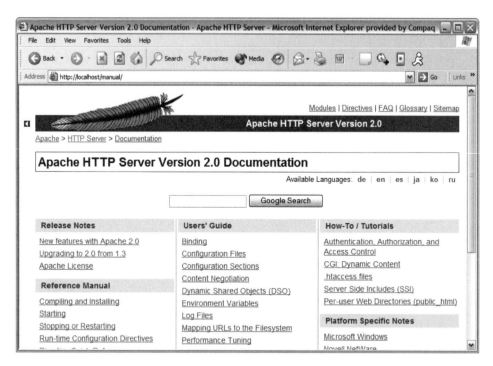

FIGURE 2.21   The Apache HTTP Server Version 2.0 Documentation page.

Configuring the `hosts` File

Within Microsoft Windows is a file named `hosts`. This is found within `C:\WINDOWS\system32\drivers\etc` or `C:\WINNT\system32\drivers\etc` (depending on the version of Windows). When attempting to open the file, the alert shown in Figure 2.22 may appear.

To get around this issue, choose Select this program from a list as shown in Figure 2.22. Choose Notepad from the list shown in Figure 2.23. This will open the `hosts` file shown in Figure 2.24.

Within the `hosts` file, there will usually be only one entry shown—`127.0.0.1 localhost`. This is how `localhost` can be typed instead of `127.0.0.1`. The IP address of `127.0.0.1` is known as the "loopback" address and is used for testing. Administrators use it to make sure the basic TCP/IP configuration on the computer appears to be working. It is not available for any Internet addresses and has been removed from the pool.

FIGURE 2.22   Windows cannot open this file prompt.

FIGURE 2.23   Selecting Notepad for opening the hosts file.

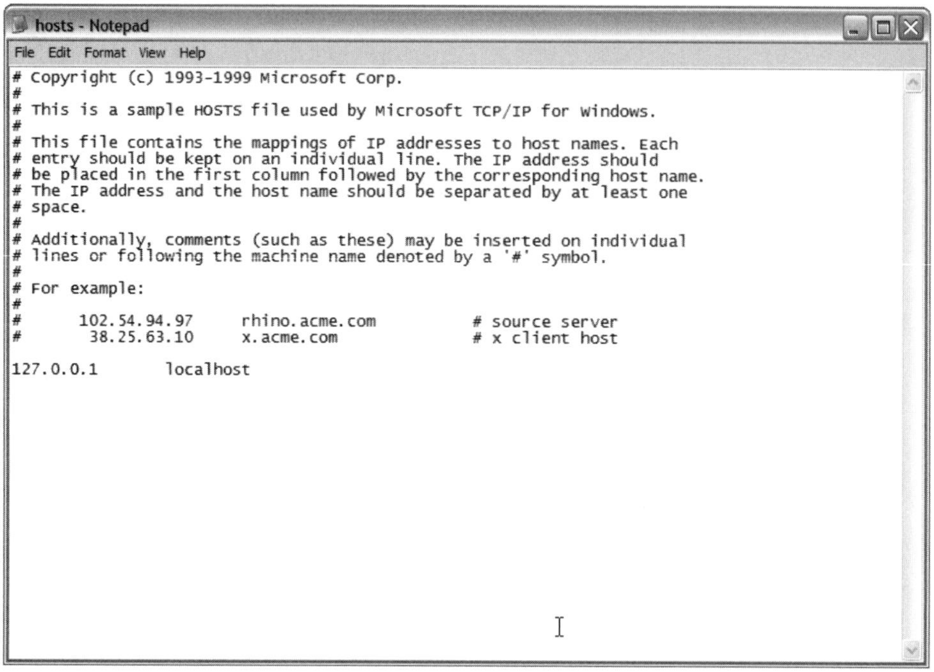

FIGURE 2.24   The hosts file.

When using the address *127.0.0.1* or *localhost*, the browser is sending out an HTTP request as it would for any site on the Web, only the operating system is looping it back to the local computer. When the request comes back into the local system, the Apache Web server is listening to port 80 (HTTP) and immediately sends back a reply. This allows the browser to display Web pages that are stored locally and serve them back in the same manner as any other client on the Internet.

The hosts file can be thought of as an internal or hardwired DNS. This is where specific server locations can be placed using whatever name the user may like. Since the directions given on the Apache installation earlier said to put firstname.*com* as the domain, two more entries should be added—firstname.*com* and *www*.firstname.*com* as shown in Figure 2.25. This will force the browser to load the Apache page whenever either of these options is typed in the address bar.

Another advantage to this method is that the Web server can be tested on other computers within the same local area network easily. As long as all of the workgroup computers are hooked up to the same switch or hub and do not have a

```
# Copyright (c) 1993-1999 Microsoft Corp.
#
# This is a sample HOSTS file used by Microsoft TCP/IP for Windows.
#
# This file contains the mappings of IP addresses to host names. Each
# entry should be kept on an individual line. The IP address should
# be placed in the first column followed by the corresponding host name.
# The IP address and the host name should be separated by at least one
# space.
#
# Additionally, comments (such as these) may be inserted on individual
# lines or following the machine name denoted by a '#' symbol.
#
# For example:
#
#      102.54.94.97     rhino.acme.com          # source server
#       38.25.63.10     x.acme.com              # x client host

127.0.0.1        localhost
127.0.0.1        eric.com
127.0.0.1        www.eric.com
```

FIGURE 2.25   The modified hosts file.

router between them, each of their host files can be modified to reflect the actual IP address of the server. This can be found by clicking on Start | Run, typing cmd, and clicking OK on Windows 2000/XP (Start | Run, command on Windows 95/98/Me). Within the command window, type ipconfig and press Enter. This will display the current IP configuration of the computer. Add this address and name to the hosts files in the other computers and they will connect to the Web server using the same name of *firstname.com* or *www.firstname.com*.

SUMMARY

In this chapter, we installed Apache 2. The basic Web server is now up and running, but there is much more to do. To make Apache more useable and robust, it needs to be configured, so let's move on to Chapter 3, "Configuring Apache."

3 Configuring Apache

In This Chapter

- Directories
- The HTTPD.CONF Configuration File
- Adding Security with OpenSSL
- Summary

In the previous chapter, we installed Apache, which should now be up and running. In this chapter, we'll configure Apache to be a more robust platform. We'll look at virtual hosts, requiring passwords for specified directory access, server-side includes, and secure socket layers.

DIRECTORIES

When Apache is installed, four directories are created by default: conf, htdocs, logs, and cgi-bin. These directories control everything that happens with Apache. Their specific functions are listed here:

conf: Contains the configuration files used for Apache HTTP Server. Of these, httpd.conf is the most important. It holds all of the main configuration settings to the Web server. Most modifications are performed in this file, which is a combination of four files previously used: access.conf, httpd.conf, srm.conf, and mime.types.

htdocs: Contains the default directory from which client files are served.

logs: All of the log files reside here. Logs are kept for both accesses and errors.

cgi-bin: This directory is created for any CGI scripts that may be run on the Web site.

The first directory to access for configuration is conf. Within, the httpd.conf file needs to be modified if the server will be doing anything other than serving up files from htdocs.

THE `HTTPD.CONF` CONFIGURATION FILE

The `httpd.conf` file is the backbone of Apache HTTP Server. A webmaster must use this file to make modifications to the Web server. It is a very long text file that is read whenever Apache is loaded. Whenever a change is made to the file, Apache needs to be restarted for it to take effect. This configuration file can be opened with any text editor and is shown in Figure 3.1 with Notepad.

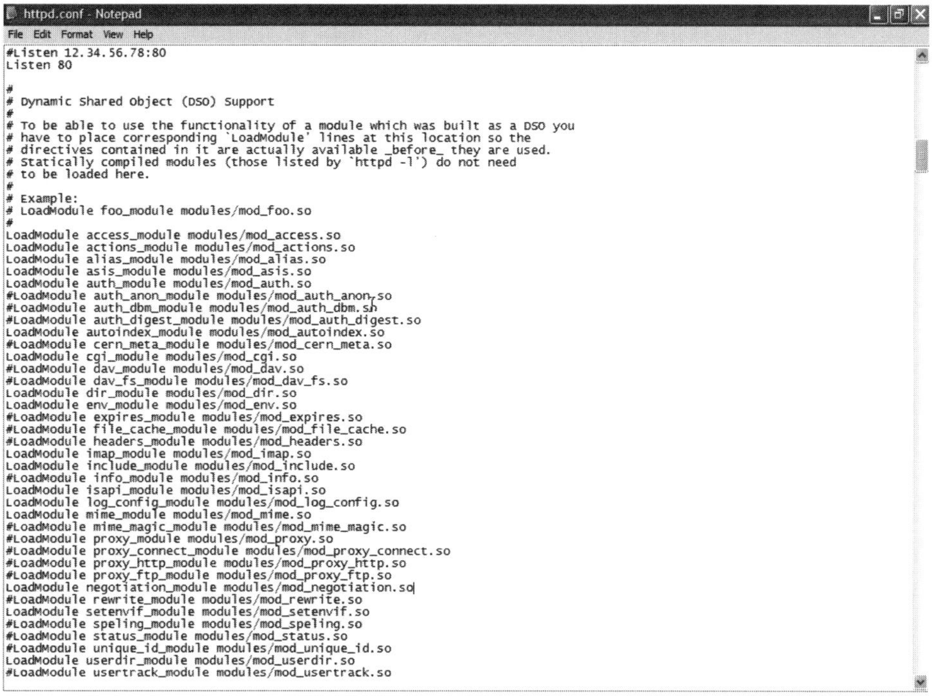

FIGURE 3.1   The httpd.conf configuration file.

As shown in Figure 3.2, the file is quite long (often running to over 1000 lines), so it is a good idea to use a text editor that has Find/Replace functionality. This will help locate directives quicker. Figure 3.2 shows the file in Crimson Editor.

Crimson Editor is a freeware text editor that can be found at *www.crimsoneditor.com/*. It offers enhancements not found in Notepad and is still small enough to fit on a 1.44 MB floppy disk. Among its features are syntax color-coding for multiple programming languages and line numbers. Both of these are very useful for modifying the `httpd.conf` file.

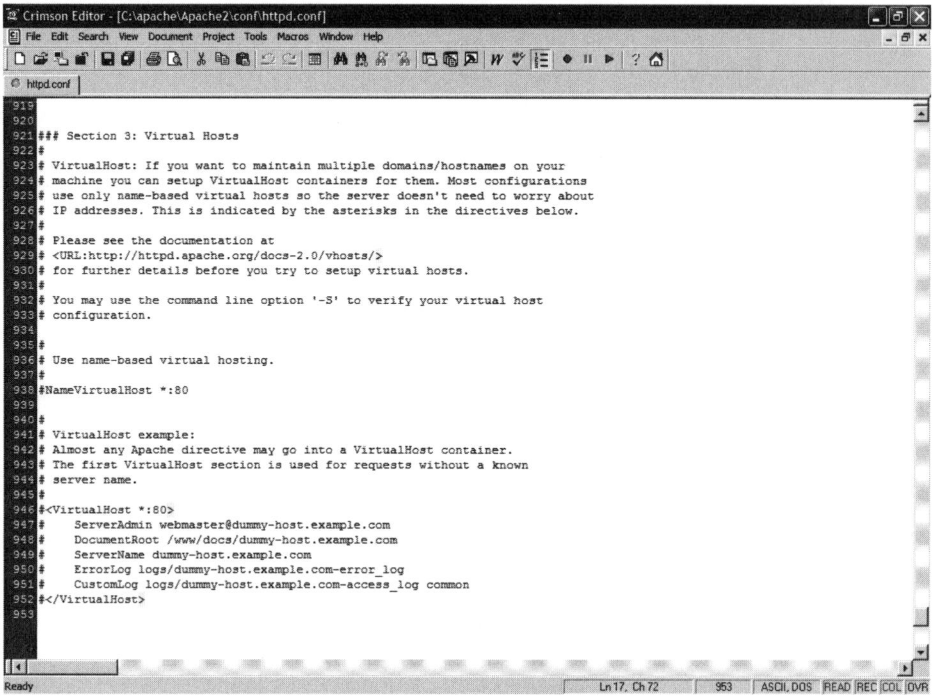

FIGURE 3.2   The httpd.conf file shown in Crimson Editor.

Directives

All configuring in the `httpd.conf` file is performed with the use of directives. These are either contained within a block, which limits them to certain conditions or virtual hosts, or are placed in the configuration file. You can find a list of all available directives online at *http://httpd.apache.org/docs/2.0/mod/directive-dict.html*.

Virtual Hosts

The first thing that will need to be modified in the `httpd.conf` file is the Virtual Hosts section, which enables a single instance of Apache HTTP server to serve up multiple Web sites using the same IP Address.

When a request comes through on port 80 in the HTTP protocol, it has two basic parts: the IP Address and the domain name. By defining Virtual Hosts for each domain name, a single server can act as multiple Web sites with each domain existing in a separate folder on the server. The `VirtualHost` portion of the configuration file will capture the request and point it to the correct location on the hard drive. An example of the necessary syntax can be found at the end of the `httpd.conf` file. It will look like the following:

```
#<VirtualHost *:80>
#     ServerAdmin webmaster@dummy-host.example.com
#     DocumentRoot /www/docs/dummy-host.example.com
#     ServerName dummy-host.example.com
#     ErrorLog logs/dummy-host.example.com-error_log
#     CustomLog logs/dummy-host.example.com-access_log common
#</VirtualHost>
```

All of these lines are *commented out* (with the pound sign) so they are not actually read by the server when it is started. The placement of commented lines throughout the configuration file is used for the purpose of providing syntactical examples as reference. While these lines can be modified, it is often a good idea to simply copy them, paste them after the commented lines, and then modify the copy. The following steps are a good start:

1. Find the line `#NameVirtualHost *:80` and uncomment it by removing the pound sign (#). This will enable the use of Virtual Hosts.
2. Copy the `VirtualHost` section starting with `#<VirtualHost * :80>` and ending with `#</VirtualHost>`.
3. Paste the section twice after the current `VirtualHost` section.
4. Modify the first `VirtualHost` section to resemble the following (`Server-Alias` may need to be added):

```
<VirtualHost *>
ServerAdmin admin@yourname.com
DocumentRoot "c:/apache2/htdocs"
ServerName yourname.com:80
ServerAlias yourname.com *.yourname.com
ErrorLog "c:/apache2/logs/error.log"
</VirtualHost>
```

If Apache HTTP Server was installed using the defaults, the file paths will be `c:\program files\apache group\apache2`.

5. This first `VirtualHost` section reflects the default Web site, which will be the carryover for any requests that do not have a specific site defined. It is common for webmasters to use the same IP address for multiple sites in Shared Web hosting. It is also very helpful if a Web site is going to be broken into sections; for example, *sales.domainname.com* and *service.domainname.com*. By having sections of a business in subdomains, they can be directly accessed by name and stored on the same server. Later, they can easily be moved to another server if necessary.

6. To facilitate multiple sites on the same computer, open Windows Explorer and create a new folder in `c:\` (or whatever drive is appropriate) called `sites`. This folder will enable easier backing up. Within `sites`, create a folder called `mojo`.

7. Inside the `mojo` folder, create two more folders—`www` and `logs`.

8. Within `logs`, right-click in Windows Explorer and choose New-Text Document as shown in Figure 3.3.

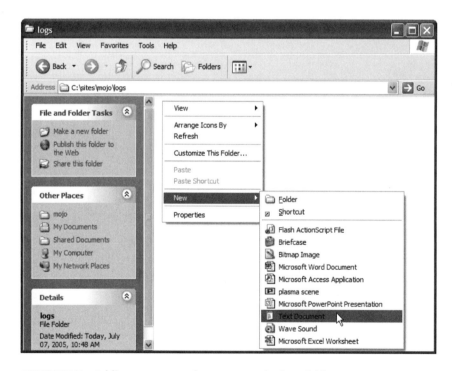

FIGURE 3.3 Adding a new text document to the logs folder.

9. Rename the new text document `error.log`. If the dialog box shown in Figure 3.4 appears, click Yes.

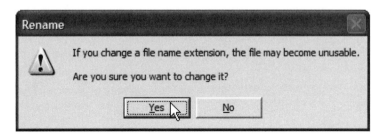

FIGURE 3.4   Rename dialog box.

10. A Web page must be created that will be served by *yournamesmojo.com*, which you can do using any text editor. Type the following into a new page saved as `index.html` in the www folder:

```
<html>
<head>
<title>yournamesmojo.com</title>
</head>
<body>
<h1>Welcome to yournamesmojo.com</h1>
</body>
</html>
```

11. Since the folders and files have been created, it is time to add it as a Web site in the `httpd.conf` file. To add this second server, modify the second `VirtualHost` to read (also shown in Figure 3.5):

```
<VirtualHost *>
ServerAdmin admin@yournamesmojo.com
DocumentRoot c:/sites/mojo
ServerName yournamesmojo.com:80
ServerAlias yournamesmojo.com *.yournamesmojo.com
ErrorLog c:/sites/mojo/logs/error.log
</VirtualHost>
```

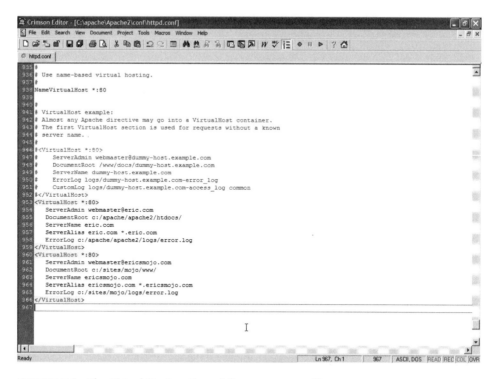

FIGURE 3.5   The Virtual Host section of the `httpd.conf` file.

12. Once the `httpd.conf` file has been modified, restart Apache by clicking on the Apache Monitor icon in the system tray and choosing Apache2—Restart.

13. After the second server has been added, a change must be made to the `hosts` file so the Web browser will point to the correct Web site when either address is typed into the address bar. Open `C:\WINDOWS\system32\drivers\etc` or `C:\WINNT\system32\drivers\etc` (depending on the version of Windows) and modify the file to reflect the two Web sites as follows (see Figure 3.6):

```
127.0.0.1                localhost
127.0.0.1                yourname.com
127.0.0.1                www.yourname.com
127.0.0.1                yournamesmojo.com
127.0.0.1                www.yournamesmojo.com
```

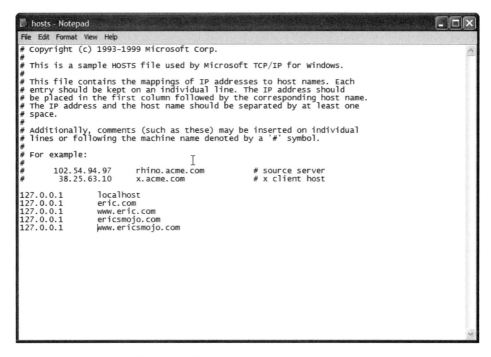

```
hosts - Notepad
File  Edit  Format  View  Help
# Copyright (c) 1993-1999 Microsoft Corp.
#
# This is a sample HOSTS file used by Microsoft TCP/IP for windows.
#
# This file contains the mappings of IP addresses to host names. Each
# entry should be kept on an individual line. The IP address should
# be placed in the first column followed by the corresponding host name.
# The IP address and the host name should be separated by at least one
# space.
#
# Additionally, comments (such as these) may be inserted on individual
# lines or following the machine name denoted by a '#' symbol.
#
# For example:
#
#       102.54.94.97      rhino.acme.com          # source server
#        38.25.63.10      x.acme.com              # x client host

127.0.0.1          localhost
127.0.0.1          eric.com
127.0.0.1          www.eric.com
127.0.0.1          ericsmojo.com
127.0.0.1          www.ericsmojo.com
```

FIGURE 3.6   The modified hosts file.

If the Web sites will be on a network that has a DNS server, the DNS server can be programmed to reflect the proper name of an IP Address as opposed to all of the local computers needing their hosts *files changed.*

14. After the hosts file has been modified, the pages can be checked. Open a Web browser and type *http://www.yourname.com* in the address bar. The page shown in Figure 3.7 should load.
15. Now the mojo site can be checked by typing *http://yournamesmojo.com* or *http://www.yournamesmojo.com* in the address bar. The page should resemble Figure 3.8.

Preventing Directory Listing

When building a Web site, you must consider security. One of the most basic levels of security is to prevent users from viewing the contents of a directory. This will

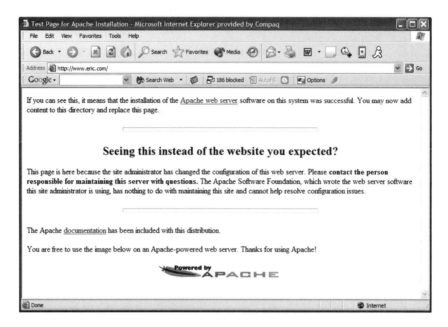

FIGURE 3.7   The default Web site.

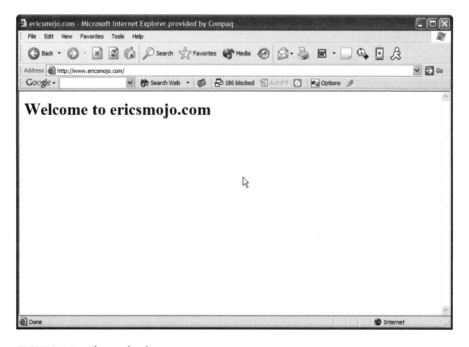

FIGURE 3.8   The mojo site.

prevent them from seeing what a webmaster has and keep them on track with the Web site.

By default, Apache HTTP server will show a directory listing of all files if there is no default page listed (see Figure 3.9). This is never a good scenario and needs to be avoided. By allowing full directory access, any user can see what files exist on a Web site. These may include administration files, authoring files (e.g., Photoshop® PSD or Flash FLA), and other important files that aren't to be shared with the general public. If a user with malicious intent is able to find an administration file or the like, it won't be long before your Web site is compromised.

Hiding the contents for directories is incredibly easy in Apache, and involves simple modification of one line. The `IndexIgnore` line should be changed to read `IndexIgnore *`. This literally translates to ignore all (the * is the wildcard used for *all*) contents of a directory when creating an index. The results will look like Figure 3.10.

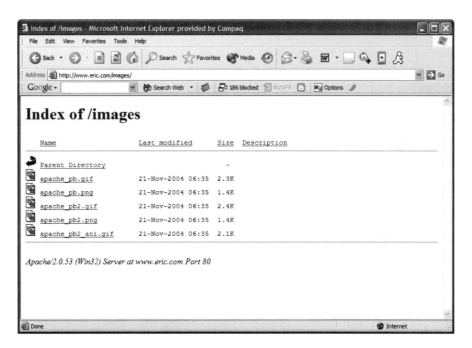

FIGURE 3.9 Directory listing in Apache.

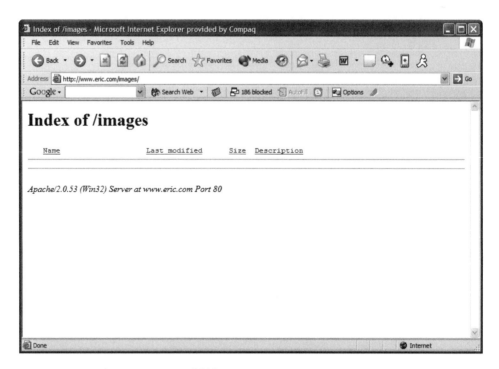

FIGURE 3.10   Directory contents hidden.

While it is effective to hide the contents of a directory from users, another step should be taken. Users may end up at a directory by accident. If they do, the screen shown in Figure 3.10 is likely to confuse them. That is where a good "oops" page may come in handy.

The "oops" page will reside at the top of any directory that does not already have a default page. A basic example is shown in Figure 3.11.

After completing the "oops" page, it should be saved as index.html and placed in any directory that doesn't have any other defaults. When the user winds up at any directory he is not supposed to traverse, the page shown in Figure 3.12 will appear.

Using .htaccess **Files to Secure a Directory**

Configuration files known as .htaccess allow webmasters to make configuration changes on a directory level. A .htaccess file placed at the root of a folder will override the httpd.conf file directives for the current directory and all those underneath.

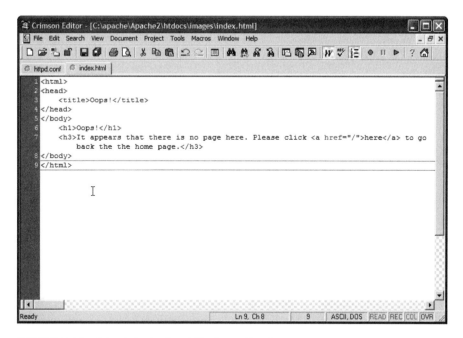

FIGURE 3.11 A basic index.html file for redirection purposes.

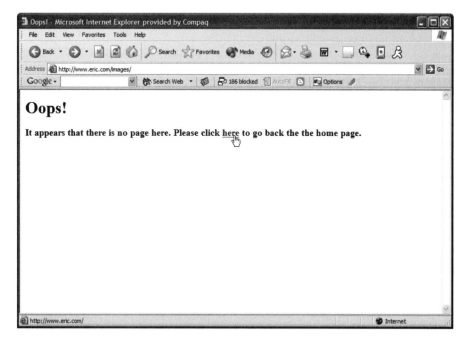

FIGURE 3.12 The index.html file has been added to the directory.

One of the most popular uses for a .htaccess file is to secure directories by requiring a username and password. There are two levels available for this process: Basic and Digest.

The easiest of the methods is Basic, which can be easily accomplished by following these steps:

1. Create a new folder within htdocs called sales.
2. Within the new folder, use a text editor to create a new text file. Save this file as .htaccess. Keep the file open.
3. Create a new folder in C:\apache\Apache2 called users.
4. Create a new text file in the folder with the name .htpasswd. Keep this file open.
5. Open the httpd.conf file and locate the line <Directory "C:/apache2/htdocs">.

Note that forward slashes are used to denote file paths in Apache, not the backslashes that are normal for Windows. This is because Apache was made to work with numerous operating systems, and Unix is its base. Unix, most operating systems, and the Internet all use forward slashes for file paths.

6. Underneath that line, find the line that reads AllowOverride None and change it to AllowOverride AuthConfig.
7. Save the httpd.conf file and restart Apache.
8. Open the .htaccess file and insert the following code:

```
AuthType Basic
AuthName "Authorization Required"
AuthUserFile C:/apache2/users/.htpasswd require valid-user
```

If there are any spaces between characters in the file path, the text must be enclosed with quotation marks.

The first part of the code is the type of authentication, followed by the realm labeled AuthName. That is what will be shown in the dialog box when it appears. Next, AuthUserFile shows the location of the password file. Last is the require statement. That can be an individual user, a group if a group file is being used, or a keyword like valid-user in this case. The valid-user keyword will allow anyone on the password list.

9. The easiest means of creating a password is to open the .htpasswd file and type *username:password* for each user (one per line). The problem with this is that anyone with directory access can simply read the password in the file. To alleviate this situation, there is a utility automatically installed with Apache called htpasswd.exe. It can be found in C:\apache2\bin.

10. Click on Start | Run and type cmd for Windows 2000/XP or command for Windows 9X/Me. This will open the command prompt. Type cd \apache\ Apache2\ \bin\ to set the path.

11. Type htpasswd -c C:\apache2\users\.htpasswd *username* and enter a password when prompted for a couple of users as shown in Figure 3.13.

If there is not a preexisting .htpasswd *file, type* htpasswd -c C:\apache2\users\ .htpasswd username, *which will create a new one and add the first user in one shot. Remove the* -c *for creating new users after the first.*

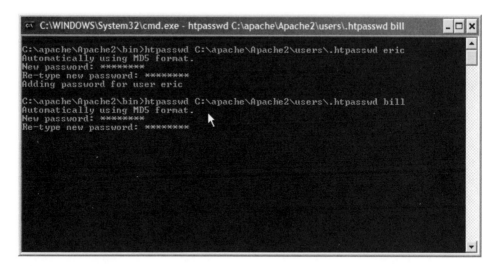

FIGURE 3.13   Creating users and passwords using the htpasswd utility.

12. By using the htpasswd utility, the passwords are encrypted in the .htpasswd file as shown in Figure 3.14.

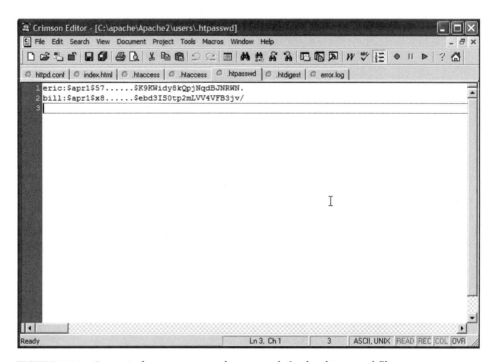

FIGURE 3.14   Encrypted usernames and passwords in the .htpasswd file.

13. When users attempt to access the sales folder now, they will see a prompt as shown in Figure 3.15.
14. After successfully entering a username and password, the Web page will load as shown in Figure 3.16.
15. If the username and/or password are incorrect more than twice, the screen shown in Figure 3.17 will appear.

While Basic authentication is a handy way to keep some people from peering into folders where they don't belong, it is by no means secure. First, the password is sent in clear text over the wire, so anyone with a Protocol Analyzer (also called a *sniffer*) can capture the packets and read username and password information.

FIGURE 3.15   User Name and Password prompt.

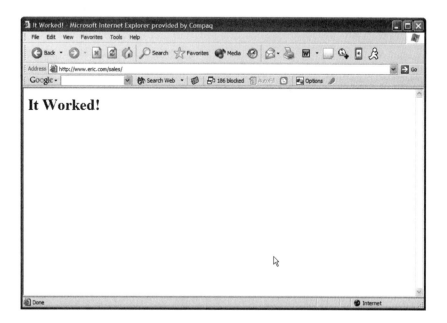

FIGURE 3.16   User Name and Password successfully entered.

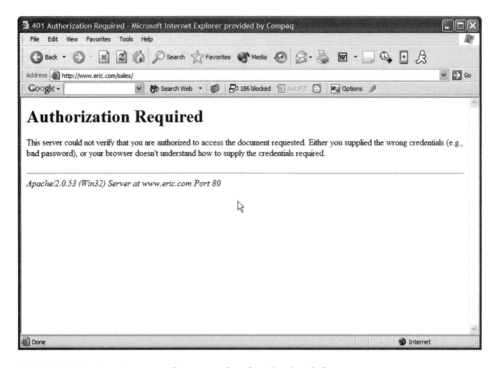

FIGURE 3.17   User Name and Password authentication failure.

Not only can the username and password be read when users first log in, but they are sent along with every request. That means it won't take too much effort to capture this information. Moreover, the information being downloaded from the site is not encrypted, which means that Basic authentication should not be used for anything that requires actual security.

Apache offers an alternative called *Digest authentication*. While this is an improvement, it too should not be used for anything requiring serious security. To use Digest authentication:

1. Open the `httpd.conf` file and uncomment the line `#LoadModule auth_digest_module modules/mod_auth_digest.so`.
2. Set up the `.htaccess` file similar to the following:

```
AuthType          Digest
AuthName          "Private"
AuthDigestFile    C:\apache2\users\digest
Require           valid-user
```

3. Place the .htaccess file in whichever directory needs to be protected.
4. Create the digest password file by clicking Start | Run and typing cmd for Windows 2000/XP or command for Windows 9X/Me. Within the command prompt window, change the directory by typing cd \apache\Apache2\bin\.
5. The command for creating a user with htdigest.exe is very similar to htpasswd.exe with a single addition of the realm parameter, which is mandatory. Type htdigest -c c:/apache/users/digest *realm username*. This will create a new file, add the username to it, and prompt for a password. To create more users, the command is the same, but the -c switch (creates a new file) should be removed.
6. After Apache has been restarted, the users will be prompted whenever they hit a directory that is using Digest authentication. The dialog box is shown in Figure 3.18.

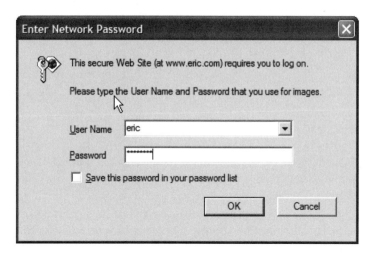

FIGURE 3.18 Prompt given when using Digest authentication.

Digest authentication is better than Basic authentication, but still should not be used if real security is needed. While it encrypts the username and password when they are sent to the server, it is not encrypting the data itself. If data truly needs to be secured, SSL (Secure Socket Layers) should be used. OpenSSL is covered later in this chapter.

Another option when using either Basic or Digest authentication is to use groups. The process is the same for both types. A group file first has to be created in the format of `groupname`: `member1 member2 member3` for each group in the file. All of the members must also be listed in the password file.

There is a common limitation of number of characters per line of 8000. If this is not sufficient for the number of users in a group, there can be more than one group listing with the same name.

If Basic authentication is being used, another line must be added to the `.htaccess` file reading `AuthGroupFile filepath`, like `AuthGroupFile C:\apache2\users\groups`. Then, the last line should read `require group name`. Digest works the same as Basic authentication, only instead of `AuthGroupFile` it uses the keyword `AuthDigestGroupFile`.

When users are authenticated using group authentication, another layer is added to the process. First, the group file is checked to see if the user is listed. If so, the password file is checked. If the user is in the password file, and the password matches, access will be granted. This is helpful for defining levels of access. All of the users are listed in one long password file, but groups separate them.

An example of how this may work is to have one master list of passwords and two groups: employees and supervisors. Within the employees group, all employees are listed (including the supervisors). On the Web site, there are two folders with `.htaccess` files. One requires employees and the other supervisors. This helps separate the levels of access. An even easier filtering method would be to only have the supervisors group file and limit one folder based on that group, while leaving the other folder available to all users in the password file.

Basic and Digest authentication are useful for keeping some areas of Web site more private than others. They will not provide real security, but when used in conjunction with OpenSSL, they can be very helpful.

While most `.htaccess` files are named as such, they do not have to be. Find the `AccessFileName .htaccess` line in `httpd.conf` and change the filename to whatever is preferable.

Using Server Side Includes

Server Side Includes technology is an extremely useful way to display Web pages enabling the use of modular Web pages. To activate their use, the following lines need to be uncommented:

```
#AddType text/html .shtml
#AddOutputFilter INCLUDES .shtml
```

Once the lines are uncommented, and `Includes` is added to the `Options` Directive, Server Side Includes will be available for use. If they are to be available as default Web pages in directories, the `DirectoryIndex` line needs to have `index.shtml` added.

Server Side Includes technology combines more than one file to make up the whole. These files each have chunks of HTML code and are not complete Web pages. This is very useful if there are recurring items on Web pages like menus that will be consistent throughout a Web site. The following steps use Server Side Includes to create a basic Web page.

Find the following lines in the `httpd.conf` file:

```
<Directory />
Options FollowSymLinks
AllowOverride None
</Directory>
```

1. Add `Includes` after `Options FollowSymLinks`.
2. Next, uncomment the following lines:

   ```
   #AddType text/html .shtml
   #AddOutputFilter INCLUDES .shtml
   ```

3. Finally, add `index.shtml` to the end of the `DirectoryIndex`.
4. Restart Apache.
5. Go inside the `C:\sites\mojo\www\` directory and either delete or rename `index.html`.
6. Create a new text document with the following code:

   ```
   <html>
   <head>
           <title>Welcome to Yourname's Mojo Site</title>
           <style type="text/css">
                   h1{
                           background-color: #00CCFF;
                           font-size: 36px;
                           font-style: italic;
                           color: #990000;
                           border: 3px solid #0000FF;
                           text-align: center;
   ```

```
                                padding: 10px;
                }
                a{
                                font-family: Arial, Helvetica, sans-serif;
                                font-size: 12px;
                                font-weight: bold;
                                }
                a:link,a:visited {
                                color: #FFFFFF;
                                text-decoration: none;
                                }
                                a:hover{
                                text-decoration: underline;
                                }
                .links{
                                text-align: center;
                                background-color: #0000FF;
                                color: #FFFFFF
                                }
            </style>
</head>
<body>
<p class="links"><a href="index.shtml">HOME</a> | <a
href="about.shtml">ABOUT</a> | <a href="contact.shtml">CONTACT</a>
| <a href="links.shtml">LINKS</a></p>
```

7. Save the document as _header.shtml in the C:\sites\mojo\www\ directory.
8. Create another document with the following code:

```
<p class="links"><a href="index.shtml">HOME</a> | <a
href="about.shtml">ABOUT</a> | <a href="contact.shtml">CONTACT</a>
| <a href="links.shtml">LINKS</a></p>
<p style="text-align: center;font-size: 10px; color: #0000CC; font-
family: Verdana, Arial, Helvetica, sans-serif">&copy;2005 Yourname
Web Designers LTD.</p>
</body>
</html>
```

9. Save the document as _footer.shtml in the C:\sites\mojo\www\ directory.
10. Now create a document with the following code:

```
<!--#include file="_header.shtml" -->
```

```
<h1>Get your Mojo Rising!</h1>
<p> </p><p> </p><p> </p><p> </p><p> </p><p
> </p><p> </p><p> </p>

<!--#include file="_footer.shtml" -->
```

11. Save the document as `index.shtml` in the `C:\sites\mojo\www\` directory.
12. Test the document by typing *http://www.yournamesmojo.com* in the address bar of the browser. The results should resemble Figure 3.19.

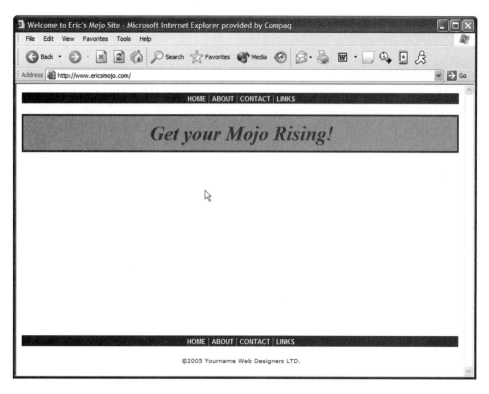

FIGURE 3.19 Web page made with Server Side Includes.

Notice that the Web page looks just like any other page. All of the components are loaded together as one. This enables Web designers to store recurring portions of code as `.shtml` files and not have to recreate them on every page. This also means that if a change has to be made, it is only made on one document and will be reflected in all pages using that document. When a page created with SHTML is loaded, the source code looks like any other Web page making it transparent to the user (see Figure 3.20).

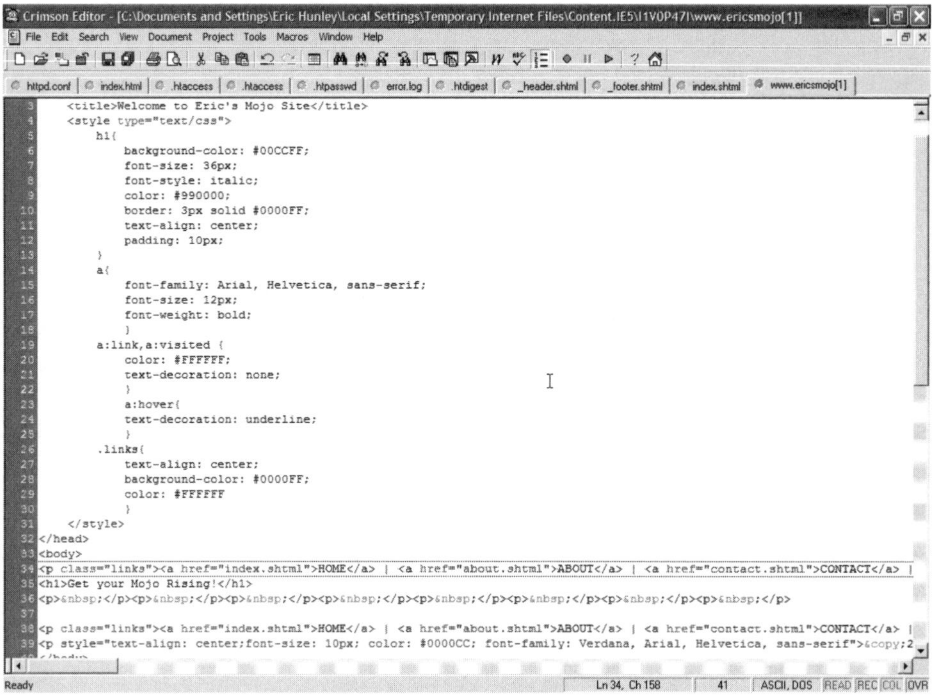

FIGURE 3.20   Source code from a loaded Web page using Server Side Includes.

ADDING SECURITY WITH OPENSSL

When creating a Web site that performs transactions or collects private information from users, there will always be the question of security. How can the information be secured in the safest possible manner? That is where Secure Socket Layers (SSL) can come to the rescue.

SSL is a protocol developed by Netscape for transmitting encrypted data over the Internet. It works by allowing the client to use a public key issued from the Web server to encrypt data. The server in turn has a private key to decrypt the data.

The following sections give instructions for adding SSL to yournames*mojo.com*.

Initial Steps

1. Open the `httpd.conf` file and find the line `Listen 80`.
2. Add `Listen 443` directly underneath.
3. Restart the Apache Service.
4. Open a Web browser, type *http://localhost:443*, and see if the page loads as shown in Figure 3.21. It is not encrypted at this point, but the port is now enabled.

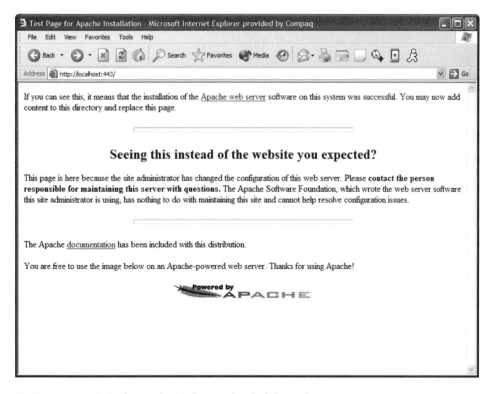

FIGURE 3.21   Default Apache Web page loaded through port 443.

ON THE CD

5. Find the `modssl` folder in the `software` folder on the companion CD-ROM and copy the `ssleay32.dll` and `libeay32.dll` files to the `System32` folder.

6. Copy `mod_ssl.so`, `mod_ssl.pdb`, and `mod_status.pdb` to the `apache2\modules` directory.
7. Copy the `openssl.exe` and `openssl.cnf` files to `apache2\bin`.
8. Copy the `ssl.conf` and `ssl.default.conf` files to `apache2\conf`.
9. Find the line `LoadModule ssl_module modules/mod_ssl.so` and uncomment it in the Apache `httpd.conf` file.

Creating a Test Certificate

The following are directions to create a certificate that can be used for encryption.

1. Open a command prompt and navigate to `C:\apache2\Bin`.
2. Type `openssl req -new > my-server.csr -config openssl.cnf` as shown in Figure 3.22. This creates a certificate signing request and 1024-bit RSA private key.

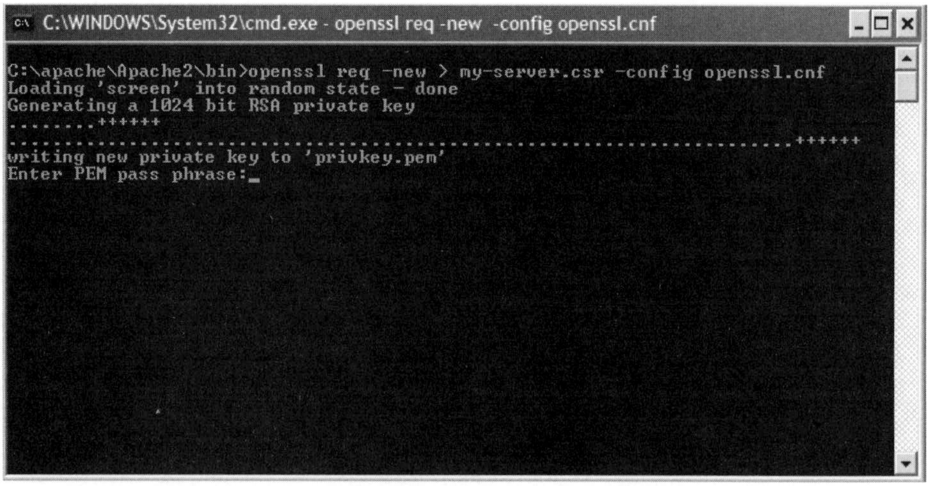

FIGURE 3.22   Creating a certificate signing request and private key.

3. When it prompts for a `PEM pass phrase`, type `password`.
4. Fill out the requested information: Country Name (two-letter code), State or Province Name (full name), Locality (e.g., city), Organization Name (e.g., company), and Organizational Unit Name (e.g., section) as shown in Figure 3.23.

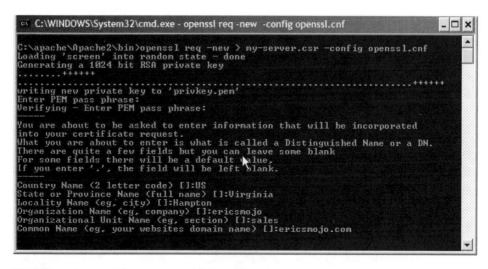

FIGURE 3.23   Providing requested information.

5. When prompted for a `Common Name`, provide the exact domain name of the Web server (in this case, yournames*mojo.com*). If the certificate doesn't match the server's domain, there may be issues with browsers.
6. When prompted for a `challenge password`, use `password` again.
7. Type `openssl rsa -in privkey.pem -out my-server.key` as shown in Figure 3.24. This removes the pass phrase from the private key, making the server key only readable to the server.

FIGURE 3.24   Removing the pass phrase from the private key.

8. Again, use `password` when prompted.
9. Next, type `openssl x509 -in my-server.csr -out my-server.cert -req -signkey my-server.key -days 365` as shown in Figure 3.25. This creates a self-signed certificate that can be used until a "real" one is purchased from a certificate authority (CA). This certificate expires after one year, but `-days 365` can be increased if needed.

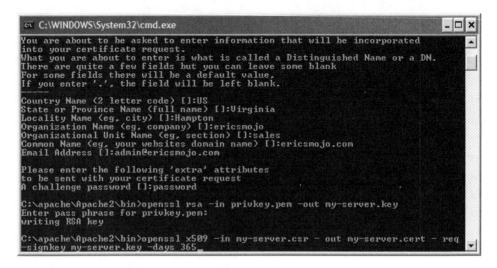

FIGURE 3.25   Completing the certificate.

Wrapping up SSL

Add the following lines to the end of `httpd.conf`, save, and restart Apache:

```
SSLMutex default
SSLRandomSeed startup builtin
SSLSessionCache none
ErrorLog logs/SSL.log

LogLevel info

<VirtualHost *:443>
    SSLEngine On
    SSLCertificateFile bin/my-server.cert
```

```
    SSLCertificateKeyFile bin/my-server.key
    DocumentRoot c:/sites/mojo/www/
    ServerName yournamesmojo.com
    ServerAlias yournamesmojo.com *.yournamesmojo.com
</VirtualHost>
```

Once the lines have been added and Apache restarted, the site can be checked by typing *https://yournamesmojo.com/* (note that it is https at the beginning to denote SSL) in the address bar. A Security Alert dialog should appear as in Figure 3.26.

FIGURE 3.26   Security Alert.

This is a normal situation. A test certificate was used that was not issued by a standard CA. Clicking View Certificate will open the Certificate as shown in Figure 3.27.

Notice that the certificate is both Issued to and Issued by *ericsmojo.com*. This shows the viewer that it matches the current domain. If Install Certificate is clicked, the alert will no longer appear.

FIGURE 3.27 The Test Certificate viewed by a user.

If OK is clicked in the Certificate window followed by clicking Yes on the Security Alert, the page will load (see Figure 3.28).

The most important part of this window is the padlock that appears in the status bar. If the status bar is not visible, click View | Status Bar. The lock tells users that communication will be secure.

While it is a good idea to go ahead and purchase a certificate from an issuing authority such as VeriSign®, the test certificate will work just as well. It is encrypting the data at a very high rate, which should work well for small Web sites.

The combination of SSL and .htaccess files discussed earlier in this chapter can be very effective when securing directories. Basic authentication can even be used successfully since all encryption is being handled by SSL and the threat of protocol analyzers capturing the information is overcome.

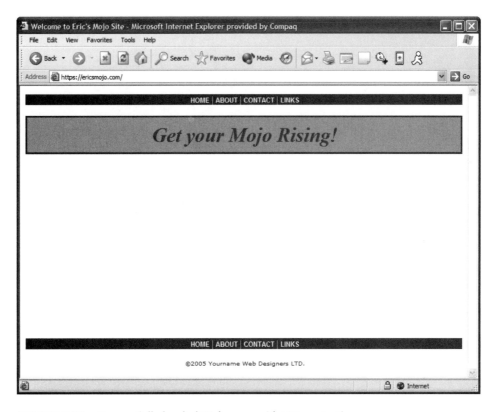

FIGURE 3.28 Successfully loaded Web page with SSL protection.

SUMMARY

This concludes basic configuration of Apache HTTP Server. Much can be done with Apache, and this chapter merely skimmed the surface. Our primary purpose here was to get the Web server up and running.

There are entire texts dedicated to Apache specifically. One of these should be purchased as a reference if Apache is being installed as a production Web server. In the meantime, there is always *http://httpd.apache.org/docs-project/* for the latest and greatest documentation, or *http://localhost/manual/* installed by default.

Now it is time to start installing programs that allow server-side scripting, so let's move on to Chapter 4, "Installing and Exploring Perl."

4

Installing and Exploring Perl

In This Chapter

- ▨ The History of Perl
- ▨ Installing ActiveState ActivePerl
- ▨ Testing the Installation
- ▨ Exploring Perl
- ▨ Summary

THE HISTORY OF PERL

Larry Wall, a Unix programmer, created Perl in 1986. He was trying to produce some reports from a collection of files for a bug reporting system, and the programming language he was using failed. He responded by writing a language he could use for this type of activity and others. This was the first version of Perl. It wasn't designed for the Web.

Perl stands for either the *Practical Extraction and Report Language* or the *Pathetically Eclectic Rubbish Lister*. Larry Wall endorses both names. Today, Perl is a full-featured programming language that can be used for both front- and back-end programming jobs.

Larry Wall's description of the language written in the original Perl 1 manual can be found at *www.perl.com/doc/FAQs/FAQ/oldfaq-html/Q1.1.html*.

INSTALLING ACTIVESTATE ACTIVEPERL

The most popular form of Perl used by Windows is ActivePerl created by Active-State. Within their distribution are the perl.exe and the Perl Package Manager. The Perl Package Manager (called Programmer Package Manager by ActiveState) enables easy downloading and installation of extra modules to enhance the program.

To install ActiveState Perl:

ON THE CD

1. For installation, ActiveState ActivePerl can be found on the companion CD-ROM in software\Perl or online at *www.activestate.com/*.
2. Click Next to start the installation as shown in Figure 4.1.

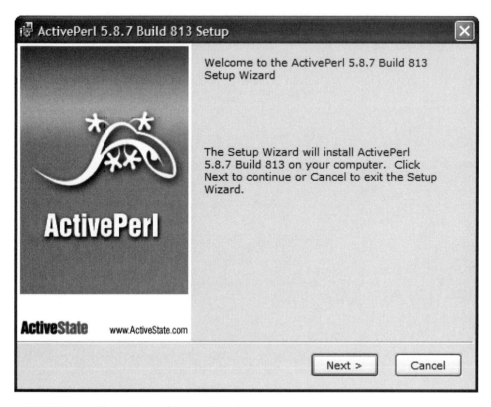

FIGURE 4.1   The ActivePerl Setup Wizard screen.

3. The License Agreement screen will appear as shown in Figure 4.2. Accept and click Next to continue.
4. The Custom Setup screen will be loaded as shown in Figure 4.3. On this screen, click Browse to change the file path.
5. The Change Current Destination Folder screen will appear as seen in Figure 4.4. Click on the top right button (Folder icon) to create a new folder. Name this folder usr, select it for the installation destination as shown in Figure 4.5, and click Next. The reason for doing this is to imitate the standard Unix path. That way, all Perl scripts will be pointing to the same path if they are moved to a Unix/Linux server later. This is especially helpful if the current computer is a development machine.

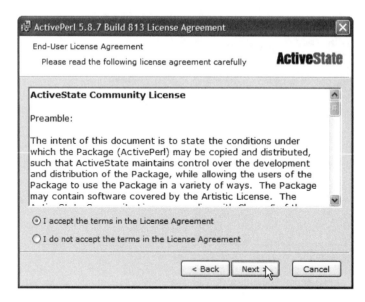

FIGURE 4.2 The ActiveState License Agreement screen.

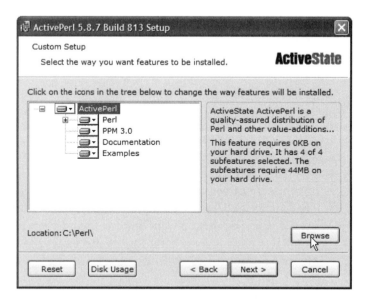

FIGURE 4.3 ActiveState ActivePerl Custom Setup screen.

6. More Setup options will appear as shown in Figure 4.6. These should remain checked, and add flexibility to the installation. Perl can be used for

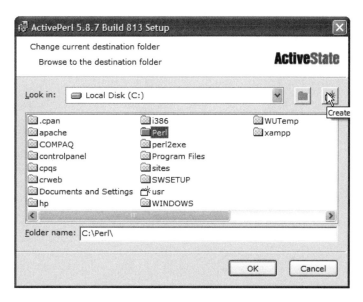

FIGURE 4.4   Change Current Destination Folder.

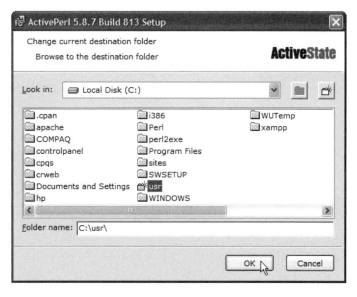

FIGURE 4.5   Changing the destination folder.

performing system tasks, which is why it was initially created. By adding
Perl to the PATH environmental variable, Perl can be run by simply typing

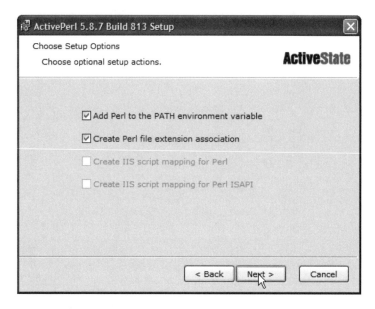

FIGURE 4.6   Setup options.

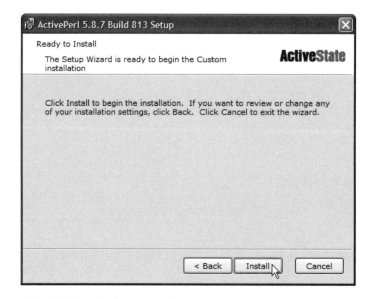

FIGURE 4.7   Ready to Install screen.

Perl, no matter what the current location is in the computer. By also creating a file extension association, any file with a.pl extension will automatically be opened by perl.exe.

7. Now that all of the options have been selected, click Install on the screen that appears next, shown in Figure 4.7.
8. Figure 4.8 shows ActiveState ActivePerl being installed. It can take a few minutes because the files are heavily compressed.
9. When the installation is complete and the screen shown in Figure 4.9 appears, uncheck Display the release notes and click Finish.

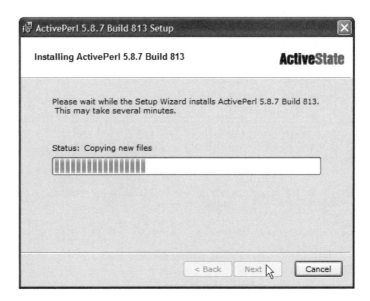

FIGURE 4.8 ActiveState installation progress.

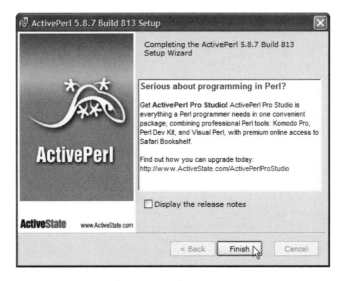

FIGURE 4.9 Installation complete.

TESTING THE INSTALLATION

Now that ActiveState ActivePerl has been installed, it needs to be tested. This is accomplished easily by changing one line in the Apache `httpd.conf` file. The following steps prepare the Apache HTTP server for Perl and test the installation:

1. Within the Apache `httpd.conf` file, find the line: `#AddHandler cgi-script .cgi`. Uncomment the line and add `.pl` to the end. The line should now be `AddHandler cgi-script .cgi .pl`.
2. The `printenv.pl` file is a sample script that prints out the environmental variables collected by the server when the client connects.
3. Modify the first line `#!c:/perl/bin/Perl.exe` to `#!/usr/bin/perl`. This needs to be done because Perl has been installed in a path to mirror Unix/Linux. The C: has been removed because Unix/Linux don't name their hard disks in that manner, and "/" literally means *root*. As long as the

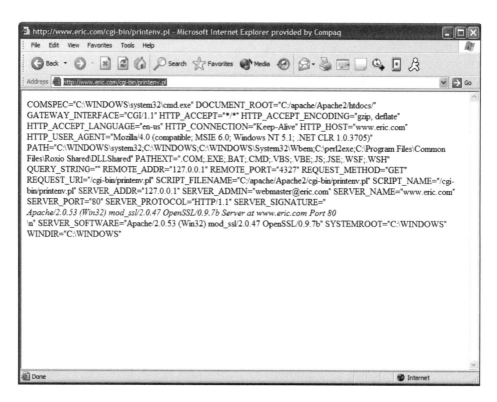

FIGURE 4.10 Environmental variables.

installation is on the same drive as the Apache HTTP Server, only "/" is needed on Windows. The `.exe` extension has been removed because it is not necessary for Windows to run the file. Unix and Linux do not use `.exe` for executable files. As the line stands modified, it is a perfect match for either operating system.

4. Now, modify the line print "Content-type: text/plain\n\n"; to read print "Content-type: text/html\n\n";. This is so the file will display as a Web page in a browser. If the line is not changed, the browser will attempt to download the file instead of displaying it as desired.

5. Type in the following path in a browser to test the configuration—http://localhost/cgi-bin/printenv.pl/. Figure 4.10 should appear. This is a printout of the Environmental variables hash. This is a collection of information about the server and the end-user computer to assist the programmer.

EXPLORING PERL

Perl is an interpreted language, meaning that there is an executable program called an *interpreter* that will run any of the scripts written. The interpreter also handles all memory management. A compiled language, on the other hand, is written and bundled into a self-contained executable that will run on any compatible system. Applications such as Microsoft Word are compiled programs.

An interpreted program will not run without an interpreter installed on a computer, which is why we had to install ActiveState ActivePerl.

While Perl is an interpreted language, it can be compiled with tools such as Perl2Exe found at www.indigostar.com/perl2exe.htm.

The Shebang, Switches, and Content-Type Line

When writing a program for Perl, the first line of any file is often called the *shebang* (#!), rumored to be short for *sharp-bang*. The #! is followed by the path to the Perl interpreter. At the end of the line, switches can often be found. Two of the most popular are -w for Warning Mode and -T (it must be capitalized) for Taint Mode.

Warning mode warns of the use of poor syntax and helps programmers clean code. It should be used while developing a script, but should be removed if on a production server. There is no reason to give users warnings about what went wrong with a script; doing so will weaken the security on a site.

Taint mode is a paranoid state. It treats all user data as if it is tainted and will not use it unless specifically referenced. This is very good because malicious users on the Internet may drop a line of code instead of what is requested into a form field, forcing a server to perform an undesirable activity. If the data is treated as tainted, the server will ignore any instructions.

The other line that every Perl script on the Web should always have is `print` "`Content-type: text/html\n\n`";. This line tells the browser that the content is in fact a Web page. As stated earlier, if it is not included, the browser will try to download the file instead of displaying the results.

Literals and Scalar Variables

When working with data in Perl, anything that is explicitly written is known as a *literal*. For example, `print "Hello World!";` contains the literal `"Hello World!"` because it is explicitly written. It is not set to change. That is where a variable comes into effect. If the script were modified to `$greeting = "Hello World!"; print $greeting;`, the result will not always be `"Hello World!"`; it will be whatever string literal (yes, the value of a variable is a literal) is contained within `$greeting`.

Perl breaks its variables into three different categories: scalars, arrays, and hashes. Scalar variables contain one piece of data, which is usually a string or number. A string is a combination of characters placed within quotation marks upon declaration. Numbers are whole, floating-point integers, or scientific notation. Examples are as follows:

```
$firstname = "Eric"; #this is a string
$address = "123 Main Street"; #another string
$phone = "757-555-1212"; #this is still a string because of the dashes
$year = 2005; #number - notice the lack of quotation marks
$distance = 1.43E+13; #number written in scientific notation
```

The # sign seen in the examples is the single-line comment symbol used in Perl. A comment is something that is placed in for informational purposes for programmers, but is not to be run by the interpreter.

All scalar variables start with a $ and can be named with any combination of letters, underscores, and numbers as long as a number is not the first digit. Perl is case-sensitive, so $Name and $name are two different variables.

Perl allows for declaration and assignment of variables to occur at the same time. This can be as simple as $variablename = value; because Perl is a loosely typed language. However, it is a good idea to add the command use strict; to the script after the shebang and switches. Doing so forces declaration of variables using the my keyword before their usage later, as in my $variablename = value;. It also will not allow a variable to determine its own scope (we'll explore variable scope later). Another option is a mass declaration like my ($firstname, $lastname, $address). The use strict declaration and my keyword will be used throughout this chapter. Every Perl script should begin as follows (the -w will be taken out when published):

```
#!/user/bin —w —T
use strict;
print "Content-type: text/html\n\n";
```

Print Statements and Quotation Marks

The most common means of output in Perl is print statements. The following is the basic "Hello World" script creating the document shown in Figure 4.11:

```
#!/user/bin —w —T
use strict;
print "Content-type: text/html\n\n";
print "<h1>Hello World!</h1>";
```

At its most basic level, the print statement will print out a literal between the quotation marks as seen in the Hello World statement. The <h1> HTML tags will work as intended because of the Content-type statement. Perl starts to show its power in how it handles quotation marks and variables. Observe the following code and the results in Figure 4.12:

```
#!/user/bin —w —T
use strict;
print "Content-type: text/html\n\n";

my $name = "Eric";

print "<h1>Hello $name!</h1>";
```

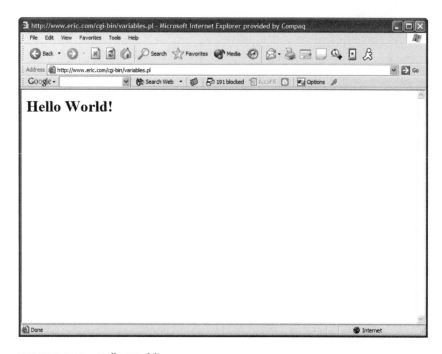

FIGURE 4.11 Hello World!

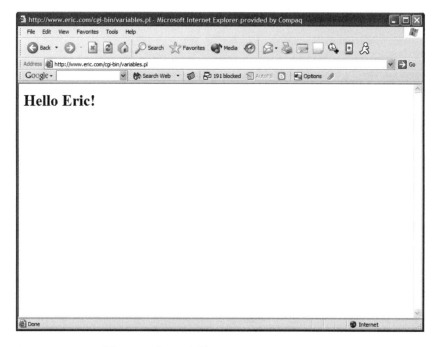

FIGURE 4.12 Adding a scalar variable.

In this version, a scalar variable is being used, so the document is now greeting the name stored in the variable. The variable is placed within the quotation marks because Perl interpolates data between double quotes before outputting. This is a handy alternative to other languages such as JavaScript, which would require the following for the same results:

```
document.write("<h1>Hello" + name + "!</h1>;.
```

This can quickly grow convoluted with all of the quotation marks needed.

What if a quote or an actual dollar sign is needed in the output? The issue must be addressed. For example, the statement `print "And Hamlet said "To be or not to be…""`; will fail. Once the quotation mark before the word `To` is read, the Perl interpreter will think that is the end of the statement and break as soon as it sees the words following since they are not keywords or functions in the language.

To add quotation marks or dollar signs within a print statement, there are a few solutions. These are explored in the following code and in Figure 4.13.

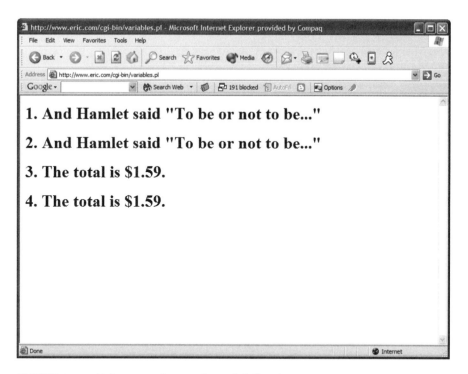

FIGURE 4.13   Using quotation marks and dollar signs.

```
#!/user/bin -w -T
use strict;
print "Content-type: text/html\n\n";

print "1. And Hamlet said \"To be or not to be…\"";
print '2. And Hamlet said "To be or not to be…"';

print "3. The total is \$1.59.";
print '4. The total is $1.59.';
```

As can be seen in Figure 4.13, all the methods achieved the desired results. In numbers 1 and 3, success was achieved by *escaping* the troublesome characters. When a character has an escape character in front of it, it is simply printed as is with no further interpolation. In numbers 2 and 4, the same result was achieved by using single quotation marks. Single quotation marks in Perl mean that data is to be output *without* interpolation. The problem with this method is that when data needs to be interpolated, it will be output literally as is. For example, look at the following script and its results in Figure 4.14:

```
#!/user/bin -w -T
use strict;
print "Content-type: text/html\n\n";

my $car = "Mazda Miata";
my $color = "blue";
my $price = 2.30;
my $tank = 11.9;
my $total = $price * $tank;

print "<h1>My $color $car costs \$$total to fill at \$$price a
gallon.</h1>";
print '<h1>My $color $car costs $$total to fill at $$price a
gallon.</h1>';
```

As shown in Figure 4.14, using single quotation marks as the only means of escaping can cause issues. The first sentence used the backslash to escape and everything came out fine. The second sentence used single quotes and does not look right.

Fortunately, Perl has other solutions available, two of which are the functions q() and qq(). The first of these, q(), quotes a string without interpolation, and qq() quotes a string with interpolation. The following code will result in Figure 4.15:

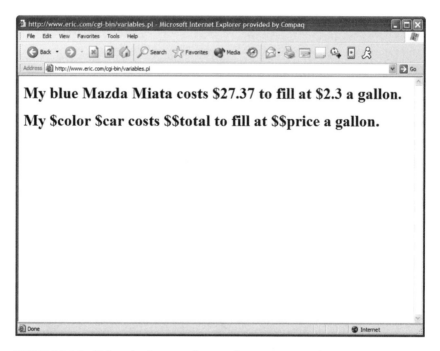

FIGURE 4.14   Using single quotation marks as a means of escape.

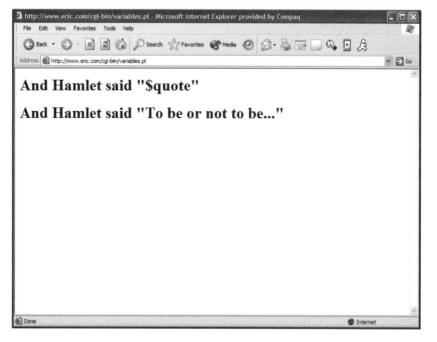

FIGURE 4.15   Using the q() and qq() functions.

```
#!/user/bin —w —T
use strict;
print "Content-type: text/html\n\n";

my $quote = "To be or not to be...";

print q(And Hamlet said "$quote");
print qq(And Hamlet said "$quote");
```

Checking Syntax

Since the scripts will be growing in complexity, it is a good idea to explore the Perl syntax checking function, or `perl -c` *filename*. Whenever there is a problem with a script that causes a failure, users will see the dreaded Internal Server Error screen shown in Figure 4.16.

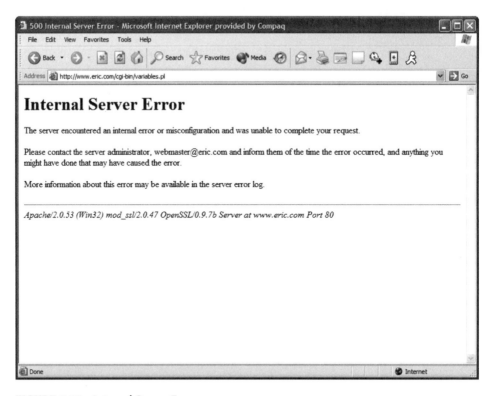

FIGURE 4.16   Internal Server Error screen.

If this screen should appear, any script can be checked with the Perl interpreter. A command prompt needs to be opened by clicking on Start | Run and typing `cmd` for Windows 2000/XP or `command` for Windows 9X/Me. Next, type `cd c:\apache2\cgi-bin\`. Since ActivePerl was installed with the PATH option selected, Perl can be accessed from anywhere. While in the directory, typing `perl -c filename` (`-c` is the switch that tells it to check) will run the interpreter and check the syntax as shown in Figure 4.17.

Whenever checking syntax with `perl -c`, *the* `-T` *(taint) switch should be removed from the shebang within the script first. Otherwise, it may fail.*

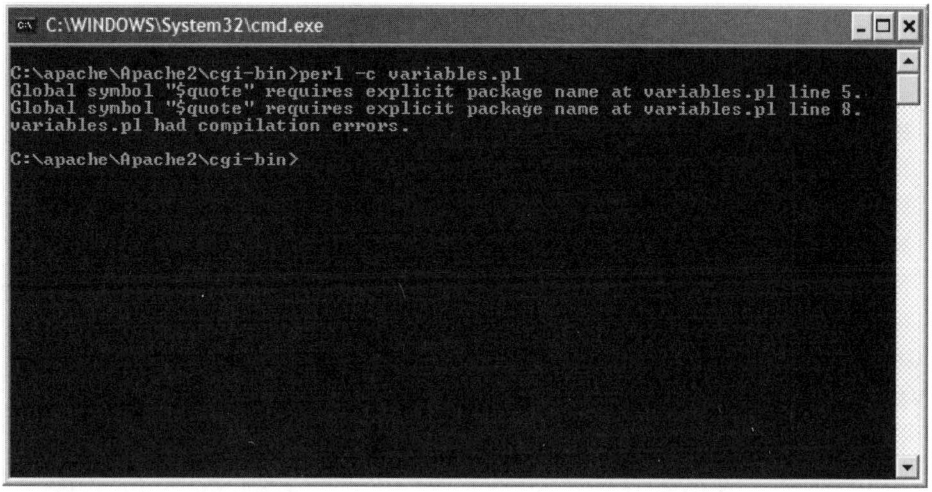

```
C:\WINDOWS\System32\cmd.exe                                          _ □ ✕

C:\apache\Apache2\cgi-bin>perl -c variables.pl
Global symbol "$quote" requires explicit package name at variables.pl line 5.
Global symbol "$quote" requires explicit package name at variables.pl line 8.
variables.pl had compilation errors.

C:\apache\Apache2\cgi-bin>
```

FIGURE 4.17 Perl syntax check.

Another option available is to check the Apache log - `c:\apache2\logs\error` as shown in Figure 4.18.

Operators

Some of the most important tools to work with in a programming language are operators. They are especially important in Perl because they manipulate data when

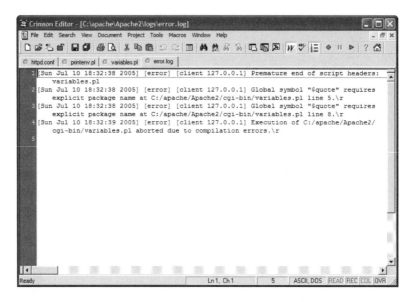

FIGURE 4.18 The Apache HTTP Server error log.

used, and help to dictate the actual data type. In Perl, it doesn't really matter how the data is declared in a variable; its type is determined by how the programmer uses it.

For example, a script could say something like $x = "1"; my $y = "2";. In this case, both $x and $y are string variables because of the quotation marks. However, if they are used mathematically like $x+$y, the result will be 2 because an arithmetical operator was applied. Since that will only work on numbers, Perl converts their type to a number and uses them accordingly.

This is an incredibly handy feature. In JavaScript, for example, the + is the addition arithmetical operator, and the concatenation operator. Concatenation is the process of appending one string to another. The same script in JavaScript would result in 11 because the concatenation operator has higher operator precedence.

Operator precedence is the process that determines what expressions will be performed in what order. A couple of issues that arise with operator precedence can be seen in the following code and Figure 4.19:

```perl
#!/usr/bin/perl

use strict;

print "Content-type: text/html; charset=iso-8859-1\n\n";

print qq(<html><head><title>Operator Precedence Examples</title><style
type="text/css">h3{margin: 0ex 0ex .5ex 0ex;}</style></head><body>);
```

```perl
my $quote = "To be or not to be...";

my $x = 10;

my $y = $x++;

print "<h3>\$x = 10;</h3>";

print "<h3>\$y = \$x++; <em>#";

print "\$x has the value of $x, and \$y has the value of
$y.</em></h3><br /><br />";

$x = 10;

$y = ++$x;

print "<h3>\$x = 10;</h3>";

print "<h3>\$y = ++\$x; <em>#";

print "\$x has the value of $x, and \$y has the value of
$y.</em></h3><br /><br />";

$x = 1; $y = 2; my $z = 3;

print q(<h3>$x = 1; $y = 2; my $z = 3;</h3>);

print q(<h3>my $result = $x+$y*$z;</h3>);

my $result = $x+$y*$z;

print qq(<h3>\$result has the value of $result</h3><br />);

$x = 1; $y = 2; my $z = 3;

print q(<h3>$x = 1; $y = 2; my $z = 3;</h3>);

print q(<h3>my $result = ($x+$y)*$z;</h3>);

my $result = ($x+$y)*$z;

print qq(<h3>\$result has the value of $result</h3>);

print qq(</body></html>);
```

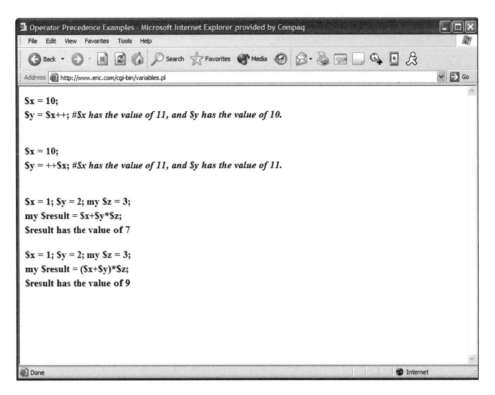

FIGURE 4.19   Operator precedence issues.

The code that created Figure 4.19 explored two of the common issues that may arise with operator precedence. The first is the issue of pre-fix and post-fix with incrementing or decrementing. Essentially, if an increment or decrement operator is used during an assignment, close attention must be paid to whether it is pre-fix (in front of) or post-fix (after). If the increment/decrement operator is pre-fix, it will increment the operand it is attached to, and then assign the results to the variable on the left of the assignment operator (=).

If it is a post-fix operator, the value will be assigned *before* the increment/decrement occurs. This is an important distinction.

The second issued explored is commonly taught as the mnemonic *My Dear Aunt Sally* (Multiplication and Division then Addition and Subtraction) in Algebra classes. This is to express the point that multiplication and division have a higher precedence than addition or subtraction. If there is a tie, the leftmost operation is performed first. To override precedence, use parentheses; the expression within parentheses will take place first. Using parentheses is a handy way to clarify expressions in code if there is any question.

Collecting User Input with CGI.pm

One of the most common purposes of server-side scripting is to collect user data, which is where the CGI.pm Perl module comes in. CGI.pm was created by Lincoln Stein and proved so popular that it has been distributed with Perl in every version since 5.004. It offers a very simple way to collect and manipulate information from users. The following code creates a basic HTML form to collect user data and will result in the page shown in Figure 4.20:

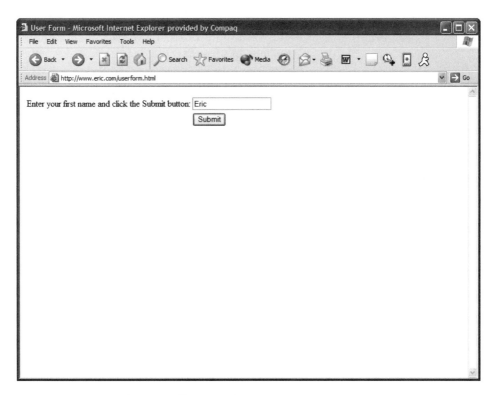

FIGURE 4.20   Basic form to collect user data.

```
<html>
<head>
    <title>User Form</title>
</head>
<body>
    <form action="cgi-bin/userform.pl" method="post">
    <table>
        <tr><td>Enter your first name and click the Submit
button:</td><td><input type="text" name="firstname"
id="firstname"/></td></tr>
        <tr><td></td><td><input type="submit" value="Submit"
/></td></tr>
    </table>
    </form>
</body>
</html>
```

The HTML acts as one-half of the process. The second half is the Perl script shown here with results displayed in Figure 4.21.

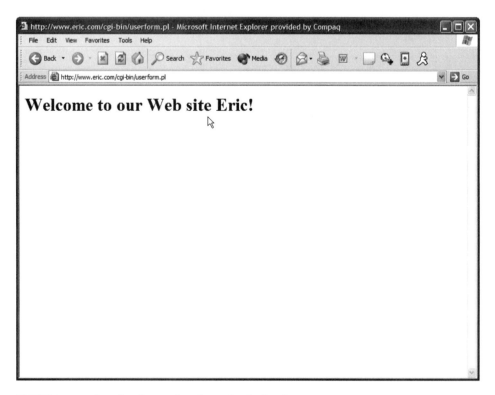

FIGURE 4.21   Results of user data from the Perl script.

```
#!/usr/bin/perl
use strict;
use CGI ':standard';
print "Content-type: text/html; charset=iso-8859-1\n\n";

my $firstname = param("firstname");

print "<h1>Welcome to our Web site $firstname!</h1>";
```

The elegance of the CGI.pm module is in the way it gathers user data. Whenever forms send data over, they send it in the fields as variables of the same name, known as *form variables*. The param("*fieldname*") function extrapolates data from the fields when their name is provided as an argument. This allows the Web developer to look for specific fields and respond only to those.

Using Arrays

In addition to scalar variables, which hold a single piece of data, Perl offers two other types of data containers, arrays and hashes, which hold more than one container of data. An array is a collection of values that are indexed by numbers starting with 0. Its name begins with an @ symbol as in @array.

The most common way to declare an array and assign values in one shot is – my @arrayname = ("item1",2,"item3");. Notice that if a value is a string, it needs quotation marks, but a number does not. To access a value in the array, the arrayname should be written as a scalar with the index number in brackets; for example, - $arrayname[2] will return item3.

The same principle can be used to modify a value in an array. The line $arrayname[1] = "item2"; will change the 2 in the array to item2. Items can also be added to an array by typing a new index number and assigning a value; for example, $arrayname[4] = "item5"; will add item5 to @arrayname at the index of 4. Keep in mind that a value will be placed at whatever index number is declared even if it is out of sequence. The following script creates and accesses arrays with the results shown in Figure 4.22:

```
#!/usr/bin/perl

use strict;

use CGI ':standard';
```

```perl
print "Content-type: text/html; charset=iso-8859-1\n\n";

my @time = localtime;

my @days = qw(Sunday Monday Tuesday Wednesday Thursday Friday
Saturday);

my @month = qw(January February March April May June July August
September October November December);

my $year = $time[5]+1900;

print "<h1>Today is $days[$time[6]], $month[$time[4]] $time[3],
$year</h1>";
```

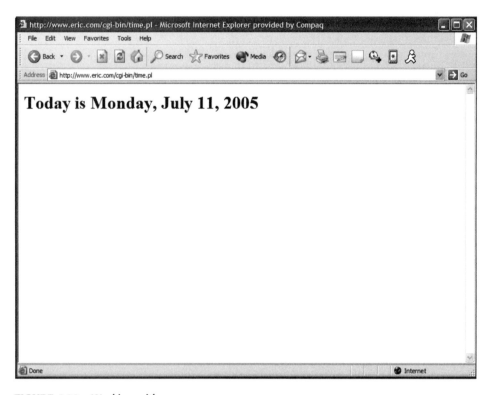

FIGURE 4.22   Working with arrays.

The line of code my @time = localtime; creates a new array by using the function localtime. This function will return a nine-part array consisting of the values - second, minute, hour, month, day, month, year, weekday, year day, and is dst - in order when it is assigned to an array. It is important to note that both month and day begin with an index of 0. In addition, year returns the number of years since 1900, so 110 will be returned for 2010.

The next two lines of code create arrays to accommodate the day and month issues and supply more meaningful data. Notice the use of the qw() function that automatically uses spaces as separations for values and will add quotation marks when processing. This is a very convenient shortcut when creating an array with all one-word values because the proper way to declare and assign values to an array in one shot requires commas for every value and quotation marks for every string. The qw() function saves a good deal of time.

The next line creates the scalar variable $year with the value of $time[5]+1900. This accesses the 6th index of $time and adds 1900 so the year will look normal.

The last line outputs the data for the user. $days[$time[6]] uses the number stored in the day index of $time to act as an index for a value in the newly created @days array. This causes an actual day name to show up as shown in Figure 4.22. $month[$time[4]] accomplishes the same task, only with a month name. The rest of the line simply accesses direct values.

Arrays also have some built-in functions to make manipulation easier. Some of these include the following based on the array @fruit = qw(apples oranges bananas strawberries grapes):

delete(): Deletes the value in a numeric array, but not the index. delete($fruit[1]); will remove the value oranges, but will still leave the space open so the array will become ("apples","","bananas","strawberries", "grapes").

join(separator, array): Returns a string with all values in the array separated by specified character. For example, print join(" | ",@fruit); will return apples | oranges | bananas | strawberries | grapes, and print join("*", @fruit); will return apples*oranges*bananas*strawberries*grapes.

pop(): Returns the last item from an array and shrinks the array by one. $pick = pop(@fruit); would return grapes, and cause @fruit to shrink to ("apples","oranges","bananas","strawberries").

push(): This function is used to add a value to the end of an array. If push(@fruits,"huckleberries"); is used, the array will be ("apples","oranges","bananas","strawberries","grapes","huckleberries").

reverse(): Reverses the order of the array. When the values are assigned to another array, the index is reversed. When assigned to a scalar variable the contents are turned into a long string and the letters are reversed.

shift(): Removes the first item from an array and shrinks it by one.

sort(): Places the contents in an array in alphabetical order. You can find more advanced options at *http://perldoc.perl.org/functions/sort.html*.

split(delimiter,string): Used to break a string into parts that can be assigned to an array. For example, my $list = "Eric, Leslie, Larry, Kitty, Jerry"; my @names = split(", ",$list); will create the five value array @names.

unshift(): The opposite of shift(). Instead of removing a value from the beginning of the list, it adds a value.

Be careful when using pop() *and* shift() *because they physically change the contents of an array. If the intention is to only return values from an array, not to change it physically, access the index directly by number.*

Form Field Arrays

Often, users may need to submit forms that will send more than one value from a field. Two of the most commonly used are the checkbox and select (with the multiple attribute) fields. Here is an example of HTML that will pass multiple values:

```
How did you hear about us? <input type="checkbox" name="referred"
id="referred" value="Internet" />Internet<input type="checkbox"
name="referred" id="referred" value="Internet" />Television <input
type="checkbox" name="referred" id="referred" value="Internet" />Radio
<input type="checkbox" name="referred" id="referred" value="Internet"
/>Newspaper
```

The only code necessary to assign the form information to an array is my @referral = param("referral");. That will create a new array with all of the values assigned to it from the submitted form.

Using Hashes

A hash is an associative array with its containers referenced by name, and all hash names begin with a percent sign; for example, %hash. Hashes are created in one of the following manners:

```
my %book =  (("Title", "Using Open Source Web Solutions with Windows"),
            ("Author", "Eric Hunley"),
            ("Publisher", "Charles River Media"),
            ("ISBN", 1584503653));

my %book= (Title=> "Using Open Source Web Solutions with Windows",
      Author=> "Eric Hunley",
      Publisher=> "Charles River Media"
ISBN=> 1584503653);
```

All that is needed to create hashes are *keys* and *values* separated by commas, which in turn are separated from one another by commas. That is where it can get confusing. `%hashname = "key","value","key","value","key","value";` is a perfectly legitimate way to create a hash, but it can be difficult to read and understand. That is why the first example has each pair in parentheses and on separate lines. The second method shown is the most popular because it is easier to read and establish the relationship between the pairs, and keys don't have to be put within quotation marks.

It is simple to add single values to hashes. The hash in question has to be written with the scalar flag at the front with the new key within curly braces, as in `$hashname{"key"} = value;`. Values are accessed in a similar manner; for example, - `$hashname{"key"}`.

Conditionals and Loops

One of the most important aspects of any programming language is the ability to make decisions, which is where conditionals and loops come into the picture. The basic conditional is "when *this* happens, do *that*," or *if… then…* Loops are nothing more than specialized conditionals.

The `if/else` is the lowest level conditional available. The following code creates a script that responds to a single value form submitted by a user and should be saved as `userform.pl`:

```
#!/usr/bin/perl
use strict;
use CGI ':standard';
print "Content-type: text/html; charset=iso-8859-1\n\n";

my $name = param("name");
```

```
if (lc($name) ne "eric"){
    print "<h1>Welcome to the site $name.</h1>";
}else {
    print "<h1>Welcome back Eric! </h1>";
}
```

The code is really quite simple. First, $name is created from the submitted form. Next, an if conditional is created. Within the argument of the conditional, $name is placed within the lc() function. This is to explore the value of the variable in a lowercase format because there is no telling how the user may have entered the text into the field. Other options available are uc() for uppercase, and ucfirst(), which capitalizes only the first letter of a string.

Next, the comparison operator can be found. In this case, it is ne or *not equal*. Checking for a negative may seem a bit odd, but there is a good reason for it. The odds are higher that the person accessing the site will not be "Eric," so the most likely match should be checked first. This makes programs run faster. Here is a basic list of comparison operators:

eq (string) Equal: Checks that the value on the left is the same as the value on the right of the comparison operators.

ne (string) Not Equal: Checks that the value on the left or the right is not equal to the other value.

gt (string) Greater Than: Checks if the value on the left is greater than the one on the right.

ge (string) Greater Than or Equal To: Checks if the value on the left is greater than or equal to the one on the right.

lt (string) Less Than: Checks if the value on the left is less than the one on the right.

le (string) Less Than or Equal To: Checks if the value on the left is less than or equal to the one on the right.

== (number) Equal: Checks that the value on the left is the same as the value on the right of the comparison operators.

!= (number) Not Equal: Checks that the value on the left or the right is not equal to the other value.

> (number) Greater Than: Checks if the value on the left is greater than the one on the right.

>= (number) Greater Than or Equal To: Checks if the value on the left is greater than or equal to the one on the right.

< (number) **Less Than**: Checks if the value on the left is less than the one on the right.

<= (number) **Less Than or Equal To**: Checks if the value on the left is less than or equal to the one on the right.

To complete the example, the following HTML code needs to be used and saved as userform.html:

```
<html>
<head>
    <title>User Form</title>
</head>
<body>
    <form action="cgi-bin/userform.pl" method="post">
    <table>
          <tr><td>Enter your first name and click the Submit
button:</td><td><input type="text" name="firstname"
id="firstname"/></td></tr>
          <tr><td></td><td><input type="submit" value="Submit"
/></td></tr>
    </table>
    </form>
</body>
</html>
```

If more than one possibility is addressed, the if/elsif/else conditional is used. It uses a similar format as an if/else, but adds an elsif for any other possible condition such as the following:

```
#!/usr/bin/perl

use strict;

use CGI ':standard';

print "Content-type: text/html; charset=iso-8859-1\n\n";

my $name = param("name");

if (lc($name) eq "eric"){
    print "<h1>Welcome back Eric! </h1>";
```

```
}elsif(lc($name) eq "leslie") {
    print "<h1>Welcome back Leslie! </h1>";
}elsif(lc($name) eq "kitty") {
    print "<h1>Welcome back Kitty! </h1>";
}else
print "<h1>Welcome to the site $name.</h1>";
}
```

As can be seen by the previous code, another elsif is added for any extra known conditional. However, there can only be one if and else per conditional.

Another type of conditional is unless, the *false* conditional. While other conditionals check for truth (if x == y), unless returns true when a condition is *not* met. For example, if(lc(name ne "eric") { print "Welcome to the Website $name!";} could just as easily be unless(lc($name) eq "eric") {print "Welcome to the Web site $name!";} and can be substituted if it is not important to have a greeting for the user named Eric—thereby saving a line of code.

After getting a handle on conditionals, loops should be mastered. Loops are a specialized conditional that will keep repeating an action while a condition is met. The two most popular loops common to most programming languages including Perl are while and for.

The while loop continues as long as a condition is true. This can be very dangerous and needs to be used with consideration. A basic while loop is written as while(condition){ actions;}. The following is an example of a while loop in Perl that gets every key and value in a hash with the results shown in Figure 4.23:

```
#!/usr/bin/perl
use strict;
use CGI ':standard';
print "Content-type: text/html; charset=iso-8859-1\n\n";

my %book= (Title=> "Using Open Source Web Solutions with Windows",
    Author=> "Eric Hunley",
    ISBN=> 1584503653,
    Publisher=> "Charles River Media");

while(($key, $value) = each(%book)){
    print "<strong>$key</strong>: $value</strong><br />";
}
```

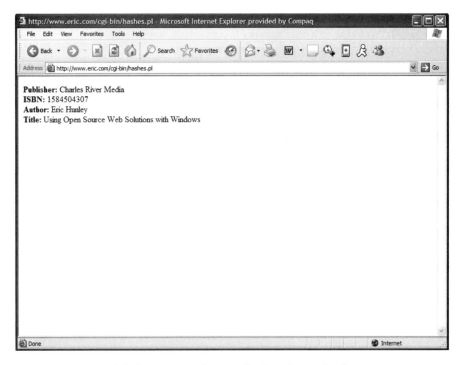

FIGURE 4.23   A while loop getting keys and values from a hash.

A `for` loop is known as the *counting loop*, and is specifically designed to run a set number of iterations. For example, the following `while` loop could be used as a countdown from 10 to 1:

```
my $x = 10;
while ($x>0){
    print "$x <br />";
    --$x;
}
```

The same task can be performed with a `for` loop:

```
for(my $x =10; $x>0;$x--){
    print "$x <br />";
}
```

The preceding uses fewer lines of code because all of the arguments and necessary counters are built in to the argument. The loop structure is for (counter; condition; iteration){actions;}. This specialized structure makes it very readable and effective for loops involving iterations.

Another type of for loop is the foreach. The foreach loop can be used to cycle through all of the values in an array, and for either keys or values in hashes. The following segments of code show how a foreach loop is written in each case:

```
@fruits =
("Apples","Oranges","Bananas","Peaches","Pears","Strawberries");
foreach (@fruits){
    print "<li>$_</li>";
}
print "</ul>";

%book = (Author => "Eric Hunley",
    Title => "Using Open Source Web Solutions with Windows",
    ISBN => 1584504307,
    Publisher => "Charles River Media");
print "<ul>";

foreach (keys %book){
    print "<li>$_</li>";
}
print "</ul>";

foreach (values %book){
    print "<li>$_</li>";
}
print "</ul>";
```

The first example shows a foreach loop that will generate all values from the @fruits array in an unordered list. The second loop generates the keys of the %book hash, while the third displays the values in an unordered list.

Like conditionals, Perl offers a negative loop known as until. Instead of the typical while or for loops, which will keep going as long as a condition is true, the until will keep going *until* a condition is true. The following demonstrates an until using a countdown:

```
my $count= 100;
until($count==0){
    print "$count... <br />";
}
```

This will count down from 100 and print each of the numbers.

Another thing to consider when working with loops is how to guarantee at least one iteration. If a condition is met when entering a loop, it will immediately stop the loop. The do, while loop is structured in such a manner that the do section is performed before the while checks the condition. The structure is as follows:

```
do {
actions;
}while (condition){
    actions;
}
```

Perl also allows a similar do, until, which is written the same way:

```
do {
actions;
}until (condition){
    actions;
}
```

The last item we'll look at regarding loops is exiting a loop early. There are two very popular options for accomplishing this task: last and next. The first, last, is used to leave the loop prematurely if a specified condition is met, and is usually written as follows:

```
while(condition){
    if(condition){
            last;
    }
    actions;
}
```

The important consideration is order. If the actions are to be performed no matter what, they should be written prior to the if conditional, because when the condition is met, the loop is ended. If the actions should not occur if the condition is met, the block should be written like the example.

The second option for leaving a loop if a condition is met is next, which allows an exit from a loop, but only for the current iteration. The actions will be skipped and the loop re-entered. For example, the following loop prints all even numbers between 1 and 100 (notice the use of the modulus):

```
for(my $i = 1;$i<=100;$i++){
    if(($i%2) == 0){
            print "$i, ";
}else{
            next;
}
}
```

Scope

Now that we've looked at conditionals and loops, it is time to explore scope, one of the concepts in programming that can be crucial to success. That is why the use of strict has been followed in this chapter. Consider the following script:

```
#!/usr/bin/perl
print "Content-type: text/html; charset=iso-8859-1\n\n";

$scope = "outside";

print "<p>$scope</p>";

if($scope){
    $scope = "inside";
    print "<p>$scope</p>";
}
print "<p>$scope</p>";
```

The script will return three lines reading outside, inside, and inside. This is because the $scope variable inside the function automatically overwrites the external with no declarations in place. Now, look at the following script:

```
#!/usr/bin/perl
use strict
print "Content-type: text/html; charset=iso-8859-1\n\n";
```

```perl
my $scope = "outside";

print "<p>$scope</p>";

if($scope){
    my $scope = "inside";
    print "<p>$scope</p>";
}
print "<p>$scope</p>";
```

When the code is run, the results will read outside, inside, and outside. This is because of the my keyword used inside the function. Because my was used, the value of $scope within the conditional is constrained to the conditional, making it local or lexical in scope. If it is desirable to modify the $scope variable from anywhere in the script, it should be declared with the keyword our, and can be written as follows:

```perl
#!/usr/bin/perl
use strict
print "Content-type: text/html; charset=iso-8859-1\n\n";

our $scope = "outside";

print "<p>$scope</p>";

if($scope){
    $scope = "inside";
    print "<p>$scope</p>";
}
print "<p>$scope</p>";
```

The script will result in outside, inside, and inside, but the intentions were very clear in the code. Improper use of the $scope variable can cause issues that are *very* difficult to track down.

Subroutines

Most programs refer to *subroutines* as *functions*, but Perl calls them *subroutines*. Essentially, subroutines are functions the programmer creates.

As a rule in programming, if an action is going to occur more than one time, a function (or in the case of Perl, a subroutine) should be written. The most basic type of subroutine is simply a list of actions that will be performed every time it is called. Here is an example:

```
hello; #subroutine call

sub hello{
    print "Hello World!";
} #subroutine creation
```

Notice that the subroutine was created after it was called. This is unusual in a programming language, but is standard practice within Perl because the interpreter reads the *entire* script before execution. In the example, the subroutine hello prints one line and is called by name. It can also be called with an ampersand in front of it, as in &hello, but is not required.

Subroutines can also have arguments passed to them, which is very important for the overall functionality of the language. Perl handles this in a unique way. Any arguments that are passed with the function call are added to the default array @_ and the values are accessed by $_[0], $_[1], and so on. The following example demonstrates the use of a subroutine that accepts arguments with the results shown in Figure 4.24.

```
#!/usr/bin/perl
use strict;
use CGI ':standard';
print "Content-type: text/html; charset=iso-8859-1\n\n";

my $fahr = 100;
my $cels = 25;

print "<p>$fahr&deg; F is equal to " . temp("c",$fahr) . "&deg;
C.</p>";
print "<p>$cels&deg; C is equal to " . temp("f",$cels) . "&deg;
F.</p>";

sub temp{
    if($_[0] eq "c"){
            return ($_[1]-32)*5/9;
    }else{
            return ($_[1]*9)/5+32;
    }
}
```

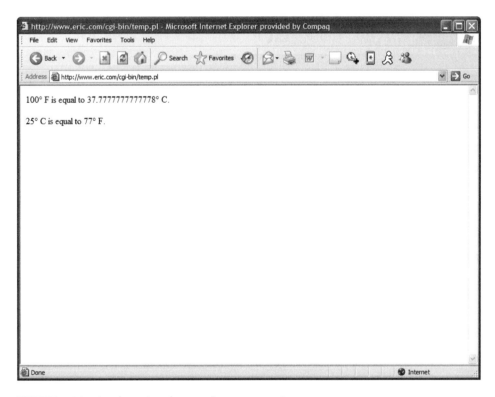

FIGURE 4.24   A subroutine that receives arguments.

The subroutine can be written more clearly as follows:

```perl
#!/usr/bin/perl
use strict;
use CGI ':standard';
print "Content-type: text/html; charset=iso-8859-1\n\n";

my $fahr = 100;
my $cels = 25;

print "<p>$fahr&deg; F is equal to " . temp("c",$fahr) . "&deg;
C.</p>";
print "<p>$cels&deg; C is equal to " . temp("f",$cels) . "&deg;
F.</p>";

sub temp{
    my ($type, $degrees) = @_;
```

```
if($type eq "c"){
        return ($degrees-32)*5/9;
}else{
        return ($degrees*9)/5+32;
}
}
```

The extra line `my ($type, $degrees) = @_;` assigns the values from the default argument array into clear variables. These variables will be disposed of when the function is complete because of the `my` keyword. By giving the values distinct variable names, the overall subroutine is much easier to read and understand.

SUMMARY

This concludes basic coverage of Perl. It is an immensely powerful language that was used early on for Web programming. We'll revisit Perl later in Chapter 9, "Communicating with MySQL." Its use on Web sites has been decreasing in recent years, as it has been outpaced by PHP, which ironically started out as a series of Perl scripts. We'll look at PHP next in Chapter 5, "Installing PHP."

5 Installing PHP

In This Chapter

- History of PHP
- Installing PHP
- PHP 5 and MYSQL
- Summary

In this chapter, we cover the three most popular installation methods of PHP on Microsoft Windows.

HISTORY OF PHP

Rasmus Lerdorf, who wanted to track visits to his online résumé, created PHP in 1994. It started out as a series of Perl scripts called Personal Home Page Tools, but he switched to C as more functionality was required. The language as written in C was originally titled PHP/FI (Personal Home Page/Forms Interpreter) and celebrated its tenth anniversary in June 2005.

As the language gained popularity, the core needed a re-write, so Zeev Suraski and Andi Gutmans created the Zend (a combination of their first names) engine. The Zend engine remains at the core of PHP to this day and is on version 2. PHP has evolved to have the recursive title of *PHP: Hypertext Preprocessor* and is on version 5 as of this writing. The full history can be found at *http://us2.php.net/history*. As of August 2005, according to Netcraft (*http://news.netcraft.com/*), PHP was on 22,267,442 domains and 1,291,738 IP Addresses.

PHP is a server-side, cross-platform, HTML-embedded scripting language. It runs on Web servers, enabling more security, and can connect to outside resources like databases and SMTP (Simple Mail Transfer Protocol) servers. It runs on several platforms, including Unix/Linux, Windows, Novell, and Macintosh, making it flexible for future development—if a client changes server platforms, PHP is likely available.

PHP is also an HTML embedded language. This is very important to developers because it adds to the ease of use. For example, as shown in the previous chapter, Perl is not an HTML-embedded language. The HTML code has to be output by Perl before being read by the Web server as shown here:

```
#!/usr/bin/perl —wT
use strict;

print "Content-type: text/html\n\n";
print q(<!DOCTYPE HTML PUBLIC "-//W3C//DTD HTML 4.01 Transitional//EN"
"http://www.w3.org/TR/1999/REC-html401-19991224/loose.dtd">);
print "<html><head><title>Hello World</title></head><body
bgcolor=\"#ffffff\">";
print "<h1>Hello World!</h1>";
print "</body></html>";
```

Every line of HTML code is written inside a `print` function because the HTML is output from Perl. This can add a good deal of overhead and may prove tedious to designers.

PHP is an embedded language that can live inside HTML, output HTML, or both. Here is the previous Hello World example written in PHP:

```
<!DOCTYPE HTML PUBLIC "-//W3C//DTD HTML 4.01 Transitional//EN"
        "http://www.w3.org/TR/1999/REC-html401-19991224/loose.dtd">
<html>
<head>
        <title>Hello World</title>
</head>
<body bgcolor="#ffffff">
    <?php
            print "<h1>Hello World!</h1>";
    ?>
</body>
</html>
```

Only the bolded lines contain PHP. PHP lives comfortably inside the HTML and can be sprinkled anywhere on the page between `<?php ?>`, making life easier for developers. Instead of worrying about how to output the final HTML, they only need to be concerned with the actual functions they wish to accomplish.

INSTALLING PHP

Apache 2 support for PHP is considered experimental. This issue makes the choice of what to use awkward, but for Windows, choose Apache 2 because of the development advances, and it should run just fine with PHP. See William Rowe's posting on the Apache project (NT Porting) at *http://www.php.net/manual/en/install. windows. apache2.php.*

There are two ways to install PHP—a CGI executable or a module. A CGI executable is similar to how Perl was installed in the previous chapter; anytime the program is needed, it will launch, process the file, and then close.

When PHP is installed as a module, it becomes an extension of Apache.exe and runs constantly, thereby resulting in a significant speed increase because you don't have to wait for the program to launch.

However, the downside is that if something goes wrong in PHP, it may well crash the entire Web server. Since the PHP module has been developed with a great deal of input and assistance from the Apache HTTP Server Project, it is fairly safe to run as a module. Instructions on both methods are provided in this chapter.

Perl can also be installed as a module on Unix/Linux, but is not recommended on Windows.

Installing PHP as a CGI Executable

ON THE CD

1. Shut down the Apache Service.
2. Copy the preferred PHP package (either php-5.0.4-Win32 or php-4.4.0. Win32) from the companion CD-ROM located in the PHP folder to C:\.
3. Rename the PHP package php.
4. Find the php.ini-dist and php.ini-recommended files in C:\php. Here, you have a choice. If the file is going to be used for a development or testing server, the php.ini-dist file should be renamed php.ini. If the server is going to be used in any form of production, the php.ini-recommended file should be renamed php.ini. The php.ini-recommended file has been configured with better security.
5. For the CGI Executable line, add one of the following lines to the Apache httpd.conf file:

   For PHP 4:
   ```
   ScriptAlias /php/ "c:/php/"
   AddType application/x-httpd-php .php
   Action application/x-httpd-php "/php/php.exe"
   ```

For PHP 5:
```
ScriptAlias /php/ "c:/php/"
AddType application/x-httpd-php .php
Action application/x-httpd-php "/php/php-cgi.exe"
```

6. Find the `DirectoryIndex` line in the Apache `httpd.conf` file and add `index.php` to the list. If PHP is going to be used frequently, it should be placed high on the list. If two default files exist in the same directory, whatever type is listed first in the `httpd.conf` will be served.
7. Restart the Apache Service.

Installing PHP as a Module

ON THE CD

1. Shut down the Apache Service.
2. Copy the preferred PHP package (either `php-5.0.4-Win32` or `php-4.4.0.Win32`) from the companion CD-ROM located in the PHP folder to C:\.
3. Rename the PHP package to `php`.
4. Modify the system path for Window NT/2000/XP:
5. Open the Control Panel and choose the System icon (in Windows XP, it is in the Performance and Maintenance Category view).
6. Within the System Properties screen, click the Advanced tab.
7. Next, click the Environment Variables button found near the bottom of the window.
8. Inside of the System variables pane, scroll until the Path line can be seen. Either double-click the line, or select it and click the Edit button.
9. Within the value, add ;C:\php to the end of what is currently written. Don't forget the semicolon preceding it.
10. Restart the computer.
11. Modify the system path for Windows 9X/Me:
12. Open the C:\autoexec.bat file with a text editor.
13. Modify the PATH line by adding ;C:\php (don't forget the leading semicolon) to the end of the line.
14. Restart the computer.

NOTE

Normally, sources recommend finding the file php4ts.dll for PHP 4, or php5ts.dll for PHP 5 and moving it to the C:\Windows directory. However, this is not the best way to go about adding support with this file. All versions of PHP, whether CGI

Executables or modules, need a php4ts.dll/php5ts.dll file, and PHP will look for it first in the current directory, then in the Web server directory, and last in any directory in the system path. That is why it is often recommended to put a copy of the file in the C:\Windows directory, which is on the system path. While this works, it is not a good idea because it involves hunting down files in directories not directly related to the Web server or previous PHP installation upon upgrade.

15. Find the `php.ini-dist` and `php.ini-recommended` files in C:\php. Here, a choice has to be made. If the file is going to be used for a development or testing server, the `php.ini-dist` file should be renamed `php.ini`. If the server is going to be used in any form of production, the `php.ini-recommended` file should be renamed `php.ini`. The `php.ini-recommended` file has been configured with better security.

16. Find the `LoadModule` section in the Apache `httpd.conf` file and add one of the following groups of lines at the end of the section:

    For PHP 4:
    ```
    LoadModule php4_module "c:/php/sapi/php4apache2.dll"
    AddType application/x-httpd-php .php
    PHPIniDir "C:/php/"
    ```

    For PHP 5:
    ```
    LoadModule php5_module "c:/php/php5apache2.dll"
    AddType application/x-httpd-php .php
    PHPIniDir "C:/php/"
    ```

17. Find the DirectoryIndex line in the Apache httpd.conf file and add index.php to the list, allowing a PHP document to be a default page. If PHP is going to be used frequently, it should be placed high on the list. If two default files like index.html and index.php exist in the same directory, whatever type is listed first in the httpd.conf will be served.

18. Restart the Apache Service.

To test the installation, type the following with a text editor:

```
<?php
        phpinfo();
?>
```

Save the file as `phpinfo.php` in the `htdocs` directory. Then, test it by typing `http://localhost/phpinfo.php` in the browser address bar. Figure 5.1 should appear.

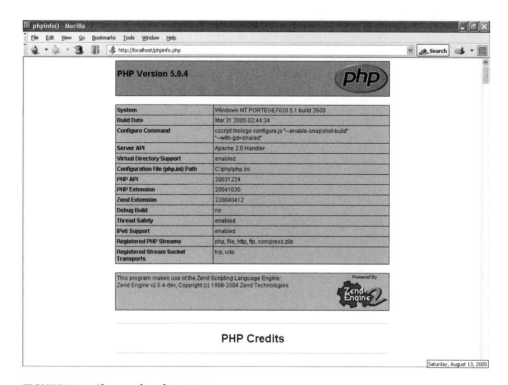

FIGURE 5.1   The results of phpinfo().

The `phpinfo()` function is a handy way to view a configuration. It lists all of the details of the operating system, loaded modules, and variables that have been passed to the script, among other things. The information can also be pared down by adding one of the following arguments to the function:

phpinfo(1) - `INFO_GENERAL`: The configuration line, `php.ini` location, build date, Web server, system, and more.

phpinfo(2) - `INFO_CREDITS`: Returns PHP credits for all the developers involved in the project. This information can also be pulled with the `phpcredits()` function.

phpinfo(4) - INFO_CONFIGURATION: Displays settings that have been made in the php.ini file. The ini_get() function returns information on these settings as well.

phpinfo(8) - INFO_MODULES: Returns loaded modules and settings. Can also use get_loaded_extensions().

phpinfo(16) - INFO_ENVIRONMENT: Environment Variable information that's also available in $_ENV.

phpinfo(32) - INFO_VARIABLES: Shows all predefined variables from EGPCS (Environment, GET, POST, Cookie, Server).

phpinfo(64) - INFO_LICENSE: PHP license information. See also the license FAQ.

phpinfo(-1) - INFO_ALL: Shows all of the above, and is the default value.

Some webmasters will to go into the php.ini file and set register_globals to on. This allows variables to be passed from forms easily, but adds some security concerns. This will be covered later in this chapter.

Installing PHP with Internet Information Services

If the machine that will be running PHP has Windows 2000 or 2003 Server installed, it is often a good idea to use Internet Information Services (IIS). It is built into the operating system and may function better.

While it is a good idea to use IIS with Windows 2000 or 2003 Server, the same does not apply to Windows 2000/XP Professional. IIS in both of these operating systems is limited to only 10 simultaneous connections and one virtual server. If the site will be serving an audience, Apache2 would be the appropriate choice for Windows operating systems other than Windows 2000 and 2003 Server.

To run PHP with IIS, use either the PHP 4 or 5 installer on the companion CD-ROM in the software\PHP\IIS\ folder, and perform the following:

1. Double-click the appropriate setup program (PHP 4 or 5) found in software\PHP\IIS\ and the Welcome screen shown in Figure 5.2 will appear. Click Next to continue.
2. The license agreement appears as shown in Figure 5.3. Click I Agree to continue.

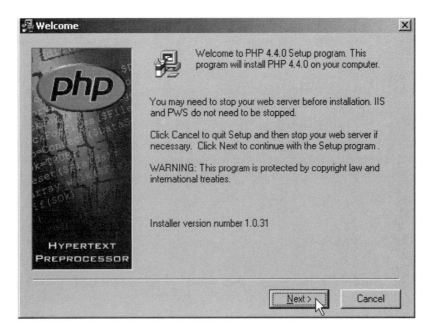

FIGURE 5.2   PHP 4 Welcome screen.

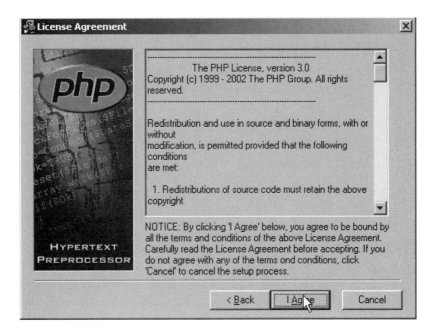

FIGURE 5.3   License agreement.

3. Choose Standard as the preferred Installation Type and click Next as shown in Figure 5.4.

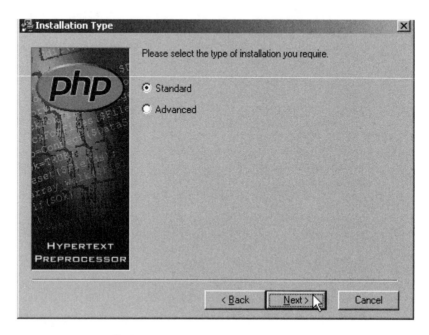

FIGURE 5.4   Installation type.

4. Figure 5.5 will appear next. Either accept the default location of C:\php, or choose a different path by clicking the Browse button. Click Next to continue.

5. The Mail Configuration screen shown in Figure 5.6 will now appear. It is advisable to leave this at the default of localhost unless another SMTP server will be used. Click Next to continue.

6. Figure 5.7 shows the Server type screen, which is where the proper version of IIS is chosen. If the computer is running Windows 2000 Server, the default of IIS 4 or higher is correct. If it is running Windows Server 2003, Microsoft IIS 6 or higher should be chosen.

7. PHP is now ready to install. Click Next to begin the installation as shown in Figure 5.8.

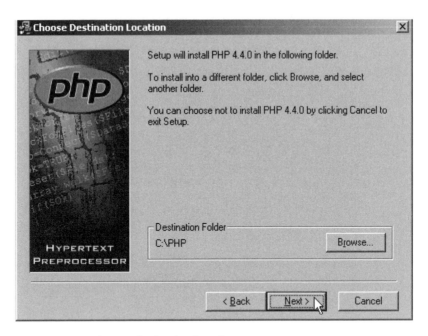

FIGURE 5.5 Choose destination location.

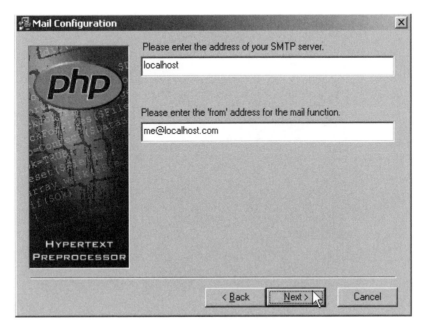

FIGURE 5.6 Mail configuration.

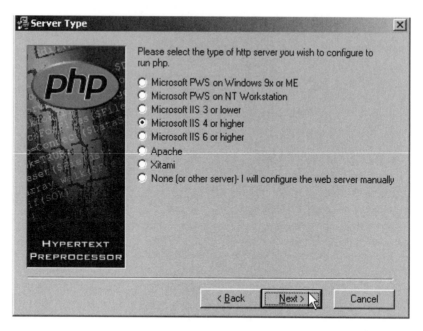

FIGURE 5.7   Server type screen.

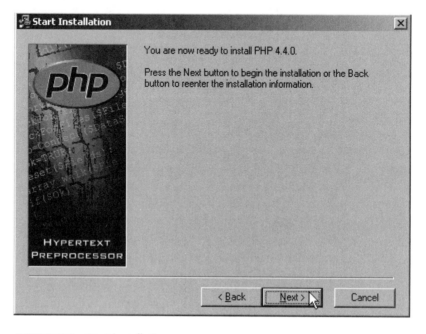

FIGURE 5.8   Start installation.

8. PHP will be installed on the computer as shown in Figure 5.9. This can take seconds or a few minutes, depending on the speed of the machine.

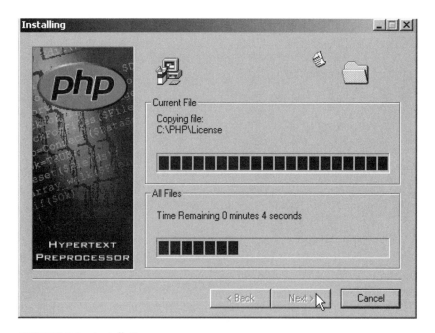

FIGURE 5.9   Installation progress.

9. If all goes well, Figure 5.10 should appear. This means that IIS has been configured with knowledge of PHP and its location. Click OK.

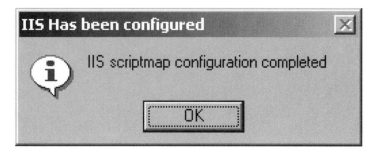

FIGURE 5.10   IIS Has been configured alert.

10. Figure 5.11 shows the Installation Complete alert. It also advises about adding proper rights for `php.exe`, `php4ts.dll`, in addition to the `uploadtmp` and session directories. These are used with PHP for collecting user information and session management.

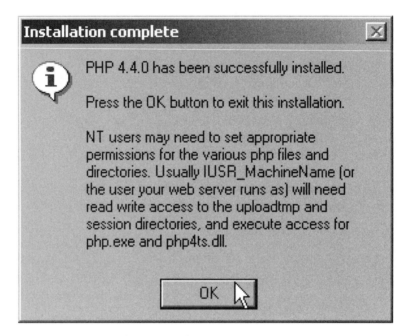

FIGURE 5.11 Installation complete.

11. Check the installation by creating a test page with the code `<?php phpinfo(); ?>` in the document. Save it as `phpinfo.php` inside the default Web (likely `wwwroot`) directory. Test the installation by typing the URL of the Web site followed by `phpinfo.php`. Figure 5.12 should appear.

Configuring IIS.

Once PHP has been installed it is likely that it will be used to create some default pages. This can be accomplished very easily.

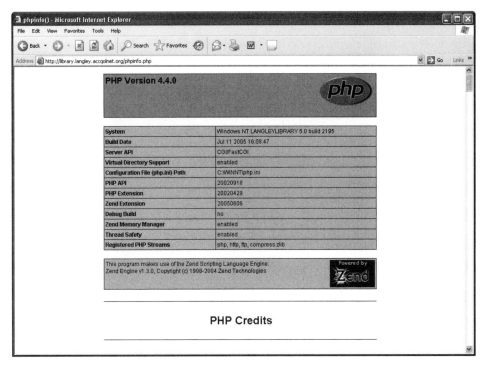

FIGURE 5.12 Testing the installation with a phpinfo() page.

1. Start by opening the Internet Services Manager found in Administrative Tools. Within the Internet Information Services MMC, right-click on a Web site and choose Properties as shown in Figure 5.13.
2. The Website Name Properties Window will open. Click on the Documents tab, and then click the Add button as shown in Figure 5.14.
3. The Add Default Document dialog box will appear as shown in Figure 5.15. Type `index.php` and click OK. The Documents screen will now reflect the addition of `index.php`.

Make sure `index.php` is selected, and click the up arrow shown to the left of the list as shown in Figure 5.16. Keep clicking the arrow until the desired placement of the document is reached. Remember that whichever document is higher on the list will be served if more than one document on the list appears in the same directory.

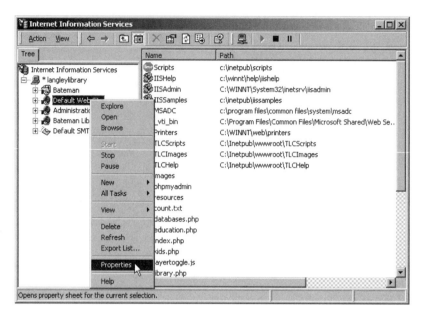

FIGURE 5.13 Choosing the Properties of a Web site in the IIS MMC.

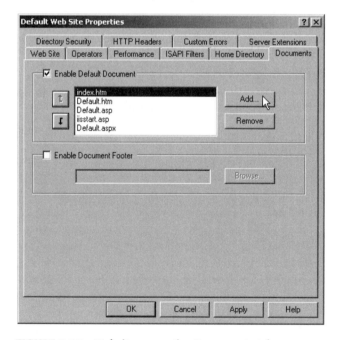

FIGURE 5.14 Website properties Documents tab.

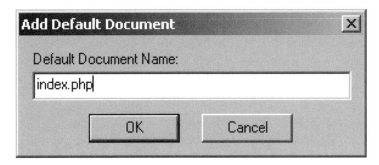

FIGURE 5.15 Adding `index.php` as a default document.

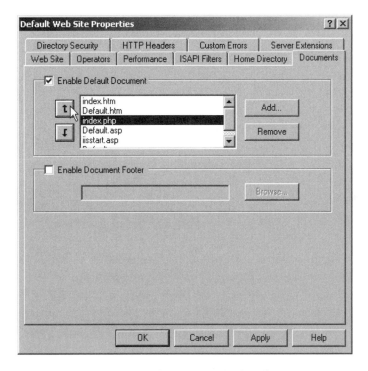

FIGURE 5.16 Advancing the priority of index.php.

PHP 5 AND MYSQL

In version 5, the MySQL libraries for PHP are no longer bundled by default, which means that any time a MySQL function is used, it will show up as undefined unless the following steps are taken:

1. Open the `php.ini` file in C:\php\.
2. Find the line `extension_dir = "./"` and change it to read `extension_dir = "./ext/"`. This line tells PHP where the extension directory is located.
3. Now, find the line `;extension=php_mysql.dll`.
4. Modify the line by removing the semicolon so it reads `extension=php_mysql.dll`.
5. Save and close `php.ini`.
6. Restart Apache if PHP is installed as a module.

There are multiple reasons for this change, which the PHP developers explain at *http://www.php.net/manual/en/faq.databases.php#faq.databases.mysql.php5*.

SUMMARY

This concludes the introduction and installation of PHP. It is actually quite easy to install and can be up and running on a server in a matter of minutes. Let's move on to Chapter 6, "Exploring PHP."

6 Exploring PHP

In This Chapter

■ PHP Syntax
■ Operators and Expressions
■ Arrays
■ Conditionals
■ Loops
■ Functions
■ Includes
■ Working with Forms
■ Creating a PHP Slideshow
■ Summary

In this chapter, we'll explore PHP as a language. The best place to begin is by looking at some of the syntactical qualities.

PHP SYNTAX

PHP as a language was designed specifically for the Web, which is apparent in its structure, efficiency, and ease of use. All actions to be performed must fall between an opening and closing tag, and more than one block can be distributed on a page.

PHP scripts most commonly open with `<?php` and close with `?>`, and can be written on a single line, or multiple lines offering flexibility. This can be handy when only a short statement is needed, like `<?php print($firstname); ?>`. All scripts on the page are handled as one larger script. Any other HTML on the page is output by PHP as a giant print statement.

Statements in PHP require the use of a semicolon. Statements are specific actions like the following:

```php
<?php
        $name = "Eric Hunley";
        print($name);
?>
```

Any block such as conditionals, loops, or functions do not have semicolons on the opening line or closing. The following code has bolded comments showing where semicolons are used:

```php
<?php
    $firstname = "Eric";  //statement – semi-colon required
    if($firstname == "Eric"){  //Conditional opens – No semi-colon
    print("Great to see you Eric!");  //statement - Semi-colon
        }else{  //opening of a conditional – No semi-colon
    print("Welcome $firstname"); //statement – Semi-colon
        }                              // Conditional close – No semi-colon
?>
```

Another output option enabled in PHP by default is the use of "short tags," where the letters php are dropped and only the <? ?> remains. This is not always considered wise because XML documents begin with a declaration, which looks something like <?xml version='1.0' encoding='iso-8859-1'?>. The similarity may cause confusion.

Anytime XML is the planned output, it is a good idea to enclose the line within a print() function or echo construct such as <?php print("<?xml version='1.0' encoding='iso-8859-1'?>"); ?> to help overcome any conflict. Short tags also enable designers to use the shortcut <?=output; ?> instead of <?php echo output; ?>, which is ideal for output in elements such as form fields. An example may look something like <input name="firstname" value="**<?=$firstname;?>**" />, with PHP fitting in the HTML tidily.

A third option for placing PHP commands in a document is using the <script language="php"></script> tags. The problem with this is that the language attribute was deprecated with plans for removal from HTML/XHTML, and there is no type attribute for PHP.

The last option is ASP style tags <% %>. These can only be used if the asp_tags Boolean is set to true in the php.ini file. If the asp_tags option is enabled, <%=output;%> can be used as a shortcut for <% echo output; %> as seen with short tags.

Using print() and echo

As seen in the previous examples, the most popular way to output data from PHP is to use either the echo construct, as in echo output;, or the print() function, as in print(output);. The results of these two options are similar, but not the same. One of the chief differences is that echo does not require parentheses; they are explicitly forbidden if there is more than one argument. Another difference is that print() as a function will return true if it has content. An echo will return nothing since it is a language construct. These differences are subtle and beyond the scope of this book, so for all examples explored, the two can be used interchangeably.

Using printf() and sprintf()

Sometimes, it is helpful to have output formatted, which is where printf() and sprintf() come in handy. They literally translate to print formatted and string print formatted. The strings can be formatted into a translation like turning an integer into its binary equivalent, or can format the appearance of the output by padding the results with leading zeros and dictating how many digits should appear.

The basic command structure of the two functions is printf("%x ", item); or sprintf("%x", item); where x is the qualifier of how the string should be formatted and item is the string that should be modified. More than one string can be modified as long as they are placed in order, as in printf("Item 1 = %x Item 2 = %x", item1, item2);.

The following code shows several options available and will return the results shown in Figure 6.1:

```php
<?php
    printf("%b - Binary<br />", 205.5);
    printf("%c - ASCII<br />", 205.5);
    printf("%d - Integer<br />", 205.5);
    printf("%e - Scientific Notation<br />", 205.5);
    printf("%u - Unsigned Positive Integer<br />", 205.5);
    printf("%u - Unsigned Negative Integer<br />", -205.5);
    printf("%f - Floating Point Number<br />", 205.5);
    printf("%o - Octal Number<br />", 205.5);
    printf("%s - String<br />", 205.5);
    printf("%x - Hexadecimal Number (lower-case)<br />", 205.5);
    printf("%X - Hexadecimal Number (upper-case)<br />", 205.5);
    printf("%+d - Signed Positive Integer<br />", 205.5);
    printf("%+d - Signed Negative Integer<br />", -205.5);
    printf("%02d/%02d/%04d - Padding added to format a date",7, 8, 2005);
?>
```

A full definition of the functions can be found online in the PHP Manual at *http://us3.php.net/manual/en/function.sprintf.php.*

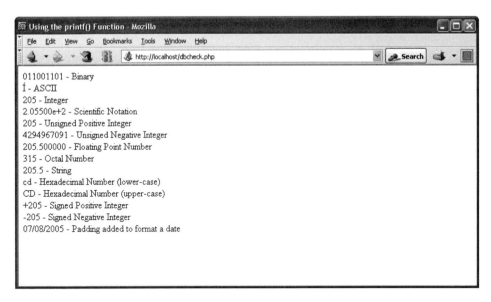

FIGURE 6.1   Using the `printf()` function.

PHP Comments

Comments are required anytime notes need to be included in a script. These allow for the addition of text that is strictly for the programmer and is not to be processed. PHP uses two types of comments: single-line and multi-line. There are two types of single-line comments: `//` and `#`. The `//` comment originally in C is also used with JavaScript, so many Web designers will be familiar with it. The `#` is also used in Perl, so designers with that background will be comfortable with this type of comment.

There is only one type of multi-line comment in PHP: `/* */` (also from C) with the commented text placed between. The following demonstrates uses of the three comment types available:

```
#This is a single line comment.

//This is also a single line comment.

/*This is a
Multi-line
comment. */
```

```
/*****************************\
*                           *
* Some programmers get fancy *
*  with multi-line comments. *
*                           *
\*****************************/
```

Variables, Literals, and Constants

Like most programming languages, PHP makes extensive use of variables. Variables can be thought of as containers, or temporary storage of data, and can change according to values assigned. A *literal* (or *constant*) is the opposite. It does not change. An example of a literal would be print("Hello $firstname!");. Within the statement, Hello and the exclamation point do not change. $firstname is a variable and will change depending on what value it holds; it is simply a placeholder that will be replaced with its value when output.

A PHP constant is created with the define() function, as in define("*constant-name*", "*constantvalue*");, and will not change over the lifespan of the script. Constants are called by name when used (e.g., echo *constantname*;) and are not surrounded by quotation marks.

Variables in PHP, as in most languages, are designed to change. They start with a dollar sign ($). Immediately following the $, a variable name must start with a letter or underscore. It can then be followed by any number of letters, numbers, or underscores.

As seen with Perl earlier, the inclusion of the $ is very important and quite useful with the language. This convention adds ease when outputting information. When dealing with some other languages such as JavaScript, outputting variables in a statement can become cluttered and difficult to read. Compare the two following examples starting with JavaScript:

```
document.write("First Name: " + firstname + "<br />Last Name: " + la
name);
```

The same example with PHP is greatly simplified:

```
print("First Name: $firstname<br />Last Name: $lastname");
```

Notice how the extra quotes have to be added to JavaScript to separate the variables from the string content. Over time, all the added quotes and JavaScript concatenation operators (+) can really add up. PHP allows the designer to focus more on the output and less on the formatting.

PHP is a loosely typed language, which means that variables can be declared and assigned a value at once. In addition, a variable does not have to be defined as a type like `number` or `string` as found in traditional programming languages such as C. In these languages, variables have to be typed so the system knows how much memory needs to be allocated to run the program. PHP is interpreted, so the PHP engine determines the memory requirements on the fly.

PHP continues a tradition from Perl in that the variable type doesn't matter. The type is determined by what the designer does with the content. The following demonstrates this principle:

```php
<?php
    $x = "10";
    $y = 10;
    print($x + $y . " is added because the addition operator (+) has
    been used.<br />");
    print($x . $y . " is concatenated with the concatenation operator
    (.).");
?>
```

The first `print()` function results in 20 because `$x` is added with `$y` with the use of the addition operator (+). The second `print()` returns 1010 because `$x` is concatenated with `$y` when the concatenation operator (.) is used.

This simplifies things a great deal. With JavaScript, string variables often have to be explicitly converted to a number to avoid unwanted concatenation (e.g., 10+10 becoming 1010 instead of 20).

In PHP, variables can hold any of the following:

string: Combination of characters between quotation marks.

integer: A whole number such as 1, 35, 99, etc.

float: A floating-point number such as 1.3.

double: Same as a `float` according to the PHP language reference at *http://us2.php.net/language.types.* All floating-point numbers will return double when the `gettype()` function is used.

boolean: Either `true` or `false`.

array: A list of values; more complex than a basic variable.

object: Used with object-oriented programming.

resource: A statement to connect to a resource like a database. For example, `$db_connect = @mysql_connect('localhost', '$username', '$password');`.

NULL – A variable that has no value.

The contents of a variable can always be checked with the gettype() function. It will return the current type of the variable demonstrated in the following code with the results shown in Figure 6.2:

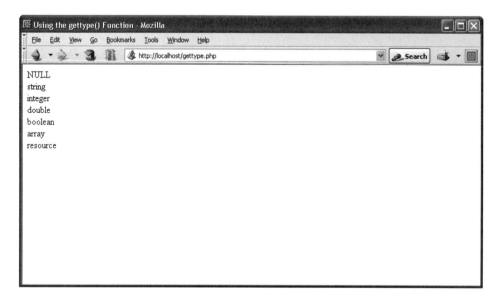

FIGURE 6.2 Results of the getype() function.

```php
<?php
    $x;
    echo gettype($x) . "<br />"; //returns NULL

    $x = "Eric";
    echo gettype($x) . "<br />"; //returns string

    $x = 10;
    echo gettype($x) . "<br />"; //returns integer

    $x = 10.3;
    echo gettype($x) . "<br />"; //returns double

    $x = true;
    echo gettype($x) . "<br />"; //returns boolean
```

```
    $x = array("item1","item2","item3");
    echo gettype($x) . "<br />"; //returns array

    $x = mysql_connect('localhost','root','password');
    echo gettype($x) . "<br />"; //returns resource
?>
```

Quotes

As shown before, in PHP, all variables begin with a $, which makes it very easy to output information from them in statements. For example, $firstname= "Eric"; echo "Hello $firstname!"; will output Hello Eric!.

This convenience is because PHP treats quotation marks in the same manner as Perl. Double quotes will process the output with *interpolation*. This means that any variable placed within double quotes will have the value swapped in when it is output.

On the other hand, as with Perl, single quotes output data *without* interpolation. Therefore, if the previous statement is written as echo 'Hello $firstname!';, the output will literally be Hello $firstname! and most likely not be the desired result.

Escape Characters

Sometimes when writing a statement, the data needs to be interpolated and have an actual dollar sign. For example, there could be a variable called $price with a value of 10. The statement print("The price is $price."); will result in "The price is 10." To put an actual dollar sign in the statement, the *escape character,* a backslash (\), needs to be added along with a second dollar sign. The statement of print("The price is \$$price."); will result in The price is $10..

Other characters that commonly need to be escaped are quotation marks, and the escape character itself. For example, the statement print("The path to the file is "c:\program files\program\myfile""); would break. When the parser sees the first quotation mark in the statement, it will think it is the end of the line. When it finds text beyond it, it will immediately break.

The statement rewritten as print("The path to the file is \"c:\program files\program\myfile\""); will function, but result in The path to the file is \"c:rogram filesrogramyfile". To display the result correctly, the statement must be rewritten to print("The path to the file is \"c:\\program files\\program\\myfile\"");.

Another method of dealing with quotes inside an interpolated print() *function or* echo *statement is to use single quotes. This is especially useful when typing HTML attribute values in the output, such as* print("<p class='dbrow'>$record</p>");.

Escape characters are not always used to prevent interpolation. They can also be used for line commands. Some of these include \n for a new-line character, which instructs the processor to drop to the next line and continue the output. The \r for a carriage return is similar to a new line, except that it will resume printing all the way to the left on the next line as opposed to the same starting point as the current line. A third option available is \t for tab.

Many people new to Web programming mistakenly think that the new-line escape character can be used for multi-line visible output in HTML. The \n *is for dropping to another line in a command-line environment, so all of the line breaks will appear in the source code of the HTML, but be invisible to the end user. For a line break in the visible output, the standard HTML/XHTML break*
 tag must be used.

OPERATORS AND EXPRESSIONS

A set of operands used in conjunction with one another to obtain a result is known as an *expression*. An example would be $x=10*10;, where the 10*10 portion of the assignment is an expression. In the example, 10 will be multiplied with 10, and the result will be assigned to $x using the assignment operator (=).

Arithmetical Operators

When devising a formula for assignment to a variable, there are several arithmetical operators from which to choose. They have basic math functionality and include add (+), subtract (-), multiply (*), divide (/), and modulus (%). Most of these work in a familiar manner—2+2 results in 4, 10*10 results in 100, and so on.

Modulus hearkens back to the days of long division, but returns the remainder as a result. For example, 10%3 will result in 1 as shown in Figure 6.3.

Modulus can be very useful for figuring out whether values are odd or even on changing variables (x%2 will always return 0 if the number is even), or for inserting commas when displaying numbers above 1000. For example:

```
$total = 10323;
$rem = $total%1000; //will result in 323
$output = ($total - $rem)/1000 . "," . $rem; //results in 10,323
print ("Final Price: \$$output");
```

FIGURE 6.3 Using Modulus.

String Operator

The concatenation operator (.) falls in this category, and is used to append one string value to another; for example, `"Eric" . " Hunley"` will result in `Eric Hunley`.

Assignment Operators

Assignment operators are used to assign values to variables in PHP. Here is a list of assignment operators used in PHP:

=: Basic assignment operator that assigns the value given on the right of the assignment operator to the left; for example, `$firstname = "Eric"`; will assign the value of "Eric" to `$firstname`.

+=: Addition assignment operator that adds the value on the right to the current value of the variable and assigns the total to the variable. For example, if `$payments` has the current value of 900, `$payments += 300`; will change the value of `$payments` to 1200. It is the same as writing `$payments = $payments + 300`.

-=: Subtraction assignment operator.

*=: Multiplication assignment operator.

/=: Division assignment operator.

.=: Concatenating assignment operator that appends the string value to the right with the current value on the left and assigns the results. For example, if `$name="Eric";, $name .= " Hunley"`; will result in `"Eric Hunley"`.

Unary Operators

Unary operators are any operator that only has a single part. Increment/decrement (++/--) operators fall in this category along with the not (!) operator, which switches the value to its opposite; for example, !true will equal false.

The negation operator (-n) can also fit in this category even though it is included as an arithmetic operator in the PHP manual. It returns the opposite value of a positive or negative integer. For example, if $x = 10, -$x will return -10.

Post- and Pre-Fix

While increment and decrement will add or subtract the value of one from an operand, their placement is important. This is critical to understand if an increment or decrement operator is being used in combination with a variable assignment.

If the operator is placed before an operand, the action will take place before the result is assigned to the variable. If it is placed after, the assignment will take place first. The following code demonstrates this:

```
$x = 10;
$y = ++$x; //$x is 11 and $y is 11
$x = 10;
$y = $x++; //$x is 11, but $y is 10
```

Comparison Operators

Comparison operators are used to compare operands. After doing so, they will return a Boolean of either true or false. They are commonly used in Conditionals (if...else). Here is a list of commonly used comparison operators:

Equality ==: Checks for equality of the value. 10 == "10" would evaluate as true.

NOTE

One of the most common mistakes new programmers make is to use the assignment operator (=) instead of the equality comparison operator (==) in a conditional block. This is very difficult to troubleshoot, because it is not syntactically wrong; it is logically wrong and may not be picked up by PHP error checking.

Strict Equality (called identical, available as of PHP 4) `===`: Checks both the contents of the value and the data type; both have to match. `10 === "10"` would evaluate as `false` because the first value is a number, but the second is a string.

Inequality `!=` **or** `<>`: Checks that the values do not match. Therefore, `10 != "10"` will evaluate as `false`.

Strict Inequality (called not identical in PHP, available as of PHP 4) `!==`: Checks both the data type and value to ensure they do not match. `10 !== "10"` will result in `true`.

Greater Than `>`: Checks if the first value is greater than the second value.

Less Than `<`: Checks if the first value is less than the second value.

Greater Than or Equal to `>=`: Checks if the first value is greater than or equal to the second value. It does not check for strict equality.

Less Than or Equal to `<=`: Checks if the first value is less than or equal to the second value.

Ternary or Conditional Operator `(condition)? true actions : false actions;`: The only operator with three *operands*. It is especially handy for a small condition such as `($age > 18)? $vote = true : $vote = false;`.

Logical Operators

Logical operators are used to combine multiple comparison operators. There are several different types:

AND `&&` **or** `and`: Requires both sides of a comparison to evaluate as `true` before returning `true`. For example, if `$x` and `$y` have the values `5` and `10`, the following will return `true`: `($x<y) && ($y == 10)`—parentheses are optional, but can be added for clarity.

OR `||` **or** `or`: Requires one of two conditions or both to be met. For example, if `$x` and `$y` have the values `5` and `10`, the following will return `true`: `($x<y) || ($y < 10)`.

XOR `xor`: Requires the first or second condition to return `true`, but *not both*.

NOT `!`: Returns the opposite of any value. For example, if `$x` and `$y` have the values `5` and `10`, `!($x<$y)` will return false while `!($x>$y)` will return `true`. The easiest way to evaluate statements with a `not` operator is to find the result of the conditions and then flip the result.

Truth Tables

Often, new programmers will use a practice method called truth tables to look at logic structure. They are good practice to see the results of statements. Here is a basic example of a truth table:

```
$x = 10;
$y = 20;
$x < $y //true
$y == 20 //true
$x != 20 //true
($x == 10) && ($y == 20) //true
($x < $y) && ($y == 10) //false
($x < $y) || ($y == 10) //true
($x == 10) xor ($y == 20) //false
```

Short-Circuit Evaluation

Whenever using comparison operators and logical operators, it is important to understand how evaluation works. PHP, like many programming languages, uses short-circuit evaluation. This means that it will only evaluate an expression long enough to come up with a true or false.

For example, if the expression is ($x < $y) && ($y == 10), PHP has to evaluate the entire expression before it can return true. On the other hand, if the expression is ($x > $y) && ($y == 10), PHP will only evaluate as far as the && before it returns false. This is because it already has a false result from the first half of the expression, so the whole thing will be false no matter how much farther it reads.

Good programmers should always write expressions in a manner where the first part of the expression is the most common and so on. This will make the code run faster.

Operator Precedence

Operator precedence determines what portion of an equation is performed first. For example, 3+3*3 will result in 12, not 18 as might be expected. This is because the multiplication operator has a higher precedence than the addition operator does. Operators with the highest precedence will be evaluated first. If there is a tie, associativity will be used. For example, multiplication * and division / have the same precedence and a left associativity. This means that in the case of $x=2*2/2;, $x will be assigned the value of 2 because the multiplication will be performed first since it is to the left.

Any time clarification is needed, or precedence needs to be overridden, use parentheses as in (3+3)*3, which will result in 18 because the addition within the parentheses will be performed first. Here is a list of some commonly used operators precedence and associativity:

Operator(s)	Associativity
()	None
++ --	None
* / %	Left
+ - .	Left
< <= > >=	None
== != === !==	None
&&	Left
||	Left
? :	Left
= += -= *= /= .= %=	Right
and	Left
xor	Left
or	Left

One advantage when using PHP is that it is a *typeless* language. This means that the type (string, integer, etc.) is loose and can be changed on the fly, and is actually often determined when used in an expression. For example, in $x="10";, the type is a string because there are quotation marks around the 10. This is important to realize because most user input that comes into the script via GET or POST will be a string, because that is how forms send single input fields.

Like Perl, PHP makes this easy to deal with because the datatype is determined by the use. If $y = $x*$x;, $y will have the value of 100 and the datatype of integer.

ARRAYS

Arrays are essentially a collection of data values organized as a list or in key/value pairs. These two array types are known as *indexed* or *associative* arrays. An indexed array contains an integer as a key for each value contained. This index starts at 0 and increments from there. An associative array has a string for a key.

There are different methods for creating and adding values to an array. The following will create the new array $names and add the values and indexes:

```
$names[0] = "Eric";
$names[1] = "Clint";
$names[2] = "Erik";
```

The example could also be written as

```
$names = array("Eric", "Clint", "Erik");
```

Both examples will create an indexed array. To create an associative array, there are also different methods:

```
$person["lastname"] = "Hunley";
$person["firstname"] = "Eric";
```

$person can also be created in the following manner:

```
$person = array(
    lastname => "Hunley",
        firstname => "Eric"
);
```

To access a value within an indexed array, use $array[index];, whereas $array['key']; will access a value in an associative array. Therefore, to access the value "Eric", $person['firstname'] should be used.

Another option with arrays is to have an array of arrays. These are known as multidimensional arrays. Here is an example:

```
$author1 = array("Hunley", "Eric");
$author2 = array("Eccher","Clint");
$author3 = array("Simmons","Erik");
$authors = array ($author1,$author2,$author3);
```

$authors[1][1]; will return the value "Clint". Multidimensional arrays are very similar to spreadsheets. The first number can be thought of as the row, while the second acts as the column. To reference a value in the multidimensional array, first type the index that holds the *sub-array*, and then its index.

When working with arrays, numerous built-in functions (known in many languages as methods) are available. These include sorting, reversing, and converting an array to a string, among many others.

To sort an array, there are a multiple options. To sort the values in standard alphabetical order, `sort()` is used. For example, if the array `$names = array("Eric", "Clint","Erik");` has the `sort()` function applied to it `sort($names);`, the new order of values would be `("Clint","Eric","Erik")`. It will also be re-indexed.

Another sort option is `rsort()`, which works as a normal `sort()` in reverse. If an associative array needs to be sorted by keys, the `ksort()` function can be used. To sort an associative array in reverse, use the `krsort()` function.

When a string needs to be converted into an array, the `explode()` function can be used. It takes two arguments: the separator and the array to be used. For example, string variable `$authors = "Eric Clint Erik";` can be turned into an array by using `explode(" ",$authors);`. Essentially, it will create the values in the array based on the spaces in the string variable.

Of course, the reverse can happen. An array can easily be converted into a string by using `implode('separator',$array);`. If the separator is left out, the values will be concatenated together.

NOTE

When using `implode()`, it does not matter what order the arguments are given. The separator argument can be placed either before or after the `array` argument. This is not the case of the `explode()` function, which must have the separator argument sent first.

Other functions commonly used with arrays are `array_push()`, `array_pop()`, `array_shift()`, `array_unshift()`, and `array_slice()`. These functions are used to either add to an array or remove a value from an array. The first two `array_push()` and `array_pop()` work with the end of an array. `array_push($array, values)` will add the value(s) sent as an argument to the end of an array, while `array_pop($array)` removes the last value from the array stack.

The `array_shift()` and `array_unshift()` functions work the same as `array_push()` and `array_pop()`, only with the beginning of the stack. To remove from the beginning of an array, `array_shift($array)` is used, while `array_unshift ($array, values)` adds to the front of the stack.

While `array_pop()` and `array_shift()` both physically change the contents of an array (they are considered *destructive*), `array_slice()` can be used to copy elements without actually changing the target array. It is written as `array_slice ($array, start, number of elements);`.

CONDITIONALS

Conditionals are used in programming to make decisions based on parameters. When used, the program will perform certain actions if a condition is met. The most basic conditional used is the `if`, which will check to see if the condition is true and perform actions when that is the case. The following is an example of the most basic type of conditional check:

```
$x = 10;
if($x){
        print("\$x has the value of $x.");
}
```

In this example, the `if` is simply checking whether `$x` has a value. If it does, the result of the value is output in the print statement. If `$x` had no value, nothing would be done. That is where `if/else` comes in. The `else` assigns what actions should take place if a condition returns `false`.

```
$x = 10;
if($x){
        print("\$x has the value of $x.");
}else{
        print("$x has no value.");
}
```

Now, if `$x` has no value, the `else` print statement will occur. Notice there are no parentheses for a condition. This is because the `else` is tied directly to the `if`. There is no condition `else` to check; it simply responds to a `false`.

When more than one value needs to be checked, `else if` can be used in the conditional block. Multiple `else if` statements can be used within a conditional block.

```
$name = "Clint";
if($name == "Eric"){
        print("Here is your <a href='eric.html'>homepage link</a>.");
}else if ($name == "Clint"){
    print("Here is your <a href='clint.html'>homepage link</a>.");
}else if($name == "Erik"){
        print("Here is your <a href='clint.html'>homepage link</a>.");
}else{
        print("Welcome to the site $name.");
}
```

In the example, the script is checking for three different names. If any of the names are matched, a customized link is presented. If none of the names is a match, a default statement is printed.

Another change in the example is within the condition itself. This time, an equality comparison operator is being used. There is a great deal of flexibility with comparison operators in if/else conditional blocks; a single comparison operator can be used, and multiple checks can be combined by using logical operators.

Another form of flow control can be found with the switch statement. With this method of flow control, a single value can be checked. It is formatted as follows:

```
switch (condition) {
      case value:
   actions;
   break;
      case value:
   actions;
   break;
      default:
   actions;
      }
```

The previous if/else block could easily be re-written as a switch statement:

```
$name= "Clint";
switch($name){
   case "Eric":
         print("Here is your <a href='eric.html'>homepage
link</a>.");
         break;
   case "Clint":
         print("Here is your <a href='clint.html'>homepage
link</a>.");
         break;
   case "Erik":
   print("Here is your <a href='erik.html'>homepage link</a>.");
   break;
      default:
   print("Welcome to the site $name.");
}
```

The `switch` statement also allows what is known as *fall-through*, which allows multiple matches to share the same result. In the previous `switch` statement, there is a `break` statement on the end of each set of actions to break out of the block should the condition be met. Fall-through is achieved through the removal of the break statements as in the following:

```
$name= "Clint";
switch($name){
    case "Eric":
    case "Clint":
    case "Erik":
    print("Welcome back $name!");
    break;
        default:
    print("Welcome to the site $name.");
}
```

In this example, if `$name` has the value of either `"Eric"`, `"Clint"`, or `"Erik"`, `"Welcome back..."` will be displayed. Using fall-through on a `switch` is sometimes a convenient way of replacing an `if` statement with logical operators, like `if (value1 || value2 || value3){actions;}`. What is important to note with a `switch` statement is that it can only check one value, whereas an `if` can check many.

LOOPS

Another method of flow control available in PHP (like most programming languages) is using loops. Loops are essentially specialized conditionals. However, instead of a normal conditional, which will perform steps when a condition is met and stop, loops will continue to repeat actions as long as the condition is met.

Three of the most popular loops used in PHP are `while`, `for`, and `foreach`. The `while` loop is one of the oldest and most basic. It will simply continue to perform actions as long as the condition evaluates as true, no matter what the condition might be. The basic structure of the `while` loop is `while(condition){actions;}`.

A very simple while loop can be written as

```
$x=1;
while($x<=100){
        print($x . ", ");
        $x++;
}
```

This will create a list of comma-separated numbers from 1–100, but could also be written very easily using a `for` loop.

A `for` loop is also known as the *counting* loop. Its conditions are all created for the specific purpose of counting, and it is not as flexible with conditions as a `while` is. A `for` loop is comprised of three parts: an index, a condition, and an counter separated by semicolons (e.g., `for(index;condition;counter)`). The `while` example would be formatted something like this:

```
for($i=1;$<=100;i++){
        print($i . ", ");
}
```

Notice how less code is involved when writing the `for` loop. That is because the counting functions are built in to the loop. The results will be identical to the `while` loop.

The last type of loop to explore here is the `foreach` loop available as of PHP 4. It is based on the `for` loop, but is especially handy for use with arrays that hold more than one piece of information. Essentially, it is based on the word *each*; for each item in the array, do these actions `foreach($array as $value){actions;}`. Here is an example of its use:

```
$colors =
array("red","white","blue","black","yellow","orange","green","purple","
gray");
foreach ($colors as $color){
        print($color . ", ");
}
```

This task can also be accomplished using a regular `for` loop:

```
$colors =
array("red","white","blue","black","yellow","orange","green","purple","
gray");
for ($i=0;$i<count($colors);$i++){
        print($colors[$i] . ", ");
}
```

Be extremely careful when using loops. If a condition is created that is possible to meet, an infinite loop will be created. This can have detrimental effects on the server, including the possibility of crashing it.

FUNCTIONS

Anytime an action needs to be performed more than once, a function should be created. This rule applies to PHP along with any other programming language.

Functions are very easy to create in PHP—even easier than subroutines in Perl. All that is required to create a function is the use of the function keyword and the function defined after that point. The following code creates a basic function:

```
function square(){
    $x = 10;
    $x *= $x;
        return $x;
}
echo square(); //prints 100
```

While the function created works fine, functions are even stronger when they can use arguments when called. To create a function with an argument, a variable parameter must be put within the parentheses of the function declaration. The same variable is then used within the body of the function as shown here:

```
function square($x){
    $x *= $x;
return $x;
}
echo square(10); //prints 100
```

This second version of the function returns 100 as well, but this time, the result is achieved with data supplied in an argument, making the function much more flexible.

Variable Scope

One handy thing about PHP is how it scopes its variables. A variable's scope is the portion of the script or application in which it can exist and be recognized. PHP keeps the scope of any variable created in a function to the function. For example, if the following code is used, the result in Figure 6.4 will be displayed:

```
<?php
    $x = "<strong>&quot;Hello World!&quot;</strong>";
```

```
function square($x){
        $x *= $x;
        return $x;
}

echo "<p>The value of \$x used in square(10) is <strong>" .
square(10) . "</strong>.</p>";
    echo "<p>But if \$x is used outside of the function, the result is
$x";
?>
```

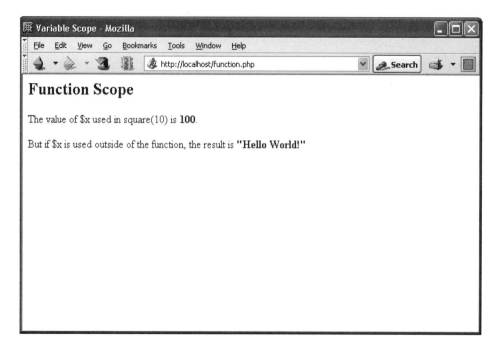

FIGURE 6.4   Exploring variable scope.

INCLUDES

The last part of PHP to be covered before moving on to working with forms is the use of includes. Includes with any language are an invaluable resource for reusable code, and PHP makes it easy with two statements: `include()` and `require()`.

Using either of these statements will bring a section of PHP code into a page as if it were natively written. The only difference between the two is that an `include` will allow the page to still load even if the `include()` fails, whereas a page will not load when a `require()` fails. The basic syntax of these two statements is `include('filepath.php');` or `require('filepath.php');`.

WORKING WITH FORMS

One of the most exciting aspects of PHP is the ability to work with forms. It is very easy to have a separate page that responds to user input from a form, or the same result can even be accomplished on the current page.

Create a Form

Creating a form for use with PHP is simple; it is just an HTML form. For this section, a very basic form will be used:

```
<html>
<head>
<title>Contact Form</title>
<style type="text/css">
table {
    border: 1px solid #000000;
    border-bottom: none;
    width: 300px;
    background-color: #CCCCCC;
    }
table td{
    padding: 5px 10px;
    font-family: Verdana, Arial, Helvetica, sans-serif;
    font-size: 14px;
    border-bottom: 1px solid #000000;
    }
</style>
</head>
```

```
<body>
<form action="readform.php">
<table cellspacing="0">
<tr><td>First Name:</td><td><input type="text" id="firstname"
name="firstname" /></td></tr>
<tr><td>Last Name:</td><td><input type="text" id="lastname" name="last-
name" /></td></tr>
<tr><td>Address:</td><td><input type="text" id="address" name="address"
/></td></tr>
<tr><td>City:</td><td><input type="text" id="city" name="city"
/></td></tr>
<tr><td>State:</td><td><input type="text" id="state" name="state"
/></td></tr>
<tr><td>Zip Code:</td><td><input type="text" id="zip" name="zip"
/></td></tr>
<tr><td>Phone:</td><td><input type="text" id="phone" name="phone"
/></td></tr>
<tr><td>E-Mail:</td><td><input type="text" id="email" name="email"
/></td></tr>
<tr><td colspan="2"><p>How would you like to be contacted?</p>
Postal Mail: <input type="checkbox" id="contact" name="contact"
value="mail" />
Phone: <input type="checkbox" id="contact" name="contact" value="phone"
/>
E-mail: <input type="checkbox" id="contact" name="contact"
value="email" /><br />
</td></tr>
<tr><td> </td><td><input type="submit" id="submit" name="submit"
value="Send" /><input type="reset" id="reset" name="reset"
value="Erase" /></td></tr>
</table>
</form>
</body>
</html>
```

Some basic CSS styles were added, and all of the form fields have both an ID and a name. This is to be sure that they are both forward and backward compatible with browsers. This form should be saved within `c:/apache2/htdocs/` as `contact.html` and is shown in Figure 6.5.

FIGURE 6.5   contact.html, a basic form.

Using GET and POST

Within the form tag, the first consideration is the action attribute. This determines where the form data will be sent. After this, the method of sending needs to be considered.

There are two possible methods available when sending a form: GET and POST. The default method is GET, so the contact.html form created previously will be sent using this method.

The GET method sends all of the form variables in the URL visible at the top of the page. If Submit is clicked on the contact form, the end of the URL shown in the address bar will read readform.php?firstname=John&lastname=Doe&address= 123+Main+St.&city=Tucson&state=AZ&zip=85710&phone=520-555- 5555&email=john%40johndoe.com&contact=mail&submit=Send. This makes all of the information available for anyone to see, and server logs often collect and publish this information. Therefore, GET is the wrong choice if the user is sending anything of a personal nature.

The second method of sending data is POST. To use the POST method, the form tag must have the method attribute added: `<form action="readform.php" method="post">`.

The POST method will cause the variables to be sent in the body of the request. This means that someone can't read the information, and it will not be logged in public server logs. Does this mean that it is secure? No. Even though it is hidden from general view, the information is sent over the Internet in clear text. The only way to secure the information is to use POST, and encrypt the data when it is sent using HTTPS (Hypertext Transfer Protocol with Secure Sockets Layer) or some other method.

You may wonder why the GET method is ever used, since it shares all of the information. The reason is that there are times that this behavior is valuable, especially when dealing with searches. Search engines store and study this information, and corporate Web sites use this information. Trends can be picked up and content can be placed in a better location. If a piece of information is searched for frequently, perhaps a link to it should be placed on the home page.

NOTE

Receiving Form Variables

Sending a form is one thing, but there must be a script ready to receive the form variables and perform actions on it. For years, it was extremely easy to access form variables with PHP. There is a switch in the `php.ini` file called `register_globals`, which allows any variable to be sent from a form and made accessible by name when it is turned on. All a designer needed to do was place a dollar sign before any form field name, and its values would be available in the script. The following code saved as `readform.php` on the companion CD-ROM would work with no problems as shown in Figure 6.6:

ON THE CD

```
<html>
<head>
   <title>Submission Results</title>
</head>
<body>
<?php
   print("<h3>Your information has been submitted $firstname. <br
```

```
/>Thank you.</h3><p>Here is what you submitted:</p>");
    print("<p><strong>First Name:</strong> $firstname<br />");
    print("<strong>Last Name:</strong> $lastname<br />");
    print("<strong>Address:</strong> $address<br />");
    print("<strong>City:</strong> $city<br />");
    print("<strong>State:</strong> $state<br />");
    print("<strong>Zip:</strong> $zip<br />");
    print("<strong>Phone:</strong> $phone<br />");
    print("<strong>E-mail:</strong> $email<br />");
    print("<strong>How to contact:</strong> $contact<br /></p>");
?>

</body>
</html>
```

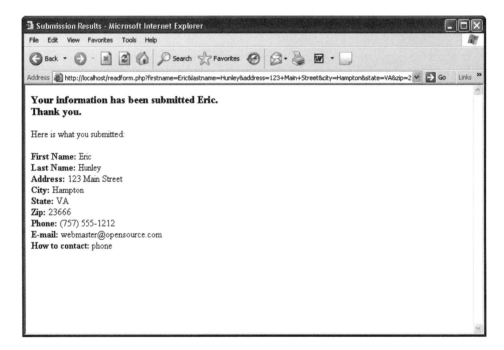

FIGURE 6.6 PHP with `register_globals` on.

While this was very convenient for designers using PHP, the default for `register_globals` was changed to `"Off"` as of PHP 4.2, because it was found to be a security issue. Details can be found at *http://www.php.net/manual/en/security.globals.php*.

With the default now being off, the same code on a server using this configuration will not show the values. The results will resemble Figure 6.7.

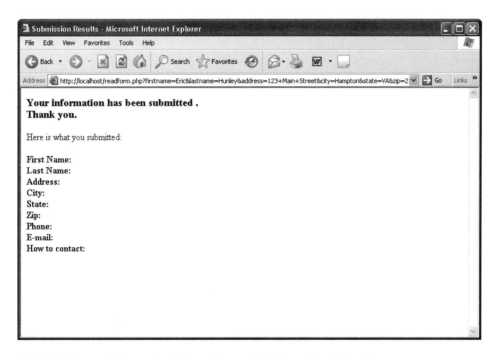

FIGURE 6.7   `readform.php` with `register_globals` set to off on the server.

Notice that no values appear. There is no error given because the variables were never set. They are being declared without values when called. They just return a `null`, and no values are printed on the page. The only thing that appears is the HTML around them.

There are multiple ways of dealing with this situation. The first is to refer to the variables using some of the built-in PHP variables, such as `$_GET` for form variables sent using the GET method, `$_POST` for the POST method, and `$_REQUEST` to receive variables from both methods. This is accomplished by treating the form variable as a key in the appropriate associative array. For example, any form field from `contact.html` can be accessed using `$_GET['fieldname'];`; `$_GET['firstname'];` will return the value of `firstname` from the submitted form.

Another method is even easier. With a simple `foreach` loop, all of the form variables needed can be accessed and set in the page as if `register_globals` is on. If the form was submitted using the GET method, the loop should read `foreach (array_keys($_GET) as $key) {$$key=$_GET[$key];}`. To receive variables from a form using the POST method, `foreach (array_keys($_POST) as $key) {$$key=$_POST[$key];}` should be used. If a page has submitted with both the GET and POST methods, both can be used. Using `contact.html`, if `foreach (array_keys($_GET) as $key) {$$key=$_GET[$key];}` is used, the results will resemble Figure 6.8.

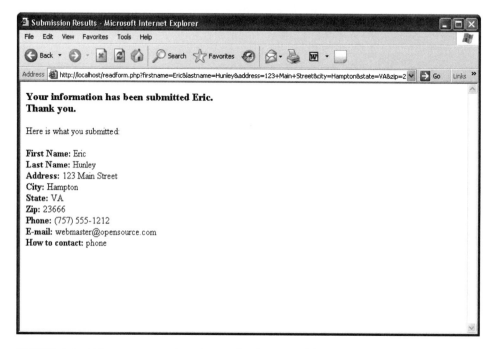

FIGURE 6.8   Using a `foreach` loop to set the form variables on a script.

As can be seen in Figure 6.8, the `foreach` loop method is a very convenient way to work around `register_globals` being set to off. This method is shown in the *User Contributed Notes* section at *http://www.php.net/manual/en/security.globals.php*.

While the foreach loop can be used for convenience, it will record any variable that is sent in via the specified method. To limit the acceptable input, $_GET['field-name'] or $_POST['fieldname'] should be used.

Submitting Array Values from Forms

When looking closely at the results from `contact.html`, you'll notice that something is wrong with the parsed data. The contact checkbox fields are only returning one value even if more checkboxes were checked. This can be resolved by submitting the data as an array.

One convenient method of appending values to an array is to simply reference the array with empty brackets and assign a new value: `$array[] = new value;`. This can be accomplished within PHP code, and from the form itself. If all of the `name` and `id` fields called `contact` are renamed to `contact[]` within `contact.html`, each checked box will append its value to the `$contact` array. This enables more than one value to be sent from a `checkbox` or `select` group. Figure 6.9 shows how the data is being received as an array by adding `phpinfo(32)` to `readform.php`.

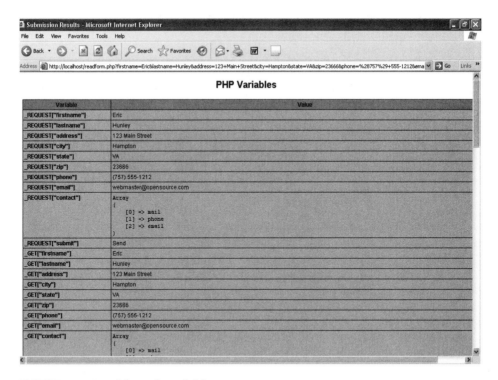

FIGURE 6.9 Receiving a form field as an array.

The next thing to consider is what to do with the data when parsed. An array cannot be output outright with `print($array);`; it will result in the word *Array* instead of the values in the array. To access the values, they have to be referenced directly by their index, using a `for` loop, or using a `foreach` loop. Another method that works particularly well is to use `implode();`, which converts the array into a string. Since the data is often going into a database, this is a good solution.

Taking the code from `readform.php`, if the line `print("<strong>How to contact:</strong> $contact<br />");` is changed to `print("<strong>How to contact:</strong> " . implode(', ',$contact) . "<br />");`, all of the checkboxes selected from the user will be recorded and displayed.

Self-Posting Forms

So far, the examples consist of two pages: an HTML page with a form, and a PHP page that parses the results. This does not have to be the case; a single PHP page can be created that accomplishes both tasks.

As the first step to demonstrate this process, move the block of PHP code from `readform.php` to `contact.html` and save `contact.html` as `contact.php`. After this has been accomplished, the combined page should look like this (the PHP is bolded):

```
<html>
<head>
<title>Contact Form</title>
<style type="text/css">
table {
    border: 1px solid #000000;
    border-bottom: none;
    width: 300px;
    background-color: #CCCCCC;
    }
table td{
    padding: 5px 10px;
    font-family: Verdana, Arial, Helvetica, sans-serif;
    font-size: 14px;
    border-bottom: 1px solid #000000;
    }
</style>
</head>
<body>
<?php
```

```
    foreach (array_keys($_GET) as $key) {$$key=$_GET[$key];}
    print("<h3>Your information has been submitted. <br />Thank
you.</h3><p>Here is what you submitted:</p>");
    print("<strong>First Name:</strong> $firstname<br />");
    print("<strong>Last Name:</strong> $lastname<br />");
    print("<strong>Address:</strong> $address<br />");
    print("<strong>City:</strong> $city<br />");
    print("<strong>State:</strong> $state<br />");
    print("<strong>Zip:</strong> $zip<br />");
    print("<strong>Phone:</strong> $phone<br />");
    print("<strong>E-mail:</strong> $email<br />");
    print("<strong>How to contact:</strong> " . implode(", ",$contact)
. "<br />");
?>
<form action="readform.php">
<table cellspacing="0">
<tr><td>First Name:</td><td><input type="text" id="firstname"
name="firstname" /></td></tr>
<tr><td>Last Name:</td><td><input type="text" id="lastname" name="last-
name" /></td></tr>
<tr><td>Address:</td><td><input type="text" id="address" name="address"
/></td></tr>
<tr><td>City:</td><td><input type="text" id="city" name="city"
/></td></tr>
<tr><td>State:</td><td><input type="text" id="state" name="state"
/></td></tr>
<tr><td>Zip Code:</td><td><input type="text" id="zip" name="zip"
/></td></tr>
<tr><td>Phone:</td><td><input type="text" id="phone" name="phone"
/></td></tr>
<tr><td>E-Mail:</td><td><input type="text" id="email" name="email"
/></td></tr>
<tr><td colspan="2"><p>How would you like to be contacted?</p>
Postal Mail: <input type="checkbox" id="contact[]" name="contact[]"
value="mail" />
Phone: <input type="checkbox" id="contact[]" name="contact[]"
value="phone" />
E-mail: <input type="checkbox" id="contact[]" name="contact[]"
value="email" /><br />
</td></tr>
<tr><td> </td><td><input type="submit" id="submit" name="submit"
value="Send" /><input type="reset" id="reset" name="reset"
```

```
value="Erase" /></td></tr>
</table>
</form>
</body>
</html>
```

After moving the PHP code, try the page. It should resemble Figure 6.10.

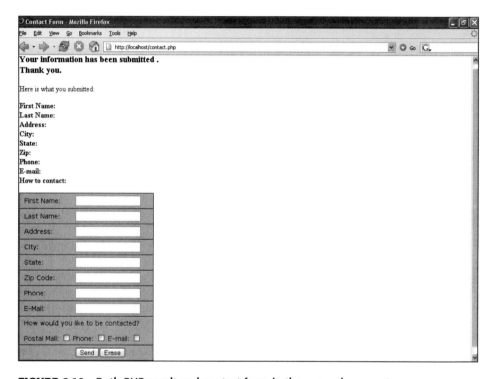

FIGURE 6.10   Both PHP result and contact form in the same document.

The key to using one page for both tasks is in determining whether the page is being entered for the first time, or is a submission of the form on the page. To accomplish this, a hidden form field can be used. Within the form on the page, place `<input type="hidden" name="submit" id="submit" value="1" />` between `<input type="reset" id="reset" name="reset" value="Erase" />` and `</td>`.

Another change that should take place is to change the action of the form and add the `method` attribute with a `post` value - `<form action="$_SERVER['PHP_SELF']" method="post">`.

The `foreach` loop within the PHP should also be changed to read `foreach (array_keys($_POST) as $key) {$$key=$_POST[$key];}`. This is to accommodate the method change. The loop could also be changed to `foreach (array_keys($_REQUEST) as $key) {$$key=$_REQUEST[$key];}`, which would make either GET or POST variables receivable, but is less secure.

Notice the use of `$_SERVER['PHP_SELF']` in the `form action` attribute. This is another built-in PHP variable that identifies the current page. By using this variable, the actual page name no longer matters, thereby adding flexibility.

Since these changes have been made, the page will no longer submit correctly. This is because there is no page called `$_SERVER['PHP_SELF']` on the server and the PHP code has not been expanded to include the form. Correcting this issue involves more steps. First, the closing PHP tag `?>` needs to be moved to include the form, and a PHP `print()` statement needs to be added, encapsulating the contents of the form.

A decision has to be made. Will all of the form appear in a print statement with all of the quotation marks escaped? That will make it work, but can be difficult to read. An alternative is to change the double quotes within the form to single quotes as follows:

```
print("
<form action=\"$_SERVER['PHP_SELF']\" method='post'>
<table cellspacing='0'>
<tr><td>First Name:</td><td><input type='text' id='firstname'
name='firstname' /></td></tr>
<tr><td>Last Name:</td><td><input type='text' id='lastname' name='last-
name' /></td></tr>
<tr><td>Address:</td><td><input type='text' id='address' name='address'
/></td></tr>
<tr><td>City:</td><td><input type='text' id='city' name='city'
/></td></tr>
<tr><td>State:</td><td><input type='text' id='state' name='state'
/></td></tr>
<tr><td>Zip Code:</td><td><input type='text' id='zip' name='zip'
/></td></tr>
<tr><td>Phone:</td><td><input type='text' id='phone' name='phone'
/></td></tr>
<tr><td>E-Mail:</td><td><input type='text' id='email' name='email'
/></td></tr>
```

```
<tr><td colspan='2'><p>How would you like to be contacted?</p>
Postal Mail: <input type='checkbox' id='contact[]' name='contact[]'
value='mail' />
Phone: <input type='checkbox' id='contact[]' name='contact[]'
value='phone' />
E-mail: <input type='checkbox' id='contact[]' name='contact[]'
value='email' /><br />
</td></tr>
<tr><td> </td><td><input type='submit' id='submit' name='submit'
value='Send' /><input type='reset' id='reset' name='reset'
value='Erase' /><input type='hidden' name='submit' id='submit'
value='1' /></td></tr>
</table>
</form>");
```

Once the quotation marks have been revised, the form will start working, but with errors, as shown in Figure 6.11.

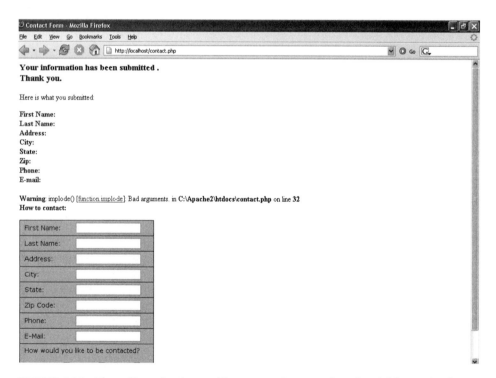

FIGURE 6.11   The self-posting form with an error due to unfound variables on load.

When examining Figure 6.11, an error can be seen in the middle of the page—**Warning**: implode() [function.implode]: Bad arguments. in **C:\Apache2\htdocs\contact.php** on line **32**. That is to be expected. The error occurs because the results have been loaded *before* the form has been submitted. The implode() function will only work on an array, and with no form data, $contact is not set. Should the completed form be submitted, it will not issue the warning.

Errors can be seen because the page is being tested on a local machine with display_errors *set to* on *in the* php.ini *file. This will normally be turned off on a production server for security reasons—another good reason to have a development machine.*

Another issue with the page, as it stands now, is that the form and results both appear all the time. This needs to be modified. A simple if/else block will resolve all remaining issues. On the line following foreach (array_keys($_POST) as $key) {$$key=$_POST[$key];}, type if($submit){.

On the line following print("How to contact: " . implode(",",$contact) . "<br />");, type }else{. This finishes the if statement surrounding the feedback area of the page and starts an else to enclose the form. Place a closing curly brace (}) on an empty line immediately above the closing ?>.

The form will now be completely functional, and is shown in Figure 6.12.

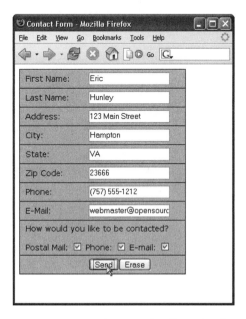 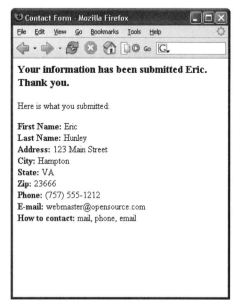

FIGURE 6.12 A functional self-posting form.

Another Self-Posting Variation

In addition to creating a giant print statement to create a form in a PHP self-posting document, HTML can be leveraged. For example, the else statement that created the form to collect user input is as follows:

```
else{
print("
<form action=\"$_SERVER['PHP_SELF']\" method='post'>
<table cellspacing='0'>
<tr><td>First Name:</td><td><input type='text' id='firstname'
name='firstname' /></td></tr>
<tr><td>Last Name:</td><td><input type='text' id='lastname' name='last-
name' /></td></tr>
<tr><td>Address:</td><td><input type='text' id='address' name='address'
/></td></tr>
<tr><td>City:</td><td><input type='text' id='city' name='city'
/></td></tr>
<tr><td>State:</td><td><input type='text' id='state' name='state'
/></td></tr>
<tr><td>Zip Code:</td><td><input type='text' id='zip' name='zip'
/></td></tr>
<tr><td>Phone:</td><td><input type='text' id='phone' name='phone'
/></td></tr>
<tr><td>E-Mail:</td><td><input type='text' id='email' name='email'
/></td></tr>
<tr><td colspan='2'><p>How would you like to be contacted?</p>
Postal Mail: <input type='checkbox' id='contact[]' name='contact[]'
value='mail' />
Phone: <input type='checkbox' id='contact[]' name='contact[]'
value='phone' />
E-mail: <input type='checkbox' id='contact[]' name='contact[]'
value='email' /><br />
</td></tr>
<tr><td> </td><td><input type='submit' id='submit' name='submit'
value='Send' /><input type='reset' id='reset' name='reset'
value='Erase' /><input type='hidden' name='submit' id='submit'
value='1' /></td></tr>
</table>
</form>");
}
?>
```

This `else` conditional can also be manipulated to work with HTML as follows:

```
else{
?>

<form action="<?=$_SERVER['PHP_SELF']; ?>" method="post">
<table cellspacing="0">
<tr><td>First Name:</td><td><input type="text" id="firstname"
name="firstname" /></td></tr>
<tr><td>Last Name:</td><td><input type="text" id="lastname" name="last-
name" /></td></tr>
<tr><td>Address:</td><td><input type="text" id="address" name="address"
/></td></tr>
<tr><td>City:</td><td><input type="text" id="city" name="city"
/></td></tr>
<tr><td>State:</td><td><input type="text" id="state" name="state"
/></td></tr>
<tr><td>Zip Code:</td><td><input type="text" id="zip" name="zip"
/></td></tr>
<tr><td>Phone:</td><td><input type="text" id="phone" name="phone"
/></td></tr>
<tr><td>E-Mail:</td><td><input type="text" id="email" name="email"
/></td></tr>
<tr><td colspan="2"><p>How would you like to be contacted?</p>
Postal Mail: <input type="checkbox" id="contact[]" name="contact[]"
value="mail" />
Phone: <input type="checkbox" id="contact[]" name="contact[]"
value="phone" />
E-mail: <input type="checkbox" id="contact[]" name="contact[]"
value="email" /><br />
</td></tr>
<tr><td> </td><td><input type="submit" id="submit" name="submit"
value="Send" /><input type="reset" id="reset" name="reset"
value="Erase" /><input type="hidden" name="submit" id="submit"
value="1" /></td></tr>
</table>
</form>

<?php
}
?>
```

In the modified code are some minor changes. First, the print statement has been removed and all HTML has been converted to a standard form. All additions to the code are in bold. What is happening in the large block is a small bit of trickery. Since PHP treats HTML between PHP blocks as a giant print statement, this section is taking advantage of that behavior. It starts with `}else{ ?>`, which closes the `if` conditional and starts an `else`. Then, the PHP block is closed with the `?>`, and the HTML `<form action="` is then output in a print statement. The PHP `<?=$_SERVER['PHP_SELF']; ?>` is processed, and all HTML until the next opening `<?php` tag is treated as another print statement. This eliminates the necessity of escaping or choosing single versus double quotes seen when the HTML is output with a `print()` function or `echo` statement.

CREATING A PHP SLIDESHOW

In this section, we'll use PHP to create a slideshow on the local Web server. While JavaScript is often used for slideshows, PHP is still a good choice. It will work whether or not JavaScript is enabled on the client, and can be dynamically created from a database. This example uses arrays to show the principle.

To begin the exercise, a new folder called `images` must be created in `C:\apache2\htdocs\`. Next, the slideshow folder from the `examples\Chapter06\` folder on the companion CD-ROM needs to be copied. It should then be pasted within `C:\apache2\htdocs\images\folder`. This makes all of the image files available for the three documents created in this exercise, the first of which is `thumbnails.php`.

ON THE CD

Creating `thumbnails.php`

The first document, `thumbnails.php`, is being created to be included in the other documents on the site. This is for the express purpose of loading thumbnails in each document. Here is the necessary code:

```
<table cellspacing="10"><tr>
<?php
    $captions = array("Blackbeard Festival: Hampton, VA. Final battle
reenactment.", "Carriage in Williamsburg, VA.","Yorktown Victory Cen-
ter: Yorktown, VA. Battle Camp.", "Yorktown Victory Center: Yorktown,
```

```
VA. Cannon Fire preparation.", "Downtown Hampton, VA seen from the
Hampton River.","Hampton&rsquo;s first fire truck. Hampton, VA","Hamp-
ton University, Hampton, Virginia","Liberty Bell 7 Capsule at the Vir-
ginia Air and Space Museum, Hampton, VA.","Osprey nest on the Hampton
River.","St. John&rsquo;s Episcopal Church founded 1610.","The Susan
Constant reproduction at Jamestown, VA.","Thatching a roof in
Jamestown,VA.");
    $gallery = array();
    for ($i=0;$i<12;$i++){
        $marker = $i + 1;
        $gallery[$i] = "gallery_$marker";
    }
    $marker = 0;
    for($i=0;$i<count($gallery);$i++){
        $marker++;
        print("<td><a href='photo.php?selected=$i'><img
src='images/slideshow/thumbs/$gallery[$i]_tn.jpg' alt='$captions[$i]'
width='40' height='40' border='0' /></a></td>");
        if($marker == 4){
            if($i<11){
                print("</tr>\n<tr valign='top'>");
                $marker=0;
            }
        }
    }
?>
<tr><td colspan="4"><p style="text-align: center; font-family: Verdana,
Helvetica, Arial; font-size: 13px; font-weight: bold"><em>Click any
image to expand.</em></p></td><tr></table>
```

No other code is needed for this document. There should be no <html>, <head>, *or* <body> *tags because this page is designed for the express purpose of being used as an include. Any extra HTML written in this page will cause duplication when* index.php *and* photo.php *(still to be made) are rendered. The excess tags will cause the pages to not validate.*

When taking a tour through the code, the first thing you see is the $captions array created. This array will be used multiple times. It will provide the information for captions on the page (photo.php) displaying the full size versions of photos, and will be used as the alt attribute value in both thumbnail and full-sized image tags.

Next, the `$gallery` `array` is created and a `for` loop is used to populate it—this is for convenience. Since all the image names (including thumbnails) for this application begin with `gallery_n`, it is easier to let a loop do the work of creating a list of names. The `$marker` variable is being used as a second counting mechanism because the image numbers start at one, but the array counts from zero.

Now that the basic arrays are created for the image information, table rows and cells need to be created for displaying the thumbnails:

```
$marker = 0;
    for($i=0;$i<count($gallery);$i++){
            $marker++;
            print("<td><a href='photo.php?selected=$i'><img
src='images/$gallery[$i]_tn.jpg' alt='$caption[$i]' width='35'
height='35' /></a></td>");
        if($marker == 4){
            if($i<11){
                    print("</tr>\n<tr valign='top'>");
                    $marker=0;
            }
        }
    }
}
?>
```

The code begins with `$marker` set to `0`. This is being used again to act as an alternate counter from the `$i` in the `for` loop.

Within the `for` loop, a couple of things are happening. First, a `<td>` is being created for each image, and the file path for each image is being created from the `$gallery` `array`. The `$caption` `array` is also being read so an `alt` attribute can be added to the `img` tag.

The second thing to notice is the `if` block, which prevents more than four images appearing in a row. If the conditional is not in place, all the images will be in a straight line and kill the design. The last nested `if` is being used to make sure a `<tr valign='top'>` is not added if the array is at its end.

Creating `index.php`

The second page to create is `index.php`, which will serve both as the home page and one of the pages that are using `thumbnails.php` as an include. The following code creates the page (the PHP include is in bold):

```
<html>
<head>
    <title>Homepage</title>
<style type="text/css">
h1 {
    text-align: center;
    background-color: #CCCCCC;
}
h1, p {
    font-family: Verdana, Helvetica, Arial;
    color: #3333FF;
}
p {
    font-size: 12px;
}
a {
    text-decoration: none;
    font-weight: bold;
}
a:hover {
    text-decoration: underline;
}
</style>
</head>
<body>
<div align="center">
<table style="text-align: left">
<tr><td colspan="2"><h1>Home Page Banner</h2></td></tr>
<tr><td><?php include("thumbnails.php"); ?></td>
<td style="width: 400px"><p>Lorem ipsum dolor sit amet, consetetur
sadipscing elitr, sed diam nonumy eirmod tempor invidunt ut labore et
dolore magna aliquyam erat, sed diam voluptua. At vero eos et accusam
et justo duo dolores et ea rebum. Stet clita kasd gubergren, no sea
takimata sanctus est Lorem ipsum dolor sit amet. Lorem ipsum dolor sit
amet, consetetur sadipscing elitr, sed diam nonumy eirmod tempor
invidunt ut labore et dolore magna aliquyam erat, sed diam voluptua. At
vero eos et accusam et justo duo dolores et ea rebum. Stet clita kasd
gubergren, no sea takimata sanctus est Lorem ipsum dolor sit amet.
Lorem ipsum dolor sit amet, consetetur sadipscing elitr, sed diam non-
umy eirmod tempor invidunt ut labore et dolore magna aliquyam erat, sed
diam voluptua. At vero eos et accusam et justo duo dolores et ea rebum.
Stet clita kasd gubergren, no sea takimata sanctus est Lorem ipsum
```

```
dolor sit amet.</p>
</td></tr>
</table>
</body>
</html>
```

By using the PHP include, some of the code has been removed from the page, trimming it a little. The page will still display the thumbnails as shown in Figure 6.13.

FIGURE 6.13   Thumbnails fed by a PHP include.

Creating `photo.php`

The `photo.php` page is being created to display the larger images referenced by the thumbnails. By using PHP, instead of having 12 separate pages (one for each image), only one is necessary. The following code can be used to create `photo.php` (all PHP is bolded):

```html
<html>
<head>
    <title>Photo Gallery</title>
<style type="text/css">
h1 {
    text-align: center;
    background-color: #CCCCCC;
}
h1, p {
    font-family: Verdana, Helvetica, Arial;
    color: #0033FF;
}
p {
    font-size: 12px;
}
a {
    text-decoration: none;
    font-weight: bold;
    color: #0033FF;
}
a:hover {
    text-decoration: underline;
}
</style>
</head>
<body>
<div align="center">
<table style="text-align: left">
    <tr><td colspan="2"><h1>Photo Gallery</h1>
    <tr valign="top">
            <td>
                    <?php
                            include("thumbnails.php");
                    ?>
            </td>
            <td valign="top" style="width: 400px; height: 350px">
                    <?php
                            $selected = $_GET["selected"];
                            if(is_null($selected)){
                                    $selected = 0;
                            }
                            $source = $gallery[$selected];
```

```
                            print("<p><img
src='images/slideshow/$source.jpg' width='400' height='300' />");
                      print("<br />$captions[$selected]</p></td></tr>");
                            $prev = $selected;
                            if($prev > 0){
                                  $prev--;
                            }else{
                                  $prev = 11;
                            }
                            print("<tr><td colspan='2'
align='right'><p><a
href='$PHP_SELF?selected=$prev'>&lt;previous</a>    
; ");
                            $next = $selected;
                            if($next < 11){
                                  $next++;
                            }else{
                                  $next = 0;
                            }
                            print("<a href=\"" . $_SERVER['PHP_SELF']
. "?selected=$next\">next &gt;</a></p>");
                            ?>
                  </td>
            </tr>
      </table>
      </div>
      </body>
      </html>
```

As can be seen in the code, there are four different PHP scripts on the page. This shows how well it embeds inside of HTML. All of these scripts work together to draw the complete page as shown in Figure 6.14.

The multiple scripts in photo.php combine to control the behavior of the gallery application. The first section of PHP code is the include, which loads the thumbnails and provides the $captions array and partial image filenames in the $gallery array.

The second section of PHP code is used to display the large image. It should be explored further:

```
<?php
    $selected = $_GET["selected"];
    if(is_null($selected)){
```

```
            $selected = 0;
        }
        $source = $gallery[$selected];
        print("<img src='images/$source.jpg' width='350' height='250' />");
    ?>
```

FIGURE 6.14 The gallery page—photo.php.

The first part of the code is the creation of the $selected variable. Its value is assigned from reading the built-in $_GET array. Immediately following the $selected declaration is an if statement, the purpose of which is to ensure that a user coming directly to the page (instead of through the normal path of index.php) will see the large image. The if checks $selected to see if it is null (no value). If it is, the if action statement assigns it the value 0. This means that $selected will always have a value when the page is loaded.

Once $selected has an assigned value, $source is created by using $selected to provide the location in the $gallery array for the partial image name. Then, $source is used within an img tag src path to load the image.

The next two sections of PHP provide the next and previous links, creating an alternate navigation method to view the images. The code that works the previous link is

```php
<?php
    $prev = $selected;
    if($prev > 0){
            $prev--;
    }else{
            $prev = 11;
    }
    print("<a href='$PHP_SELF?selected=$prev'>&lt; previous</a>");
?>
```

Within the code, a new variable is created—$prev. It is given the value from $selected, which holds the array marker of the current image source being displayed. Next, an if/else conditional is used to determine if the value of $prev is greater than zero. If it is, $prev is decremented; otherwise, it is set to 11 to prevent any negative number from being assigned. There are no negative values in the $gallery array, and the link will cycle through all of the images and start over when it hits the end.

Once $prev has a value, it is assigned to the previous link. $PHP_SELF is also used because the link will be pointing to the current page.

The next link is created the same way as the previous link; only everything is reversed. In addition, another variable is created called $next that is used instead of $prev.

SUMMARY

That completes our brief tour of PHP coding and syntax—there is much more to explore. In the upcoming chapters, PHP will be used even more starting with Chapter 7, "PHP and the File System."

7 | PHP and the File System

In This Chapter

- Creating a Web Counter
- Working with Images in PHP
- Generating E-Mail
- Summary

In the previous chapter, we introduced PHP. It is now time to explore more of its features. In this chapter, we will use PHP to access the file system to create a basic Web counter and generate e-mail. We'll also explore creating images with the GD Library.

CREATING A WEB COUNTER

One commonly found feature on Web pages is a counter, which is used to advertise the popularity of a site, or for site owners to track the number of hits. Web counters are not an exact science. Most of the basic ones simply track every time a page is loaded, which means results can be skewed by a single person continuously refreshing a page.

It takes a great deal of programming to create an accurate tracking system—that will not be happening in this chapter. This chapter is about creating a simple Web counter. While it will not be the most accurate tracking system out there, it can still be useful to get a general sense of people visiting the site. It can also be handy for tracking particular pages, to help inform site operators if a page is getting traffic.

To create a basic Web counter, all we need is a text file and some PHP code. The text file is commonly referred to as a "flat file" because it is not a database, and its storage is rudimentary—which in the case of a counter, is perfect.

When creating the text file, take note of the permissions. If the file is going to be loaded onto a Unix/Linux server later, the rights have to be changed to allow read and write permissions for everyone. On a Windows server, it can be left alone.

After creating the text file, create a new file called `counter.php` in `C:\Apache2\htdocs\` with the following code:

```php
<?php
    $fp = fopen("count.txt","r");
    $count = fread($fp,filesize("count.txt"));
    fclose($fp);
    $count++;
    $file = fopen("count.txt","w");
    fwrite($fp,$count);
    fclose($file);
?>
```

The counter can now be used in any page. To experiment with the counter, add an echo statement or print() function using the $count variable before the ?> like:

```php
echo "<h1>The current count is $count</h1>";
```

Try the page in a browser by typing *http://localhost/counter.php*. The screen shown in Figure 7.1 will appear.

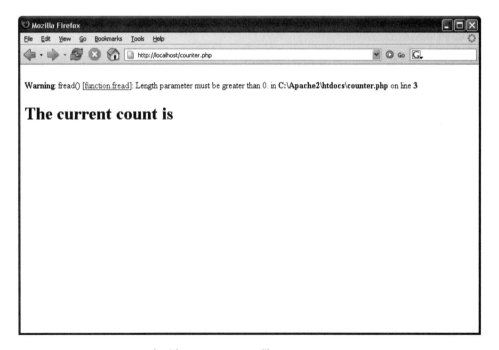

FIGURE 7.1 Error created with an empty text file.

The error shown in Figure 7.1 is caused by the fact that count.txt is an empty text file. There are no characters within, so the filesize("count.txt") function is returning NULL. To resolve the issue, simply type a single 0 within the text file; that will add a character making the file size 1 byte. The count will also start correctly reflecting the first visitor because $count is incremented before being reported. Figure 7.2 shows the results.

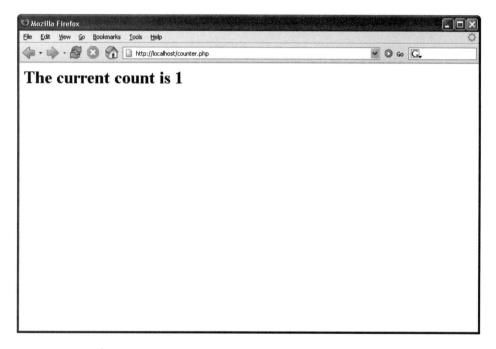

FIGURE 7.2 Using counter.php.

PHP File System Functions

There are several functions available when working with PHP and the file system:

fopen(file,mode): Opens a file for access. The mode determines what is allowed. Several modes are available: r for read only (places the file pointer at the beginning of the file); r+ for read and write access; w for write only (places the pointer at the beginning, truncates the file size to zero, and will attempt to create a file if it does not exist); w+ for write and read; a for append (adds to the end of a file and attempts creation if the file does not exist); and a+ for append and read.

The fopen() function is often used to create a resource handle called a file pointer, as in $fp = fopen(file,mode); ($fp is a commonly used variable name for file pointers and will be used throughout this section). Upon creation of $fp in the example, the file is open and $fp is used as the resource handle or file pointer to it. This file pointer can then be referenced in other functions as shown previously in the page counter. The file will remain open to the script until it is explicitly closed with the fclose() function.

Be careful when using the r+ mode. If a file is read before any data is to be written to it, the data may be appended instead of overwritten. This is because in the r+ mode, the file pointer acts in a similar manner to a playhead on a VCR. Where it leaves off after reading with the r+ function will be where it will start to record.

fclose($fp): Used to close the file identified with the resource handle.

fread($fp, *length*): Used to read an arbitrary amount of information in a file. Save the following line of text in a file called test.txt in the htdocs directory:

This is a line of text within a text file.

The following code can be saved as test.php in htdocs:

```
<?php
    $fp = fopen("text.txt","r");
        $contents = fread($fp, 13);
        fclose($fp);
    echo "<h1>$contents</h1>";
?>
```

The result of *http://localhost/test.php* is shown in Figure 7.3.

Notice how the contents have not been completely read, which is because the length argument is set to 13. This means fread() will stop reading after it has reached 13 bytes and return the results.

The filesize() function can be used to make sure all of the data is received as shown previously in the page counter, but there must be data within the text file or there will be an error.

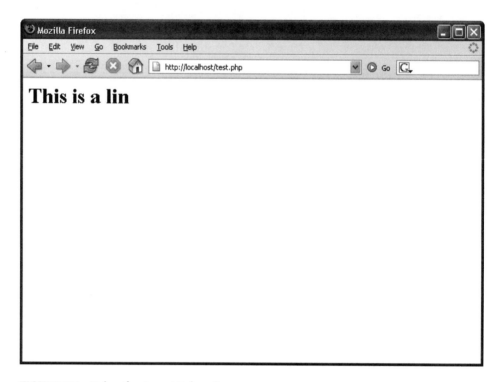

FIGURE 7.3 Using the `fread()` function.

fgets($fp): Retrieves a single line from a file pointer. This is commonly used in conjunction with a loop and the `feof()` function. The following two parts show this in use with the results shown in Figure 7.4.

The text file `billofrights.txt`:

```
Congress shall make no law respecting an establishment of religion, or
prohibiting the free exercise thereof; or abridging the freedom of
speech, or of the press; or the right of the people peaceably to assem-
ble, and to petition the government for a redress of grievances.
A well regulated militia, being necessary to the security of a free
state, the right of the people to keep and bear arms, shall not be
infringed.
No soldier shall, in time of peace be quartered in any house, without
the consent of the owner, nor in time of war, but in a manner to be
prescribed by law.
```

The right of the people to be secure in their persons, houses, papers, and effects, against unreasonable searches and seizures, shall not be violated, and no warrants shall issue, but upon probable cause, supported by oath or affirmation, and particularly describing the place to be searched, and the persons or things to be seized.

No person shall be held to answer for a capital, or otherwise infamous crime, unless on a presentment or indictment of a grand jury, except in cases arising in the land or naval forces, or in the militia, when in actual service in time of war or public danger; nor shall any person be subject for the same offense to be twice put in jeopardy of life or limb; nor shall be compelled in any criminal case to be a witness against himself, nor be deprived of life, liberty, or property, without due process of law; nor shall private property be taken for public use, without just compensation.

In all criminal prosecutions, the accused shall enjoy the right to a speedy and public trial, by an impartial jury of the state and district wherein the crime shall have been committed, which district shall have been previously ascertained by law, and to be informed of the nature and cause of the accusation; to be confronted with the witnesses against him; to have compulsory process for obtaining witnesses in his favor, and to have the assistance of counsel for his defense.

In suits at common law, where the value in controversy shall exceed twenty dollars, the right of trial by jury shall be preserved, and no fact tried by a jury, shall be otherwise reexamined in any court of the United States, than according to the rules of the common law.

Excessive bail shall not be required, nor excessive fines imposed, nor cruel and unusual punishments inflicted.

The enumeration in the Constitution, of certain rights, shall not be construed to deny or disparage others retained by the people.

The powers not delegated to the United States by the Constitution, nor prohibited by it to the states, are reserved to the states respectively, or to the people.

The billofrights.php code:

```
<html>
<head>
    <title>The United States Bill of Rights</title>
</head>
<body>
<h2>The U.S. Bill of Rights</h2>
<dl>
```

```php
<?php
    $fp = fopen("billofrights.txt","r");
    $num = 1;
    while(!feof($fp)){
        $line=fgets($fp);
        echo "<dt><strong>Amendment $num</strong></dt>";
        echo "<dd>$line</dd>";
        $num++;
    }
    fclose($fp);
?>
</dl>
</body>
</html>
```

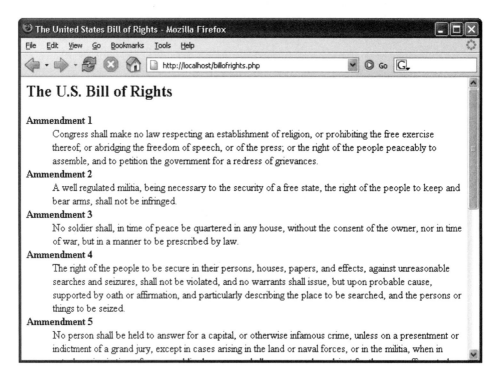

FIGURE 7.4 The Bill of Rights file.

This same principle can be used for creating a file called states.php. When collecting address information from users, often webmasters want to be as accurate and consistent as possible. When asking for state information, it is unknown whether the users will type out the entire state, the U.S. abbreviation, or some other approach.

Within the states file will be a state name followed by a comma and its abbreviation per line, as in Arizona, AZ. The upcoming code can be then used to create states.php. This file includes a function creating a <select> menu for users to choose the appropriate state in a form.

```php
<?php
    function states(){
        echo "<select name=\"state\">";
        $fp = fopen("states.txt","r");
        while(!feof($fp)){
            $line=fgets($fp);
            $state = explode(", ",$line);
            echo "<option value=\"$state[1]\">$state[0] -
            $state[1]</option>";
        }
        echo "</select>";
    fclose($fp);
}
?>
```

After states.php has been created and saved, it can be used in any PHP file with the following code:

```php
<?php
include("states.php"); //change the path to match the proper directory
states();
?>
```

The file states.php should only be included once in any given PHP script. For example, if there will be sections for both billing and shipping addresses, make sure that include("states.php"); is written only once on the page, or use include_once("states.php"); to overcome any oversight. This will cause the PHP engine to ignore any other include_once() requests. The states() function call can be used as often as needed after the include statement.

On Windows, PHP 4 is case insensitive, which can lead to an odd occurrence with the include_once() *function. If a second* include_once() *calls the same file, but the case is different, the file will be reloaded. For example,* include_once ("file.php"); *followed by* include_once("File.php"); *will cause* file.php *to be loaded twice. This behavior has been corrected in PHP 5.*

The result of the function is shown in Figure 7.5.

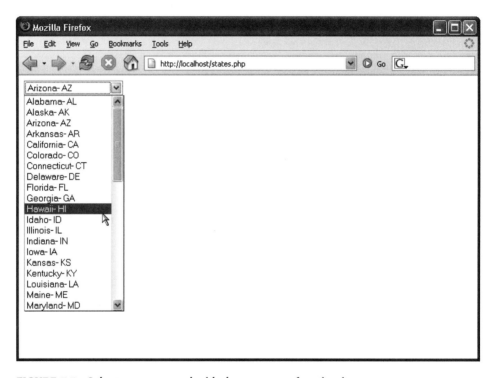

FIGURE 7.5   Select menu created with the states() function in states.php.

fgetc($fp): Works in a similar manner to fgets(), only it returns a single character.

fputs() and **fwrite():** These two functions are formed the same way and deliver identical results. They are used to add information to an external file. How that information will be added depends on what arguments were used with the fopen() function. Compare the following script with its results shown in Figure 7.6 to see the effect of the arguments:

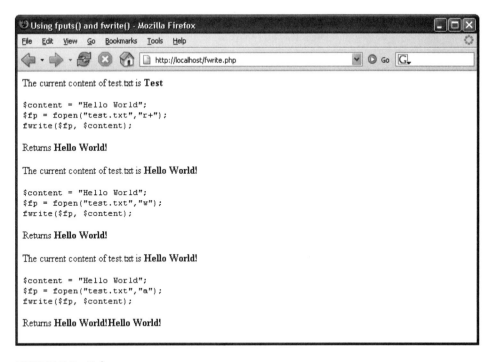

FIGURE 7.6   Using fwrite().

```
<html>
<head>
<title>Using fputs() and fwrite()</title>
<style type="text/css">
.code {
    font-family: monospace;
}
</style>
</head>
<body>
<?php
    $fp = fopen("test.txt","r");
    $content = fgets($fp);
    echo "<p>The current content of test.txt is
    <strong>$content</strong></p>";
    $content="Hello World!";
    fclose($fp);
```

```
$fp = fopen("test.txt","r+");
fwrite($fp, $content);
fclose($fp);
$fp = fopen("test.txt","r");
echo "<p class='code'>\$content = \"Hello World\";<br />";
echo "\$fp = fopen(\"test.txt\",\"r+\"); <br />fwrite(\$fp,
\$content);</p>";
echo "<p>Returns ";
$content = fgets($fp);
cho "<strong>$content</strong></p>";
fclose($fp);

$fp = fopen("test.txt","r");
$content = fgets($fp);
echo "<p>The current content of test.txt is
<strong>$content</strong></p>";
$content="Hello World!";
fclose($fp);
$fp = fopen("test.txt","w");
fwrite($fp, $content);
fclose($fp);
$fp = fopen("test.txt","r");
echo "<p class='code'>\$content = \"Hello World\";<br />";
echo "\$fp = fopen(\"test.txt\",\"w\"); <br />fwrite(\$fp,
\$content);</p>";
echo "<p>Returns ";
$content = fgets($fp);
echo "<strong>$content</strong></p>";
fclose($fp);

$fp = fopen("test.txt","r");
$content = fgets($fp);
echo "<p>The current content of test.txt is
<strong>$content</strong></p>";
$content="Hello World!";
fclose($fp);
$fp = fopen("test.txt","a");
fwrite($fp, $content);
fclose($fp);
$fp = fopen("test.txt","r");
echo "<p class='code'>\$content = \"Hello World\";<br />";
```

```
        echo "\$fp = fopen(\"test.txt\",\"a\"); <br />fwrite(\$fp,
        \$content);</p>";
        echo "<p>Returns ";
        $content = fgets($fp);
        echo "<strong>$content</strong></p>";
        fclose($fp);
    ?>
    </body>
```

flock($fp, *operation*): Anytime external files are being accessed, there is a risk of corruption if too many script instances are trying to access them at the same time. The flock() function helps prevent too much access when a file is open. There are three commonly used operations. The first of these is shared, written as flock($fp,LOCK_SH). It allows other scripts to read the file at the same time, but prevents writing to the file. The second option is exclusive, written as flock($fp, LOCK_EX), and prevents any other access and is commonly used while writing to the file. The last option is release or flock($fp, LOCK_UN). A file lock will also be released if the resource handle is closed using the fclose() function.

fseek($fp,*int_offset*,*[whence]*): Used to move the pointer around a file. For example, fseek($fp, 100); will set the pointer to 100 bytes from the start of the file. If the third argument of whence is to be used, there are three options: SEEK_SET, SEEK_CURR, and SEEK_END. SEEK_SET is the default, and sets the position to the number of bytes specified from the beginning of the file. SEEK_CURR sets the offset from the current position, and SEEK_END sets the position from the end of the file (a negative integer can be used, but is not required).

ftell($fp): Used to determine the current position in the file. Will return the byte number.

touch(*filename*, *[modtime]*,*[accesstime]*): Technically, its purpose is to set the access and modification times of a file, but it is more commonly used to create files. If a file does not exist to modify the times (which are optional arguments anyway), PHP attempts to create the file. Remember that proper rights to the directory have to exist on Unix/Linux machines.

unlink(*filename*): Used to delete files.

file(*filename*): Puts each line of a file into an array. This works well if the file is a list of items.

`file_get_contents(`*`filename`*`)`: Available in PHP 5. Will read all of the contents within a file in a single operation. This is handy to use, as it only requires the filename as an argument.

`file_put_contents(`*`filename`*`,`*`values`*`)`: Available in PHP 5. Writes the contents of the second argument to an external file. Usually, the second argument will be a variable. This function will also attempt to create a file if the file does not currently exist.

Revisiting the Counter

As you can see, there are many ways to access external files using PHP. To help demonstrate this point, consider the following three scripts:

```
<?php
    $fp = fopen("count.txt","r");
    $count = fread($fp,filesize("count.txt"));
    fclose($fp);
    $count++;
    $file = fopen("count.txt","w");
    fwrite($fp,$count);
    fclose($file);
?>
```

The first example shows the original script used to create a counter previously. This is a perfectly fine version, and many similar scripts can be found in use on the Internet. However, the script can be trimmed down a little more and revised as follows:

```
<?php
    $fp = fopen("count.txt","r+");
    $count = fgets($fp);
    rewind($fp);
    fwrite($fp,++$count);
    fclose($fp);
?>
```

In this second version of the counter, the script line count has shrunk from seven to five. However, more importantly, the new version only opens and closes the external file once. It accomplishes this with the r+ mode. Notice how rewind($fp) is included; that is to prevent the script from appending. The script also uses fgets() instead of fread(), removing the need for the filesize() function. Moreover, instead of having $count increment on a separate line, it is happening as it is being sent as an argument in the fwrite() function.

When sending a variable that should be incremented as it is being sent, remember to write it as prefix—++$variable. If you do not, the value of the variable will be sent, and the variable will be incremented. Therefore, in the case of the counter, if the fwrite() *function is written as* fwrite($fp,$count++), *the counter will never change. This is because when looking at the structure of the function, the count is read from* count.txt. *Then, that value is incremented as it is sent to the file again. If it is written as $count++, the original value will be sent right back to the text file unchanged, and the increment will be irrelevant.*

The next variation of the counter script is as follows:

```php
<?php
    $count = file_get_contents("count.txt");
    file_put_contents("count.txt",++$count);
?>
```

Notice that only two lines of code are used. Unfortunately, this version can only be used in PHP 5 and later. However, it is worth using if that is what is installed on the server.

A last consideration is to use the counter as a function in an include file. This offers the greatest flexibility and can be done very easily. The second version may look like the following:

```php
<?php
    function counter($file){
        $fp = fopen($file,"r+");
        $count = fgets($fp);
        rewind($fp);
        fwrite($fp,++$count);
        fclose($fp);
        return $count;
    }
?>
```

After being included in a script, the function can be called simply with counter(*filename*). Making the filename an argument makes the function more flexible still. This way, there can be a counter on more than one page if needed. Each counter can be made unique by having a different text file. The same function can be created on the third counter variation for PHP 5 using the following code:

```
<?php
    function counter($file){
        $count = file_get_contents($file);
        file_put_contents($file,++$count);
        return $count;
        }
?>
```

WORKING WITH IMAGES IN PHP

PHP doesn't only work with text and forms. With the addition of the GD Library, it can also be used to create dynamic images. This section will explore the basic functionality of the GD Library, and later it will be used to create dynamic graphs.

Enabling GD Support

The first thing to do when using PHP and Windows is to enable the GD Library, which is done in the `php.ini` configuration file. The process is different depending if PHP 4 or 5 is being used.

For PHP 4, find the line `extension_dir = "./"` and modify it to `extension_dir = "./extensions"`. Next, find the line `;extension=php_gd2.dll` and remove the semi-colon. Finally, restart the Apache HTTP Server if PHP is being used as a module.

For PHP 5, make certain the `extension_dir` line has been modified to read `extension_dir = "./ext/"`. Next, remove the semicolon from `;extension=php_gd2.dll` and then restart Apache if PHP has been installed as a module.

Creating Shapes

There are several shapes available with the GD Library, including lines, rectangles, ellipses, polygons, and arcs. Here is a list of some commonly used functions for the GD Library:

imagecreate(*width*, *height*): Creates the initial image and its width and height. This is assigned to a variable, as in `image=imagecreate(300,300);`. All shapes are then added to the base image.

imagedestroy(*image*): Destroys the image to save server memory. If this function is not used, the images created will accumulate on the server.

imagecolorallocate(*image*, *R*, *G*, *B*): Used to create colors for use in the image. These colors are assigned to variables as follows: `$white = imagecolorallocate($image, 255,255,255);`. The first allocated color will be the default background color of the image.

`imageline(`*`image`*`,` *`x`*`,` *`y`*`,` *`x`*`,` *`y`*`,` *`color`*`)`: Creates a line defining the x (left to right) and y (up and down) coordinates for the beginning and ending points. GD draws a straight line to connect these points.

`imagerectangle(`*`image`*`,` *`x`*`,` *`y`*`,` *`x`*`,` *`y`*`,` *`color`*`)`: Creates the strokes for an empty rectangle by defining first the top left, and then bottom right corners (or vertices). PHP adds the lines to connect these together.

`imagefilledrectangle(`*`image`*`,` *`x`*`,` *`y`*`,` *`x`*`,` *`y`*`)`: Creates a rectangle fill. `imagerectangle()` creates the strokes (lines).

`imageellipse(`*`image`*`,` *`center_x`*`,` *`center_y`*`,` *`width`*`,` *`height`*`)`: Creates an ellipse by providing the center points, width, and height. This function is more recent. Earlier versions of PHP and GD used the `imagearc()` function for creating ellipses.

`imagefilledellipse(`*`image`*`,` *`center_x`*`,`*`center_y`*`,`*`width`*`,`*`height`*`)`: Creates an elliptical fill using the center coordinates, width, and height. Like `imageellipse()`, functionality was previously served by another function—`imagefilledarc()`.

`imagefilledpolygon(`*`image`*`,`*`point_array`*`,`*`sides`*`,`*`color`*`)`: This shape is much more complex than a basic rectangle or ellipse. One difference between it and other shapes is that it requires an array for its coordinates, and an argument for the number of sides.

`imagearc(`*`image`*`,` *`center_x`*`,` *`center_y`*`,` *`width`*`,` *`height`*`,` *`start_degree`*`,` *`end_degree`*`,` *`color`*`)`: This was initially used for creating arcs and ellipses. It adds the starting and ending degree arguments to what is found in the ellipse functions. This is how the amount of an ellipse is covered.

`imagefilledarc(`*`image`*`,` *`center_x`*`,` *`center_y`*`,` *`width`*`,` *`height`*`,` *`start_degree`*`,` *`end_degree`*`,` *`color`*`,` *`style`*`)`: This is the same as the `imagearc()` function, only with the added style argument. There are four options available with this argument: `IMG_ARC_PIE` creates a rounded edge, `IMG_ARC_CHORD` connects the points, `IMG_ARC_NOFILL` outlines a section, and `IMG_ARC_EDGED` connects the beginning and ending edges.

`imagestring(`*`image`*`,` *`text_size`*`,` *`x`*`,` *`y`*`,` *`text`*`,` *`color`*`)`: Used to add text to images. There are five default font sizes available numbered appropriately 1 through 5. Custom fonts can be loaded, but is beyond the scope of this book.

`imagesetthickness(`*`image`*`,` *`int`*`)`: Sets the thickness of all strokes in shapes following the command. To change thickness, it needs to be typed again with a new value. It takes two arguments: the image requiring the change, and an integer representing the pixel thickness, such as `imagesetthickness($image,5);`.

Adding the Header

One of the first steps in creating an image file in PHP is to use the `header()` function. This informs the browser what type of file is coming. One of three lines are commonly used: `header("Content-type: image/png");` for creating a PNG (Portable Network Graphics) file, `header("Content-type: image/gif");` for creating a GIF (Graphics Interchange Format), or `header("Content-type: image/jpeg");` for creating JPEG (Joint Photographers Expert Group) files. The most commonly used of the three is `header("Content-type: image/png");` because it was designed for the Web and offers features of both JPEG and GIF, and will be used for all examples in this chapter.

Creating the Image

After the header has been created identifying what type of image is being used, the image itself needs to be created. This is an easy process requiring a variable name for the image, and the `createimage()` function with the width and height as arguments like `$image = createimage(400,400);`.

Whenever creating an image, other lines of code should be added automatically toward the end of the script. First, there should be one of the three output functions (they should match the header file type): `imagepng(image,[filename])`, `imagejpeg(image,[filename])`, or `imagegif(image,[filename])`. An example would be `imagepng($image);`. If the results are to be used in creating a separate file, the filename argument will need to be provided as a string. Otherwise, the results are formatted for a browser.

The other line that must be added is `imagedestroy(image)` so the created image will be removed from memory. The following code can be considered a template for creating any `.png` style image for use in browsers:

```php
<?php
    header("Content-type: image/png");
    $image = imagecreate(400,400);

    //colors and shapes go here

    imagepng($image);
    imagedestroy($image);
?>
```

It is very important that there are no extra lines or space before the opening `<?php` and closing `?>`. Any extra space or HTML can make the graphic fail.

Adding Colors

Before any colors can be added to an image, they must first be defined. This is done with the `imagecolorallocate()` function. A variable is created with the preferred name of the color, and `imagecolorallocate()` is used with the image variable name and RGB (Red, Green, Blue) values as arguments, as in – `$gray = imagecolorallocate($image,175,175,175);`. The RGB color values can be written as either base 10 numbers `0-255`, or hexadecimal `0x00–0xFF` (the `0x` is required as a flag showing the numbers as hexadecimal). Color allocations are usually created together in a list for clarity. The first color will act as a background color of the image.

Creating a Line

The most basic of all graphic shapes created with the GD Library is the line, which requires six arguments. These are broken down to the image, four coordinate arguments, and the color of the line, as in `imageline($image,75,100,185,190,$black);`. The four coordinate arguments are really two pairs; one pair is for the first point, and the second is for the second point. GD connects these two points with a stroke, and a straight line is created as shown in Figure 7.7.

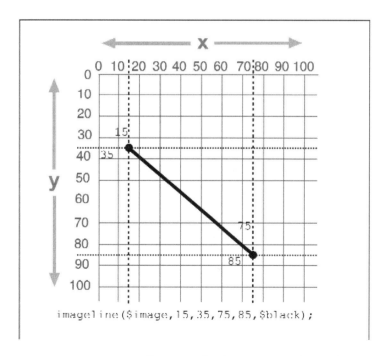

FIGURE 7.7   How coordinates work when creating a line with PHP and the GD Library.

The easiest way to look at the coordinate system is to imagine the graphic as a grid. Figure 7.7 shows it as 100 pixels width and height. To figure the first x coordinate, think of an imaginary straight line running up and down at the number of pixels from the left. The second coordinate is on the y-axis, or up and down. If a second line is imagined, a point will be created where the two lines intersect. This principle is repeated for the second point.

The following code creates an image containing a single line with its result shown in Figure 7.8:

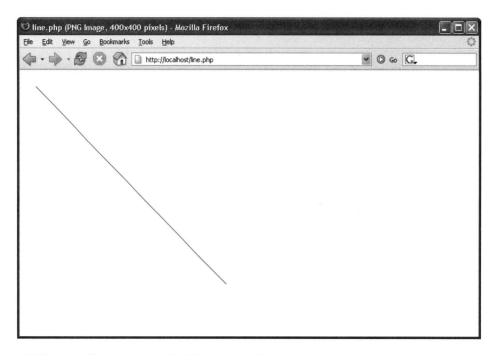

FIGURE 7.8 Line creation with PHP and the GD Library.

```php
<?php
    //image definition
    header("Content-type: image/png");
    $image = imagecreate(400,400);

    //color allocation
    $white = imagecolorallocate($image,255,255,255);
    $black = imagecolorallocate($image,0,0,0);
```

```
//shape creation
imageline($image,20,20,350,350,$black);

//image creation and cleanup
imagepng($image);
imagedestroy($image);
?>
```

Creating Rectangles

Rectangles use one of two functions: imagerectangle(*image*, *x*, *y*, *x*, *y*, *color*) or imagefilledrectangle(*image*, *x*, *y*, *x*, *y*, *color*). The first creates the lines, and the second the fill. Rectangles take the same number of arguments as lines. Figure 7.9 shows how it works.

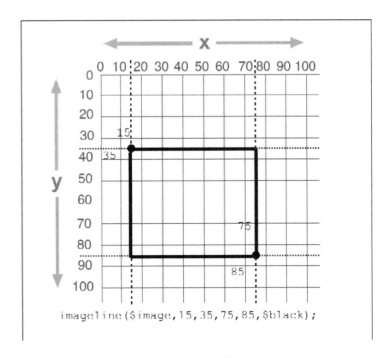

FIGURE 7.9   Exploring rectangle coordinates.

Like lines, rectangles require two pairs of coordinates; only for rectangles, these coordinates create the top-left and bottom-right corners. These pairs are all that are needed to create a complete rectangle. Remember visualizing an imaginary line for each of the coordinates and placing a point at each vertex? Rectangles work with the imaginary lines to calculate the edges. The following code creates some rectangles with the results shown in Figure 7.10:

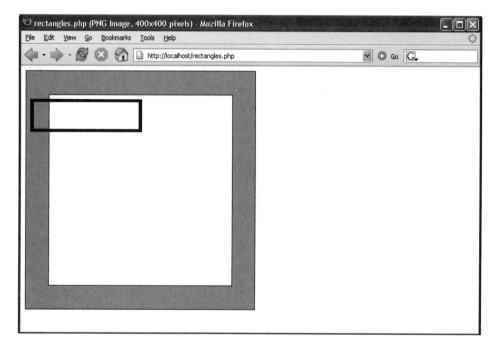

FIGURE 7.10 Creating rectangles.

```php
<?php
    header("Content-type: image/png");
    $image = imagecreate(400,400);

    $white = imagecolorallocate($image,255,255,255);
    $black = imagecolorallocate($image,0,0,0);
    $gray = imagecolorallocate($image,175,175,175);

    imagefilledrectangle($image, 0,0,399,399,$gray);
    imagerectangle($image, 0,0,399,399,$black);
```

```php
imagefilledrectangle($image, 40,40,359,359,$white);
imagerectangle($image,40,40,359,359,$black);

imagesetthickness($image,5);
imagerectangle($image,10,50,200,100,$black);

imagepng($image);
imagedestroy($image);
?>
```

This image has five rectangles; three comprised of strokes, and two are fills. There is also a imagesetthickness() slipped in to show how it works for images. One thing to notice is the order of the functions. For example, the first line is image-filledrectangle($image, 0,0,399,399,$gray);, followed by the line imagerectan-gle($image, 0, 0, 399, 399, $black);. This may seem odd because most envision a border declared before a fill.

The reason the order has to be reversed is due to the way shapes are displayed. The image can be seen as a stack; the first listed items are placed first with all subsequent shapes set on top. For example, if imagerectangle($image, 0, 0, 399, 399, $black); were declared first, it would be buried under imagefilledrectangle($image, 0,0,399,399,$gray);. Remember that order counts for all shapes.

Creating Ellipses

Ellipses are very easy to create. The following code creates four ellipses (two strokes and two fills) and is shown in Figure 7.11:

```php
<?php
    header("Content-type: image/png");
    $image = imagecreate(400,400);

    $white = imagecolorallocate($image,255,255,255);
    $black = imagecolorallocate($image,0,0,0);
    $gray = imagecolorallocate($image,175,175,175);

    imagefilledellipse($image, 100, 200, 200, 200, $gray);
    imageellipse($image, 100, 200, 200, 200, $black);
    imagefilledellipse($image, 250, 200, 200, 200, $white);
    imageellipse($image, 250, 200, 200, 200, $black);

    imagepng($image);
    imagedestroy($image);
?>
```

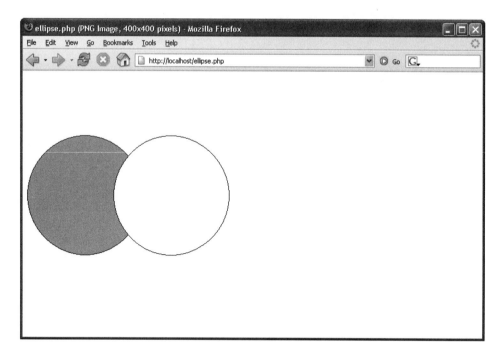

FIGURE 7.11 Using ellipses.

In this example, there are four ellipses created. They are all perfect circles, but they don't have to be. Again, order counts, and this allows the white filled "disc" to cover the gray.

Creating Arcs

Arcs are more complex than ellipses, and previously were used as such in addition to their arc functionality. The following code and Figure 7.12 demonstrate arcs in action:

```php
<?php
    header("Content-type: image/png");
    $image = imagecreate(400,400);

    $white = imagecolorallocate($image,255,255,255);
    $black = imagecolorallocate($image,0,0,0);
    $gray = imagecolorallocate($image,175,175,175);
```

```
imagefilledarc($image, 200, 200, 300, 300, 0, 250, $gray,
IMG_ARC_PIE);
imagefilledarc($image, 200, 200, 300, 300, 250, 300, $white,
IMG_ARC_PIE);
imagefilledarc($image, 200, 200, 300, 300, 300, 360, $black,
IMG_ARC_PIE);
imagearc($image, 200, 200, 300, 300, 0, 360, $black);

imagepng($image);
imagedestroy($image);
?>
```

In this image, four arcs are used; three fills with the IMG_ARC_PIE style and one line. PHP calls an arc a partial ellipse, and the diagram in Figure 7.12 shows why. The three fills are all incomplete, with each continuing where the last left off to complete the ellipse. The line acting as a border is a complete ellipse created with the arc function degrees running from 0 to 360.

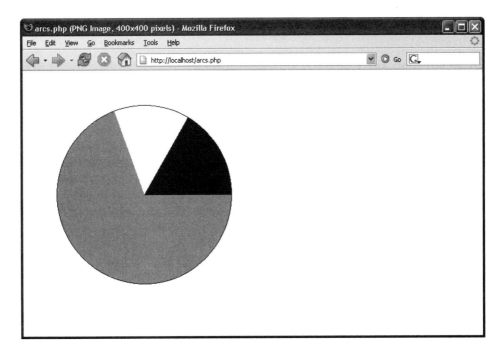

FIGURE 7.12   Using arcs with PHP and the GD Library.

Creating Polygons

The more coordinates involved, the more complex shapes become. Polygons are a case and point of this phenomenon. They require an array that includes all of the necessary points to work correctly. The following code with the results shown in Figure 7.13 displays two polygons used in the same image:

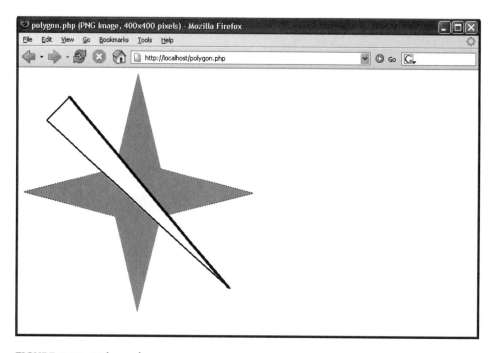

FIGURE 7.13 Using polygons.

```php
<?php
    header("Content-type: image/png");
    $image = imagecreate(400,400);

    $white = imagecolorallocate($image,255,255,255);
    $black = imagecolorallocate($image,0,0,0);
    $gray = imagecolorallocate($image,175,175,175);

    $points = array(200, 1, 240, 160, 399, 200, 240, 240, 200, 399, 160,
    240, 1, 200, 160, 160);
    imagepolygon($image,$points,8,$black);
```

```
    imagefilledpolygon($image,$points,8,$gray);

    $points = array(80,40,40,80,359,359);
    imagesetthickness($image,5);
    imagefilledpolygon($image,$points,3,$white);
        imagepolygon($image,$points,3,$black);

    imagepng($image);
    imagedestroy($image);
?>
```

Polygons must be used if more sides or an angle are needed with rectangles. Traditional rectangles with PHP and the GD Library are straight across the horizontal and vertical plane. If any skewing is required, or more sides, a polygon must be used, because each point to be plotted must be explicitly stated. Figure 7.13 shows two such polygons. The first in the background is a four-pointed star, which requires eight points in its array. This can get very complex. The second shape is a three-point polygon; three sides is the lowest number available with polygons.

Combining Shapes

If it is not clear that PHP and the GD Library offer powerful possibilities the following code should prove enlightening. It is a combination of different shapes showing that they are not mutually exclusive.

```
<?php
    header("Content-type: image/png");
    $image = imagecreate(400,400);

    $white = imagecolorallocate($image,255,255,255);
    $black = imagecolorallocate($image,0,0,0);
    $lightgray = imagecolorallocate($image, 0xCC,0xCC,0xCC);
    $gray = imagecolorallocate($image,175,175,175);

    $points = array(75,100,185,190,210,190,325,100);
    imagefilledpolygon($image,$points,4,$lightgray);
    imagearc($image, 200, 100, 250, 30, 0, 360, $black);
    imagefilledellipse($image, 200, 100, 250, 30, $lightgray);
    imagearc($image, 200, 100, 245, 25, 0, 360, $black);
    imagefilledellipse($image, 200, 100, 245, 25, $gray);
    imageline($image,75,100,185,190,$black);
    imageline($image,325,100,210,190,$black);
    imagearc($image, 200, 335, 130, 50, 0, 190, $black);
    imagefilledarc($image, 200, 335, 130, 50, 0, 190, $gray,IMG_ARC_PIE);
```

```
imagearc($image, 200, 330, 130, 50, 280, 255, $black);
imagefilledarc($image, 200, 330, 130, 50, 280, 255, $lightgray,
IMG_ARC_PIE);
imagefilledrectangle($image,185,190,210,330,$lightgray);
imageline($image,185,190,185,330,$black);
imageline($image,210,190,210,330,$black);
imagestring($image, 5, 140, 380, "Martini Glass", $black);

imagepng($image);
imagedestroy($image);
?>
```

There is a lot happening in the code used to create Figure 7.14. First is the typical code to define the image and allocate colors. Notice that $lightgray has its RGB values determined using hexadecimal numbers.

FIGURE 7.14 Using a combination of shapes.

```
header("Content-type: image/png");
    $image = imagecreate(400,400);

    $white = imagecolorallocate($image,255,255,255);
    $black = imagecolorallocate($image,0,0,0);
    $lightgray = imagecolorallocate($image, 0xCC,0xCC,0xCC);
    $gray = imagecolorallocate($image,175,175,175);
```

Next, the $points array is created followed by a four-point polygon:

```
$points = array(75,100,185,190,210,190,325,100);
imagefilledpolygon($image,$points,4,$lightgray);
```

This polygon creates the fill within the bowl part of the martini glass. It has to be placed first so the arcs, ellipses, and lines that make up the rim and edges appear on top of the shape. These are created next:

```
imagearc($image, 200, 100, 250, 30, 0, 360, $black);
    imagefilledellipse($image, 200, 100, 250, 30, $lightgray);
    imagearc($image, 200, 100, 245, 25, 0, 360, $black);
    imagefilledellipse($image, 200, 100, 245, 25, $gray);
    imageline($image,75,100,185,190,$black);
    imageline($image,325,100,210,190,$black);
```

Following the bowl components, the base is created with four more arcs:

```
imagearc($image, 200, 335, 130, 50, 0, 190, $black);
    imagefilledarc($image, 200, 335, 130, 50, 0, 190,
$gray,IMG_ARC_PIE);
    imagearc($image, 200, 330, 130, 50, 280, 255, $black);
    imagefilledarc($image, 200, 330, 130, 50, 280, 255,
$lightgray,IMG_ARC_PIE);
```

Last within the image is the code that creates the stem. It is made up of two lines and a rectangle. It has to be made with lines instead of a rectangle for the edges because it would be undesirable to have lines going across the ends of the stem.

```
imagefilledrectangle($image,185,190,210,330,$lightgray);
imageline($image,185,190,185,330,$black);
imageline($image,210,190,210,330,$black);
```

The last code used within the image is an `imagestring()` function, which adds a text label for the martini glass.

It may seem odd to use arcs instead of ellipses in multiple locations, but there is a reason for this. If all fills are commented out like the upcoming code, the results will resemble Figure 7.15. Ellipses will cause overlapping lines, whereas arcs allow for more flexibility.

FIGURE 7.15   The glass image without fills.

Creating a Dynamic Poll

Now that basic shapes have been covered, it is time to take the lesson even further. In this section, a dynamically fed poll will be created using a combination of file system functions and the GD Library.

Create the Results File

To start the poll, there must be a file created containing the results. Within this file, simply type 55,18,16,12,9 (don't add any spaces within the file) and save the file as `poll.txt`. This creates a results file with some results already within so they will show up when testing the poll image.

Creating the Image

Now that the results file is created, the image itself should be created. The following code will display the results shown in Figure 7.16. Save this file as `results.php`.

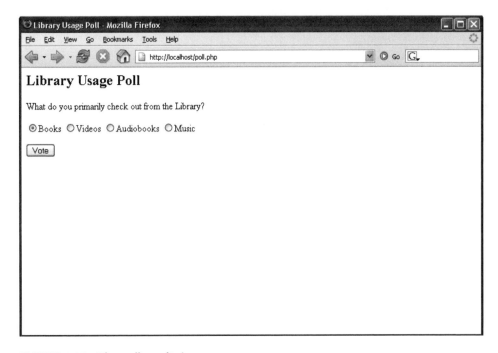

FIGURE 7.16   The poll results image.

```php
<?php
    //Image declaration
    header("Content-type: image/png");
    $image = imagecreate(300,250);

    //Data retrieval and text
    $title = "Library Poll Results";
    $fp = fopen("poll.txt","r");
    $results = fgetcsv($fp,1000);
    fclose($fp);
    $votes = trim($results[0]) . " responses.";
```

```php
$books = "Books - " . $results[1] . " votes";
$videos = "Videos - " . $results[2] . " votes";
$audiobooks = "Audiobooks - " . $results[3] . " votes";
$music = "Music - " . $results[4] . " votes";

//Colors
$white = imagecolorallocate($image,255,255,255);
$black = imagecolorallocate($image,0,0,0);
$gray = imagecolorallocate($image,150,150,150);
$red = imagecolorallocate($image,255,0,0);
$green = imagecolorallocate($image,0,255,0);
$blue = imagecolorallocate($image,0,0,255);
$yellow = imagecolorallocate($image,255,255,0);
$purple = imagecolorallocate($image,150,0,255);

//Shapes and text
imagerectangle($image, 0,0,299,249,$black);
imagestring($image, 5, 50, 1,$title, $black);
imageline($image, 1, 225, 299, 225, $gray);
imagestring($image, 2, 50, 230,$votes, $black);
imagestring($image, 3, 20,20,$books,$black);
imagefilledrectangle($image, 20,35, ($results[1]/$results[0]
*100*3+20),60,$purple);
imagerectangle($image, 20,35,($results[1]/$results[0]
*100*3+20),60,$black);
imagestring($image, 3, 20,70,$videos,$black);
imagefilledrectangle($image, 20,85,($results[2]/$results[0]
*100*3+20),110,$red);
imagerectangle($image, 20,85,($results[2]/$results[0]
*100*3+20),110,$black);
imagestring($image, 3, 20,120,$audiobooks,$black);
imagefilledrectangle($image, 20,135,($results[3]/$results[0]
*100*3+20),160,$blue);
imagerectangle($image, 20,135,($results[3]/$results[0]
*100*3+20),160,$black);
imagestring($image, 3, 20,170,$music,$black);
imagefilledrectangle($image, 20,185,($results[4]/$results[0]
*100*3+20),210,$yellow);
imagerectangle($image, 20,185,($results[4]/$results[0]
*100*3+20),210,$black);

//image creation and cleanup
imagepng($image);
imagedestroy($image);
?>
```

As can be seen by the code, there is a lot happening to create this image. The shapes and text are relatively simple, but they have to be changed according to input. After the image declaration section, the data is retrieved and first assigned to some text variables:

```
//Data retrieval and text
    $title = "Library Poll Results";
    $fp = fopen("poll.txt","r");
    $results = fgetcsv($fp,1000);
    fclose($fp);
    $votes = $results[0] . " responses.";
    $books = "Books - " . $results[1] . " votes";
    $videos = "Videos - " . $results[2] . " votes";
    $audiobooks = "Audiobooks - " . $results[3] . " votes";
    $music = "Music - " . $results[4] . " votes";
```

This section of the file creates all string variables supplying text to be used in the image. It is receiving much of its data from poll.txt using the fgetcsv() function. This works especially well because it receives comma-separated values and places each in an array. If another method of storing the different values in the text file is used, more functions may be needed to modify the data before it can be used. Stripping extra space, line breaks, and return characters would likely be part of the process.

Once this data is received, it is concatenated with strings and assigned to each appropriate variable. These in turn are used in imagestring() functions as shown in the following section of code:

```
//Shapes and text
imagerectangle($image, 0,0,299,249,$black);
imagestring($image, 5, 50, 1,$title, $black);
imageline($image, 1, 225, 299, 225, $gray);
imagestring($image, 2, 50, 230,$votes, $black);
imagestring($image, 3, 20,20,$books,$black);
imagefilledrectangle($image,20,35,($results[1]/$results[0]*100*3+20),60
,$purple);
imagerectangle($image,
20,35,($results[1]/$results[0]*100*3+20),60,$black);
imagestring($image, 3, 20,70,$videos,$black);
imagefilledrectangle($image,20,85,($results[2]/$results[0]*100*3+20),11
0,$red);
imagerectangle($image,
20,85,($results[2]/$results[0]*100*3+20),110,$black);
imagestring($image, 3, 20,120,$audiobooks,$black);
```

```
imagefilledrectangle($image,20,135,($results[3]/$results[0]*100*3+20),1
60,$blue);
imagerectangle($image,
20,135,($results[3]/$results[0]*100*3+20),160,$black);
imagestring($image, 3, 20,170,$music,$black);
imagefilledrectangle($image,20,185,($results[4]/$results[0]*100*3+20),2
10,$yellow);
imagerectangle($image,
20,185,($results[4]/$results[0]*100*3+20),210,$black);
```

In addition to the assignment of text in the imagestring() functions, information from the $results array is being used to create rectangles. This is based on a calculation added within each of the rectangle functions—($results[*num*]/$results[0]*100*3+20). This calculation is the same for all rectangles; the only variance between each is the index number within the first $results array. What is being calculated is the width of the overall rectangle.

After the calculations have been completed, creation and cleanup are needed. This is done with two lines: imagepng($image); to create the image, and destroyimage($image); to free memory used.

Creating Display Page

Now that an image has been created that displays results read from poll.txt, a file must be created tying everything together. The new file poll.php has a form that allows users to vote. It will take these votes and update poll.txt. Last, it will display the results image after the vote has been recorded. The following code creates poll.php, which can be seen in both states in Figures 7.17 and 7.18:

```
<html>
<head>
    <title>Library Usage Poll</title>
</head>
<body>
<?php
    if(!$_POST['process']){
?>
<h2>Library Usage Poll</h2>
<p>What do you primarily check out from the Library?</p>
<form action="<?=$_SERVER['PHP_SELF']; ?>" method="post">
<p><input type="radio" name="update" value="1" checked="checked"
/>Books <input type="radio" name="update" value="2" />Videos <input
type="radio" name="update" value="3" />Audiobooks <input type="radio"
name="update" value="4" />Music</p>
<input type="submit" value="Vote" />
```

```
<input type="hidden" name="process" value="1" />
</form>
<?php
    }else{
        $update = $_POST['update'];
        $fp = fopen("poll.txt","r+");
        $items = fgetcsv($fp,1000);
        $items[0]++;
        $items[$update]++;
        rewind($fp);
        fwrite($fp,implode($items,','));
        fclose($fp);
?>
<img src="results.php" width="300" height="250" alt="Library Poll
Results" />
<?php
    }
?>
</body>
</html>
```

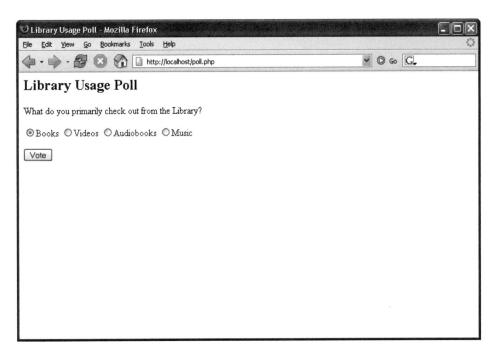

FIGURE 7.17 Library usage poll form.

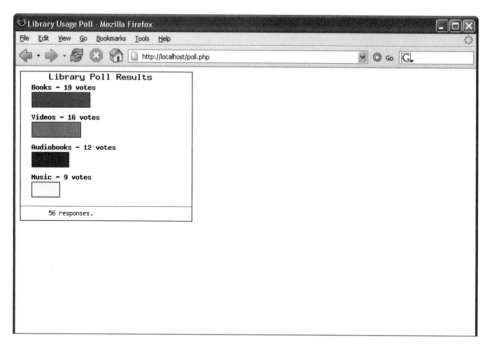

FIGURE 7.18 Library poll results.

Bar charts are not the only way dynamic results can be displayed. The following code modifies results.php into using a pie chart to display the poll results shown in Figure 7.19:

```php
<?php
    //Image declaration
    header("Content-type: image/png");
    $image = imagecreate(300,250);

    //Data retrieval and text
    $title = "Library Poll Results";
    $fp = fopen("poll.txt","r");
    $results = fgetcsv($fp,1000);
    fclose($fp);
    $votes = $results[0] . " responses.";
    $books = "Books - " . $results[1];
    $videos = "Videos - " . $results[2];
    $audiobooks = "Audiobooks - " . $results[3];
    $music = "Music - " . $results[4];
```

```
//Colors
$white = imagecolorallocate($image,255,255,255);
$black = imagecolorallocate($image,0,0,0);
$gray = imagecolorallocate($image,150,150,150);
$red = imagecolorallocate($image,255,0,0);
$green = imagecolorallocate($image,0,255,0);
$blue = imagecolorallocate($image,0,0,255);
$yellow = imagecolorallocate($image,255,255,0);
$purple = imagecolorallocate($image,150,0,255);

//Shapes and text
imagerectangle($image, 0,0,299,249,$black);
imagestring($image, 5, 50, 1,$title, $black);
imageline($image, 1, 225, 299, 225, $gray);
imagestring($image, 2, 50, 230,$votes, $black);
imagestring($image, 3, 10, 20, $books, $black);
imagefilledrectangle($image, 10, 35, 50, 60,$purple);
imagerectangle($image, 10, 35, 50, 60,$black);
imagestring($image, 3, 10, 70, $videos, $black);
imagefilledrectangle($image, 10, 85, 50,110,$red);
imagerectangle($image, 10,85,50,110,$black);
imagestring($image, 3, 10,120,$audiobooks,$black);
imagefilledrectangle($image, 10,135,50,160,$blue);
imagerectangle($image, 10,135,50,160,$black);
imagestring($image, 3, 10,170,$music,$black);
imagefilledrectangle($image, 10,185,50,210,$yellow);
imagerectangle($image, 10,185,50,210,$black);
$books = floor($results[1]/$results[0]*100*3.6);
$videos = floor(($results[2]/$results[0]*100*3.6) + $books);
$audiobooks = floor(($results[3]/$results[0]*100*3.6) + $videos);
imagestring($image, 5, 60, 230, $videos_end, $black);
imagefilledarc($image, 200, 125, 150, 150, 0, $books, $purple,
IMG_ARC_PIE);
imagefilledarc($image, 200, 125, 150, 150, $books, $videos, $red,
IMG_ARC_PIE);
imagefilledarc($image, 200, 125, 150, 150, $videos, $audiobooks,
$blue, IMG_ARC_PIE);
imagefilledarc($image, 200, 125, 150, 150, $audiobooks, 360, $yellow,
IMG_ARC_PIE);

//image creation and cleanup
imagepng($image);
imagedestroy($image);
?>
```

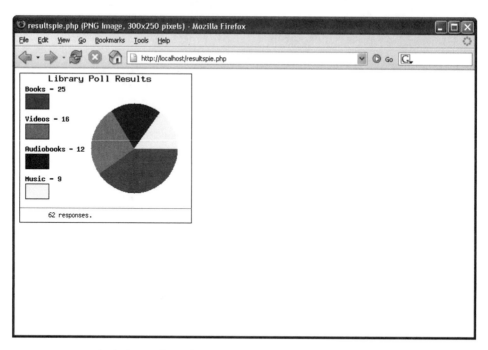

FIGURE 7.19 Displaying poll results using a pie chart.

GENERATING E-MAIL

One of the most popular tasks in PHP is generating e-mail, which can be used as a feedback mechanism, or even a mass mailer. Unfortunately for some users, this section must be used with Windows 2000 Professional, Server, XP Professional, or Windows Server 2003, all of which have a built-in SMTP Server.

Enabling SMTP

Before any mail can be sent with PHP, SMTP has to be enabled. This is done in Internet Information Services found in Control Panel | Administrative Tools. Follow these steps to enable SMTP:

1. Open Internet Information Services, right-click on SMTP Server, and choose Properties as shown in Figure 7.20.
2. Within the Default SMTP Virtual Server Properties window, click the Access tab (see Figure 7.21).

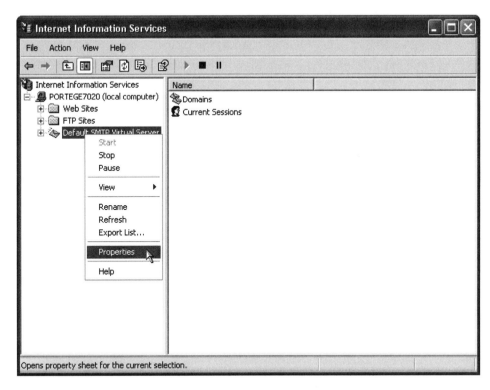

FIGURE 7.20   Choosing properties on the SMTP Server.

FIGURE 7.21   Default SMTP Virtual Server Properties.

3. Click the Relay button, and the Computer button shown in Figure 7.22 will open.

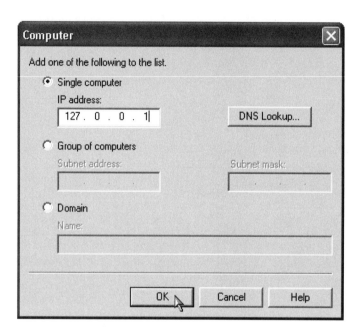

FIGURE 7.22 Adding the local IP Address.

4. With Single computer selected, type `127.0.0.1` in the IP address field and click OK. This is the loopback (the computer itself) and will limit all SMTP (outgoing) mail requests to the computer.
5. The Relay Restrictions screen shown in Figure 7.23 will now appear, showing 127.0.0.1 as the only computer on the access list. Click OK to return to Default SMTP Virtual Server Properties.
6. Click OK once more to finish configuration of the SMTP Server.
7. The last step to be taken is within the `php.ini` file. Make sure the following lines are in place:

```
[mail function]
; For Win32 only.
SMTP = localhost
smtp_port = 25
```

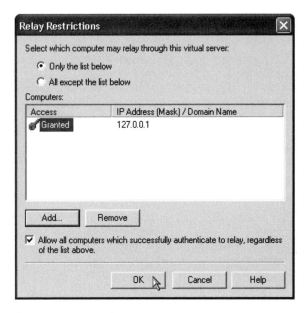

FIGURE 7.23   Relay Restrictions.

Creating an E-Mail Script

Now that the SMTP Virtual Server is enabled, it is time to create an e-mail script. The following code creates the basic form shown in Figure 7.24:

```
<html>
<head>
    <title>E-Mail Form</title>
    <style type="text/css">
        h2,h3,p{
            font-family: verdana;
        }
        input {
            font-family: verdana;
            font-size: 10px;
        }
        p{
            font-weight: bold;
            font-size: 12px;
        }
        .data{
            width: 300px;
```

```php
        }
    </style>
</head>
<body>
<?php
if(isset($_POST['process'])){
    $to = $_POST['to'];
    $subject = $_POST['subject'];
    $message = $_POST['message'];
    $from = $_POST['from'];
    if (eregi('\r',$from) || eregi('\n',$from)){
    die("<h2>Security Alert!</h2><h3>IP Address: " .
$_SERVER["REMOTE_ADDR"] . "</h3><p>This script is for the use of the
current Web site exclusively. It appears that an attempt has been made
to hijack this script, so the mail function has failed. If this message
has appeared in error, please try again.</p>");
    }else{
        if (mail($to,$subject,$message,"From: $from\n")){
        // success
        echo "<h2>Success</h2><h3>Your message was successfully sent to
        $to.</h3><p>Send <a href=\"" . $_SERVER['PHP_SELF'] .
        "\">Another</a>?</p>";
        }else{
        // failure
        echo "<h1>Error</h1><p>The e-mail failed to be sent. Please try
        again later.";
        }
    }
}else{
?>
<h2>Send An E-mail</h2>
<form action="<?= $_SERVER['PHP_SELF'];?>" method="post">
    <table style="text-align: left; width: 350px">
        <tr><td><p>To: </p></td><td> <input type="text" name="to"
        class="data" /></td></tr>
        <tr><td><p>From: </p></td><td> <input type="text" name="from"
        class="data" /></td></tr>
        <tr><td><p>Subject: </p></td><td> <input type="text" name="
        subject" class="data" /></td></tr>
        <tr><td valign="top"><p>Message: </p></td><td> <textarea
        name="message" rows="6" cols="20" class="data"></textarea>
        </td></tr>
        <tr><td></td><td><input type="submit" value="Send" /> <input
        type="reset" value="Erase" /></td></tr>
```

```
        </table>
        <input type="hidden" name="process" value="1" />
    </form>
    <?php
    }
    ?>
    </body>
    </html>
```

FIGURE 7.24   E-mail form.

When the e-mail is sent successfully, Figure 7.25 will appear. If there is something wrong with the SMTP Virtual Server, or it is turned off, an error message will appear, as shown in Figure 7.26.

When looking at the overall structure of the form, it is yet another self-posting document. There is an overall if/else conditional. The first half determines if the process form field has been submitted, while the second returns a form if it has not. If process has been submitted, there is a nested if/else conditional. This conditional is written for the purposes of a security issue known as *E-mail injection*, where spammers hijack e-mail scripts on servers for the purposes of sending out bulk mail.

FIGURE 7.25 E-mail sent successfully.

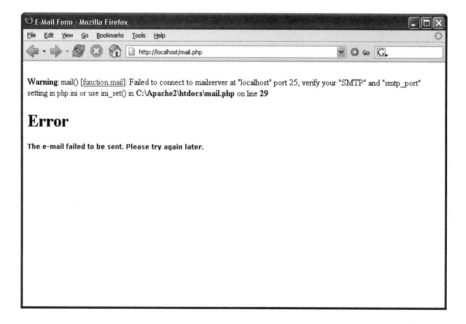

FIGURE 7.26 Failure to send message.

The excellent article located at *http://securephp.damonkohler.com/index.php/ Email_Injection* influenced the conditional used in the script. This article explains the issue itself, and steps to overcome it. Here is the conditional:

```
if (eregi('\r',$from) || eregi('\n',$from)){
    die("<h2>Security Alert!</h2><h3>IP Address: " .
$_SERVER["REMOTE_ADDR"] . "</h3><p>This script is for the use of the
current Web site exclusively. It appears that an attempt has been made
to hijack this script, so the mail function has failed. If this message
has appeared in error, please try again.</p>");
    }else{
        if (mail($to,$subject,$message,"From: $from\n")){
            // success
            echo "<h2>Success</h2><h3>Your message was successfully sent to
            $to.</h3><p>Send <a href=\"" . $_SERVER['PHP_SELF'] .
            "\">Another</a>?</p>";
        }else{
            // failure
            echo "<h1>Error</h1><p>The e-mail failed to be sent. Please try
again later.";
        }
    }
```

The check for e-mail injection is found in the initial if—if (eregi("\r",$from) || eregi("\n",$from)). This statement is using two regular expressions. Regular expressions are used to check for patterns within data and are shown in Appendix A, "An HTML Primer." These expressions are looking for any \r (carriage return) or \n (new line) characters in the $from variable. A common form of injection is to add more fields to the from field on the form in SMTP; the fields are separated by either the new line or carriage return characters like myname@blah.com\nCc:spamvictim@site.com,spamvictim2@site.com. By disallowing these characters, it is more difficult for spammers to inject other addresses into the code. They can even send a different header and place the entire message within. The filtering of these characters will make the e-mail a smaller target and return the screen shown in Figure 7.27.

If no suspect characters are filtered, the following code is executed:

```
if (mail($to,$subject,$message,"From: $from\n")){
        // success
        echo "<h2>Success</h2><h3>Your message was successfully
        sent to $to.</h3><p>Send <a href=\"" . $_SERVER['PHP_SELF']
        . "\">Another</a>?</p>";
    }else{
        // failure
        echo "<h1>Error</h1><p>The e-mail failed to be sent. Please
        try again later.";
    }
```

First, it attempts to use the `mail()` function to send the message within the `if` argument. If it is successful, a message is returned reflecting the success. If the `mail()` function fails, it will return `false`, which will engage the false statement that displays a statement informing the user.

The e-mail script may fail if the ISP providing Internet access for the server has the SMTP port blocked. There will be no sign of this from the script itself, and it will report a successful send. The only way to know of the failure is if the messages sent are not received. Check with the ISP FAQs or customer/technical support if this is happening.

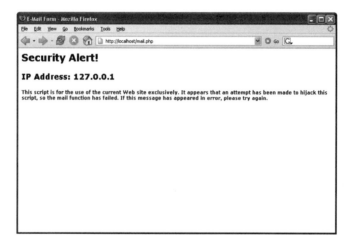

FIGURE 7.27   A foiled spam attempt.

SUMMARY

This concludes coverage of PHP and the file system. Now it is time to shift focus, so let's move on to Chapter 8, "Introducing MySQL" and learn about the most popular Relational Database Management System used with PHP. We will revisit PHP and Perl in Chapter 9, "Communicating with MySQL."

8 Introducing MySQL

In This Chapter

- History of MySQL
- Installing MySQL
- Using the MySQL Monitor
- Using phpMyAdmin
- Summary

MySQL is an open source Relational Database Management System. MySQL is not a database, but rather a program that manages databases. There can be multiple databases attached to one MySQL server, which uses SQL to communicate with the databases.

IBM created SQL in the 1970s to make it easier for users to communicate with databases using an easier understood programming syntax. The original name of the language was Structured English Query Language (SEQUEL), but was later modified to SQL to solve a copyright issue. SQL was adopted by the ANSI (American National Standards Institute) in 1986, followed by the ISO (International Standards Organization) in 1987, and has become the de facto standard of communication with databases. There have been five ANSI revisions to the standard with the latest in 2003, but most databases primarily concentrate on meeting the ANSI '92 standard.

MySQL uses SQL as a means of communication to simplify working with it. Whether users choose the MySQL monitor utility, or to communicate from a programming language such as PHP or Perl, SQL queries are the commands used.

HISTORY OF MYSQL

A consulting firm in Sweden called TcX developed MySQL, because they were in need of a database system that was extremely fast and flexible. MySQL is loosely based on another database management system called mSQL. In 2001, TcX became MySQL AB (AB being Swedish for Incorporated).

The name MySQL is usually pronounced in one of two ways: MY ESS QUE ELL, or My Sequel, with the first being correct. The origin of the name is unclear. According to historical information on *mysql.com*, the name either comes from the fact that "my" was used as a prefix for the base directory and many of the tools used with the program, or after co-founder Monty Widenius' daughter who is named My.

INSTALLING MYSQL

Installing MySQL on Windows is simple. A copy of MySQL can be found on the companion CD-ROM in the software folder. The following instructions and figures use that version as an example.

1. Open `mysql-essential-4.1.13a-win32.msi` on the CD-ROM in the software folder. If Windows XP with Service Pack 2 is installed, Figure 8.1 may appear—just click Run. Otherwise, the MySQL Server 4.1 Setup Wizard will load as shown in Figure 8.2. Click Next to continue.

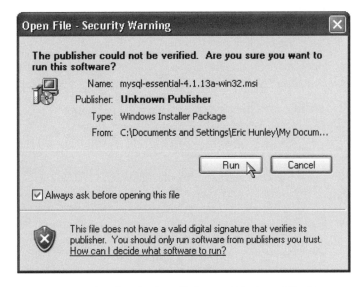

FIGURE 8.1 Starting the installation on Windows XP with Service Pack 2.

2. Now, the setup type can be chosen as shown in Figure 8.3. Typical is fine, so click Next.

The default path for a MySQL installation is C:\Program Files\MySQL\MySQL Server 4.1\. If another path is desired (e.g., C:\MySQL), a Custom installation should be chosen.

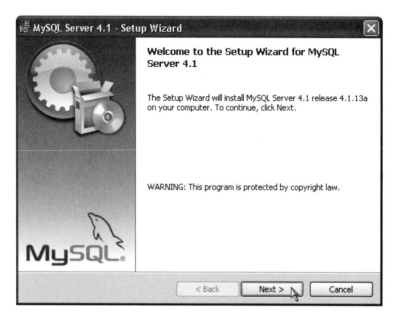

FIGURE 8.2 The MySQL Server 4.1 Setup Wizard.

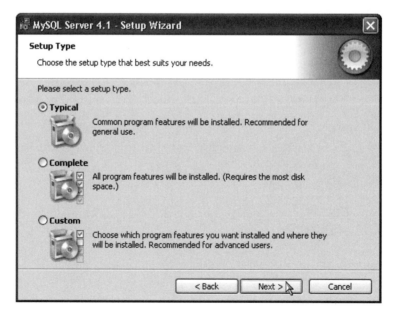

FIGURE 8.3 Setup type.

3. The Ready to Install screen shown in Figure 8.4 will appear. Click Install.
4. The progress of the installation can be seen in Figure 8.5. It can take some time.

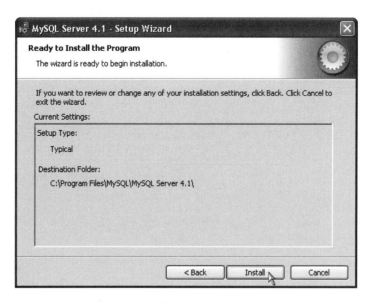

FIGURE 8.4 Ready to install the program.

FIGURE 8.5 Installation status.

5. When the installation is complete, an option to create a MySQL.com account is available as shown in Figure 8.6. This subscribes users to a monthly newsletter, allows for comment addition to the online manuals, and bug reporting. For now, choose Skip Sign-Up and click Next. You can create an account online later at *http://www.mysql.com/register.php*.

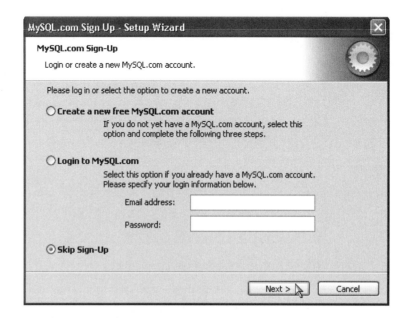

FIGURE 8.6   MySQL.com Sign-Up screen.

6. This completes the basic setup. Make sure to leave "Configure the MySQL Server now" checked as shown in Figure 8.7 and click Finish.

MySQL Instance Configuration Wizard

Brand new to MySQL is the MySQL Instance Configuration Wizard shown in Figure 8.8. This was created for version 4.1 to use with the updated Windows Installer. Full details along with the following steps can be found at *http://dev.mysql.com/tech-resources/articles/4.1/installer.html*:

FIGURE 8.7   Setup Wizard completed.

1. Figure 8.8 shows the Welcome screen in the MySQL Instance Configuration Wizard. Click Next to continue.

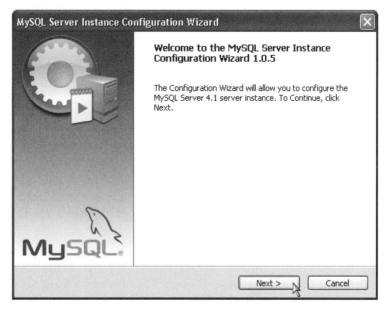

FIGURE 8.8   MySQL Instance Configuration Wizard.

2. The Configuration type screen in Figure 8.9 will appear. Choose Standard Configuration if MySQL is not already installed on the computer.

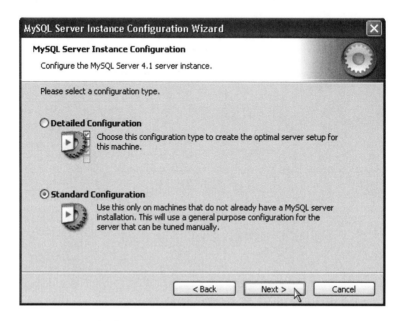

FIGURE 8.9 Configuration type.

3. Figure 8.10 will appear. This is where Windows options are chosen, and is a very handy tool. Here, the Install As Windows Service option and the ability to include the `bin` directory in the system path are available. Previously, to install as a Windows service, `mysql-nt --install` had to be typed from the bin directory. Leave Install As Windows Service checked, Include Bin Directory in Windows PATH unchecked, and click Next.
4. Figure 8.11 will appear. Here, the root password is set. Type `password` in New Root Password, retype it in Confirm, and click Next to continue.
5. The configuration utility is now ready to execute as shown in Figure 8.12. Click Execute to apply the changes. Figure 8.13 shows the progress of changes being made.

The configuration can always be changed later. Simply open the `MySQL Server Instance Config Wizard` found on the Start menu under `MySQL – MySQL Server 4.1`.

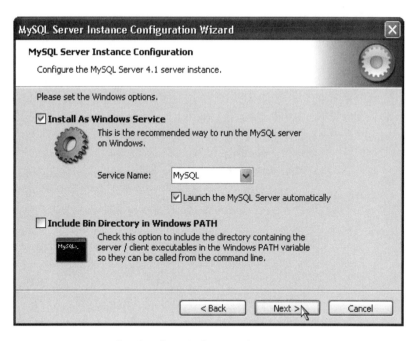

FIGURE 8.10   Configuring the Windows options.

FIGURE 8.11   Setting the root password.

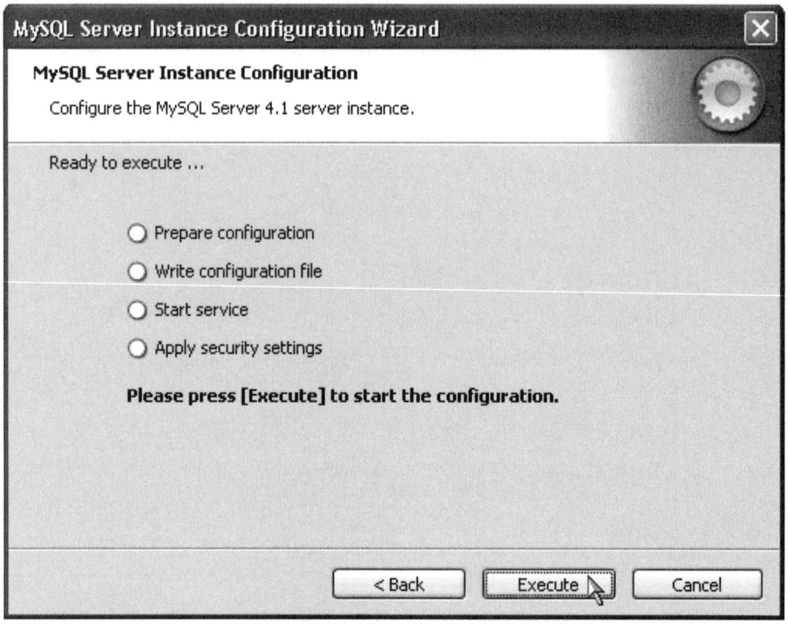

FIGURE 8.12   Ready to execute.

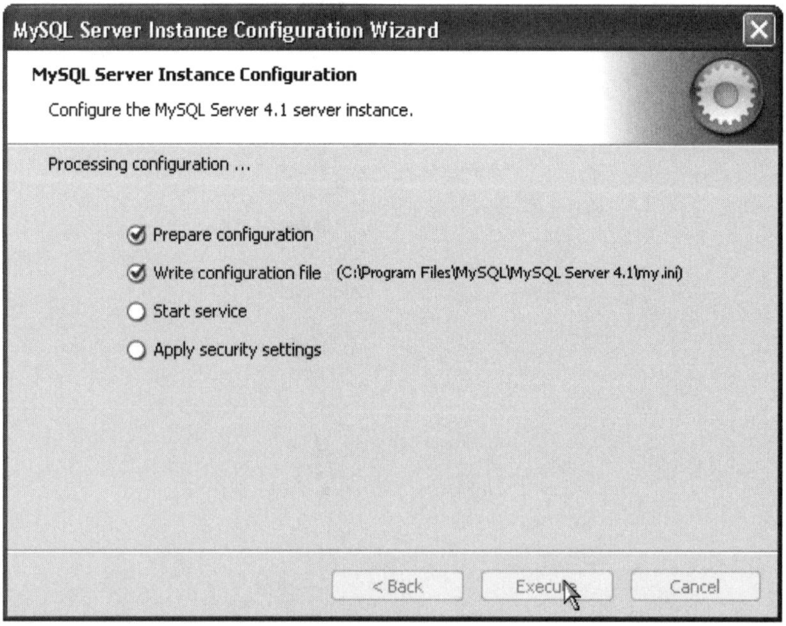

FIGURE 8.13   Processing configuration.

USING THE MYSQL MONITOR

Many tasks to be performed in MySQL can be done in the MySQL monitor. This command-line tool is a direct interface for the relational database system. The version included on the companion CD-ROM will add a shortcut to the Windows Start menu with a typical installation. Access it by clicking MySQL – MySQL Server 4.1 – MySQL Command Line Client as shown in Figure 8.14.

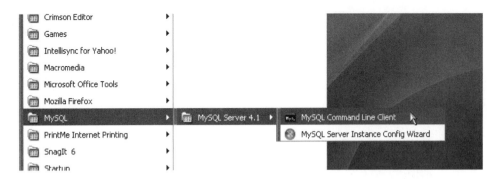

FIGURE 8.14   Opening the MySQL Command Line Client.

Upon opening the client, a password prompt will appear. After the password is typed in, MySQL monitor will open. Notice the advice Commands end with ; or \g (go). This is very important to note because it is often forgotten. A command will not be executed unless one of these two symbols is used before the Enter key is pressed. This is due to the number of character limitation in command lines. For example, in Windows NT and 2000, the character limitation for a single line in cmd.exe is 2047. The limitation for Windows XP is 8191 characters. It is possible to have very long queries typed into MySQL monitor. When this occurs, they can be carried from line to line in the command prompt window, but will not actually execute until either \g or ; has been typed. The MySQL monitor is shown in Figure 8.15.

If either \g or ; have not been typed before the Enter key is pressed, simply type one or the other on the next line and press Enter again.

One of the first commands used when entering the MySQL monitor is SHOW DATABASES (see Figure 8.16). This will list all databases that are currently attached to the MySQL server. By default, there will be two: mysql and test.

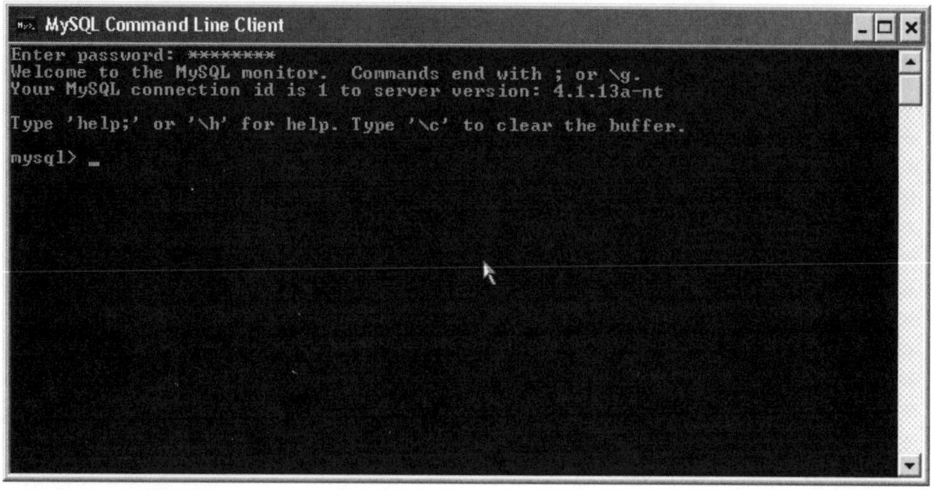

FIGURE 8.15 The MySQL monitor.

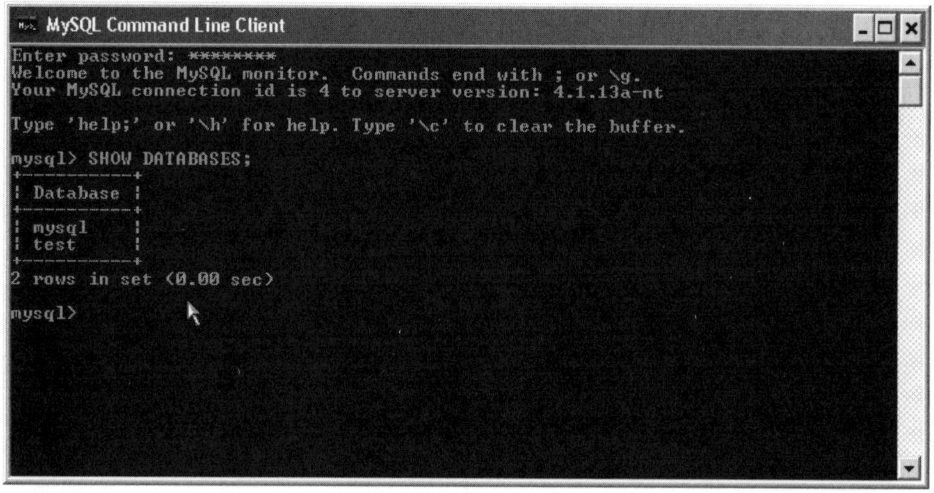

FIGURE 8.16 Executing the SHOW DATABASES; command.

Once the MySQL monitor has been entered, users have the ability to create, delete, and manipulate database structure. This is done with the use of Data Definition Statements.

Data Definition Statements

Data Definition Statements are part of the SQL Data Definition Language used to manipulate the structure of databases. They do not change the data itself, but rather the structure of the database containing it. The following are some SQL Data Definition Statements most commonly used in MySQL:

CREATE DATABASE: Creates a new database with the provided name—CREATE DATABASE *dbname*;. Figure 8.17 demonstrates this in use.

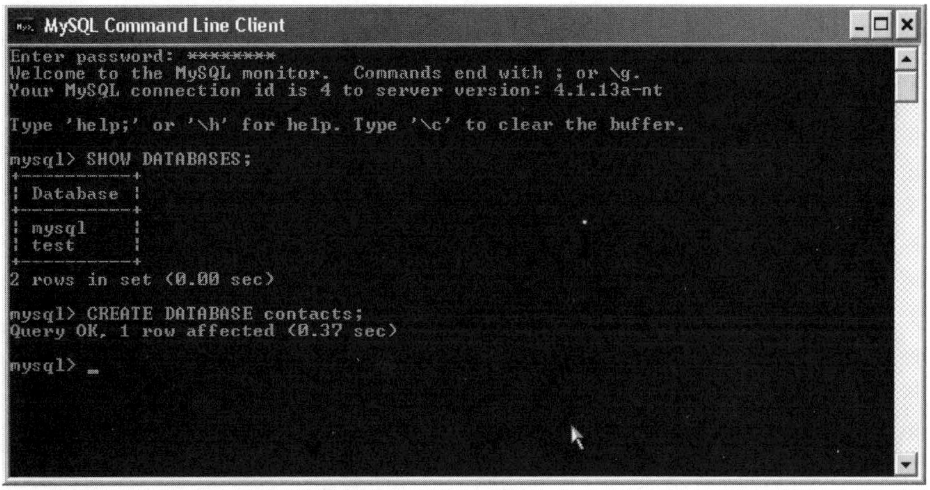

FIGURE 8.17 Creating a new database.

Once the database has been created, it can easily be seen along with all pre-existing databases with the SHOW DATABASES; command. This is shown in Figure 8.18.

DROP DATABASE: Deletes a database—DROP DATABASE *dbname*;. While the term *drop* seems odd, it makes sense when looking at the database server model. With MySQL, all databases are attached to a server. If they are "dropped," they are no longer associated with the server. Figure 8.19 shows the command in use, and Figure 8.20 shows the result of a SHOW DATABASES; command.

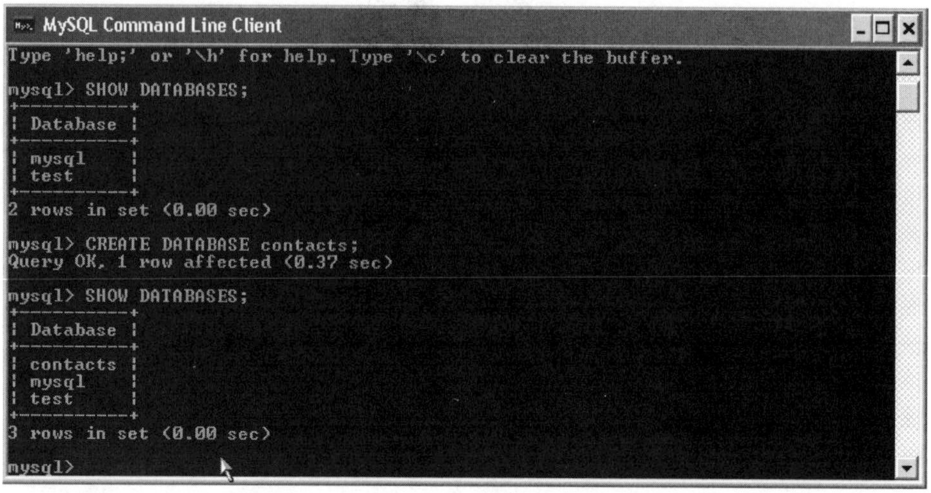

FIGURE 8.18 Checking for the new database contacts.

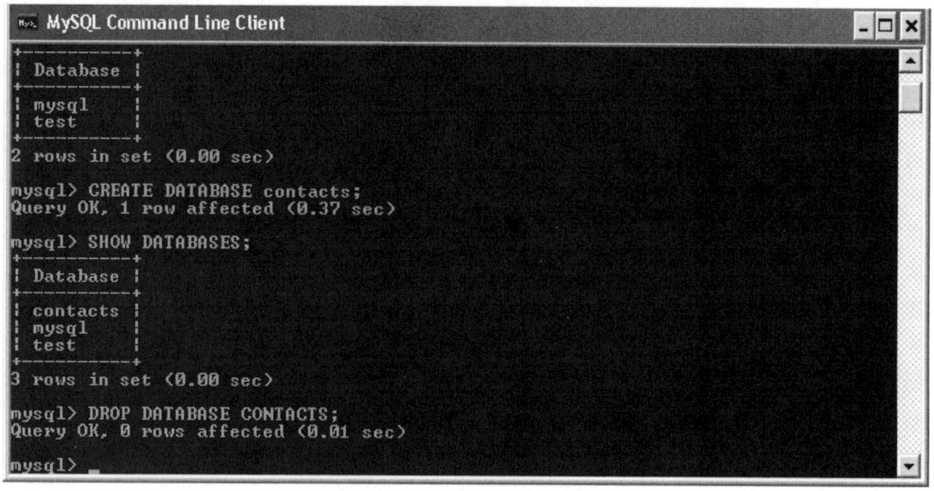

FIGURE 8.19 Dropping a database.

For the remaining commands, the contacts database needs to be recreated. This is accomplished with CREATE DATABASE contacts; displayed in Figure 8.21. The contacts database should also be set as the default database for future commands. This is done with the USE command also shown in Figure 8.21.

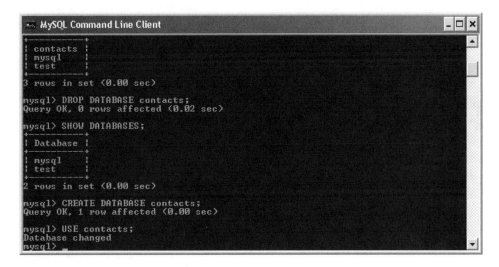

FIGURE 8.20   Checking to see if the contacts database has been dropped.

FIGURE 8.21   Creating and using contacts.

MySQL also offers two utility statements, each of which has a single purpose. DESCRIBE tablename; is used to view information about columns on a table in MySQL. USE databasename; is used to determine which database will act as the default for subsequent statements.

CREATE TABLE: Creates a new table—CREATE TABLE *tablename (columns)*;. Creating a table is a bit more complex than creating a database. While a database is simply a container that can contain one or more tables, a table must contain at least one column upon creation. This means that the table has to be created along with any columns that will be used. Figure 8.22 shows a table being created in the contacts database.

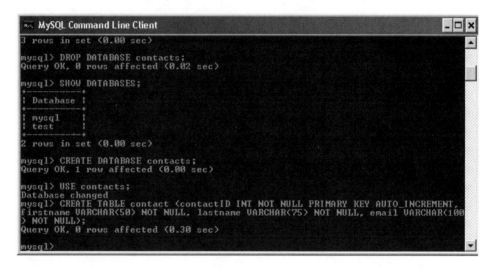

FIGURE 8.22 Creating a table in contacts.

To see whether a table has been created, SHOW TABLES FROM databasename; can be used. If the current default database (determined with the USE databasename; utility command) has the tables in question, just the truncated command SHOW TABLES; will suffice. Both methods are shown in Figure 8.23.

While SHOW TABLES; will list all tables within a database, it will not show the columns. This can be done in two ways. The first is the self-explanatory SHOW COLUMNS FROM tablename; shown in Figure 8.24. The second method is with the MySQL utility command DESCRIBE also shown in Figure 8.24.

DROP TABLE: Deletes a table – DROP TABLE tablename;.

ALTER TABLE: Used to change the structure of a table. This can include many activities, such as adding and removing columns, adding and removing indexes,

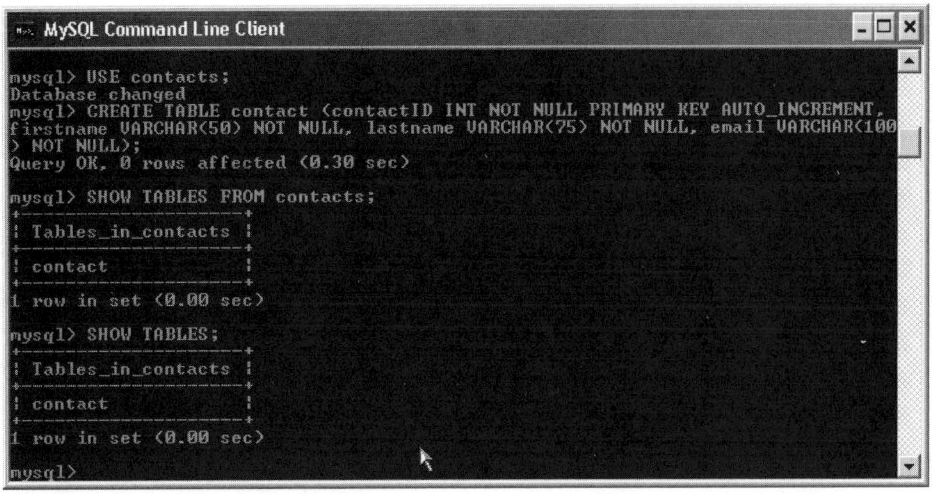

FIGURE 8.23 Viewing tables.

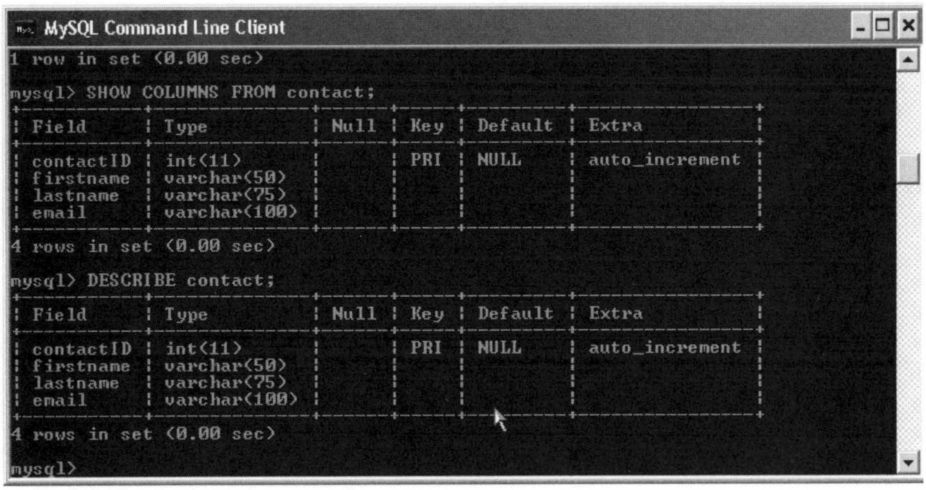

FIGURE 8.24 Two methods of viewing columns.

adding primary and foreign keys, and more. Figure 8.25 shows a new column being added to the contact table, and Figure 8.26 shows it being dropped. Both figures show a describe statement so the changes are reflected.

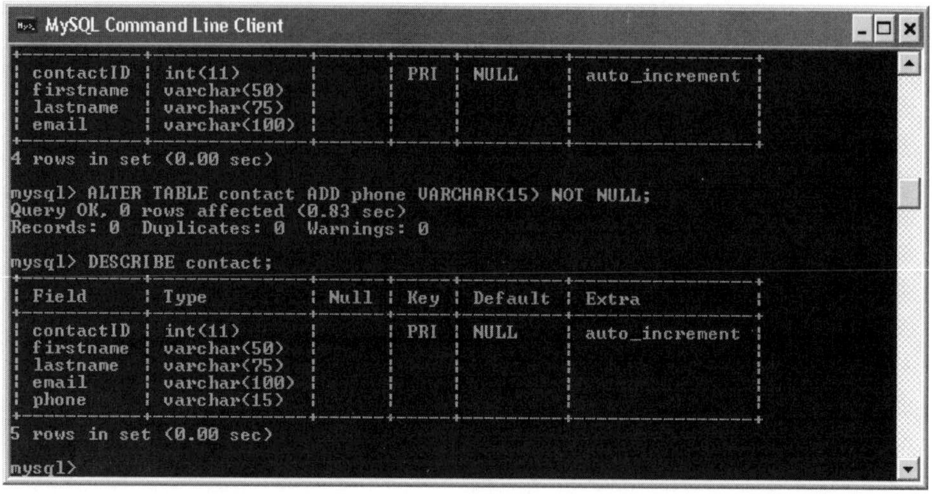

FIGURE 8.25 Altering a table.

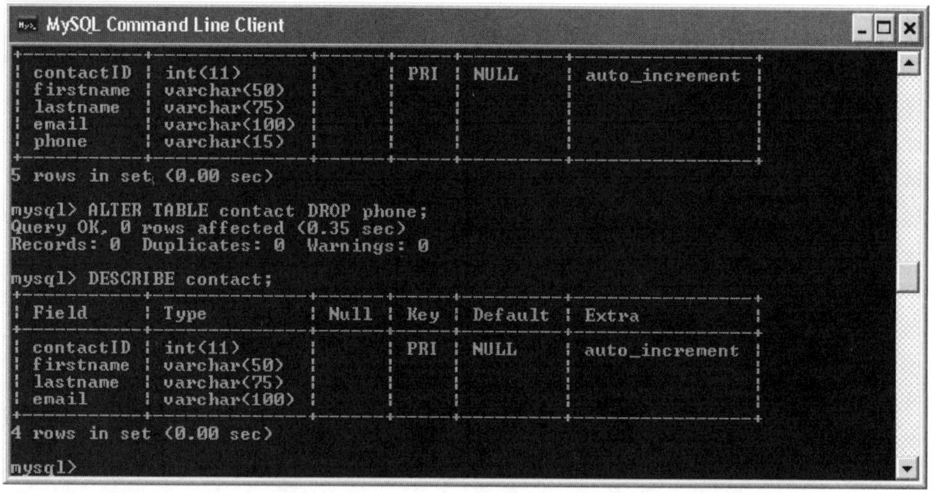

FIGURE 8.26 Dropping the new column.

RENAME TABLE: Creates a new table with the name provided, transfers data to it, and deletes the old table. Used in conjunction with ALTER TABLE – ALTER TABLE *tablename* RENAME *newname*;.

CHANGE: Enables changing a column name, data type, or both. The basic format is ALTER TABLE *tablename* CHANGE *columnname newname datatype*;. For example, in the current table, the column `firstname` could be changed to allow more characters with the line `ALTER TABLE contact CHANGE firstname firstname VARCHAR(75) NOT NULL;`.

CREATE INDEX: Adds an index to a given column. Indexes are a handy tool for speeding up data retrieval, but should be used carefully. While they speed up data retrieval, it takes longer to insert or update data, because the index has to be changed along with the data.

The format for creating indexes is `CREATE INDEX indexname ON tablename(columnnames);`. An index can span more than one column. Another method for creating indexes on tables is `ALTER TABLE tablename ADD INDEX (column);` to add an index to a single column.

DROP INDEX: Deletes an index — `DROP INDEX indexname ON tablename;` or `ALTER tablename DROP INDEX indexname;` (if the `ALTER` method was used to create the index, the index name will be the same as the column).

Data Manipulation Language

While the Data Definition language defines the structure of the database, the SQL Data Manipulation language manipulates the data within. This is primarily done with queries.

SQL Verbs

All SQL queries begin with a verb. The four most commonly used verbs in the Data Manipulation language are as follows:

INSERT: Used to add a row of data into a table. Written as `INSERT INTO tablename(columns) VALUES(values);`. Figure 8.27 demonstrates its usage with the `contacts` database by inserting two records.

Figure 8.27 shows two methods for adding data to `contacts`. The first line is `INSERT INTO contact VALUES(NULL, 'John','Smith','john@johnsmith.com');`, which inserts an entire row of data into the database. Notice the `NULL`. This is put in as a marker. Because the field was defined as a primary key field with an Auto-increment, nothing should be added to the field—doing so can cause an issue. The `NULL` keyword literally adds nothing to the field.

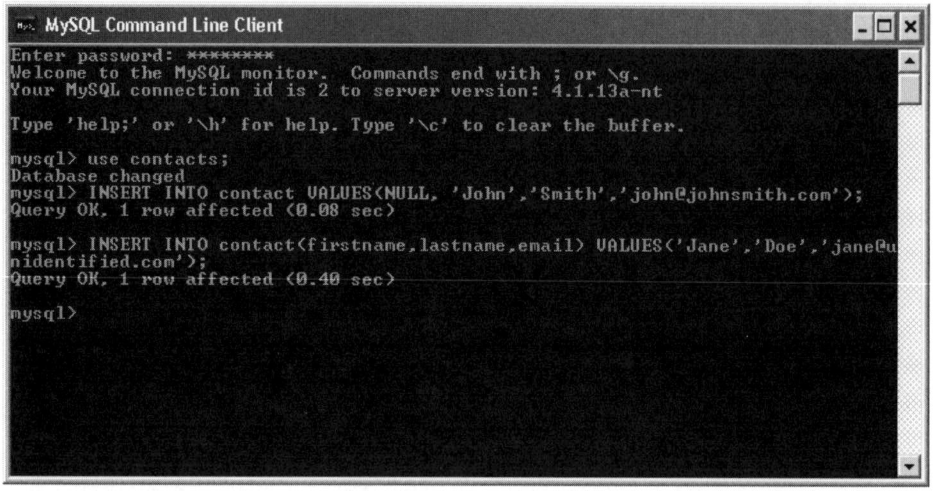

FIGURE 8.27   Inserting records into `contacts`.

The next command is `INSERT INTO contact(firstname,lastname,email) VAL-`
`UES('Jane','Doe','jane@unidentified.com');`. This time, there is no `NULL` used.
That is because in the parentheses next to `contact`, the columns to be used are specified. The columns to the right of the table name can be in any order, but the order
of the `VALUES` must correspond or data will be inserted into the wrong fields.

> *Notice that all values being inserted into the database are surrounded by single
> quotation marks. This is because they are strings (mixed characters). If a value is
> a number or a keyword like the NULL shown before, quotation marks are not
> needed. This also applies to UPDATE, which is coming up.*

SELECT: Used to view data from within the database. Format is `SELECT` *quali-*
fier `FROM` *tablename*`;`. Figure 8.28 shows a basic `SELECT` statement used to display data from the `contact` table.

Figure 8.28 demonstrates the most basic of all `SELECT` statements. It uses the
wildcard `*`, which means *all*. The statement returns all records and all fields from
the table. If fewer fields are required, the columns need to be specified in the query.
For example, `SELECT lastname,firstname FROM contact;` will return a list of only
the lastname and firstname fields (in that order). This is useful if not every field is
required, or the order should be modified.

FIGURE 8.28 Using SELECT to view data.

If the number of results is going to be filtered at all, more has to be added to the query. The WHERE clause is the primary method used to specify which records should be shown. For example, if the select statement was written as SELECT * FROM contact WHERE contactID=1; the only record returned would be John Smith.

Another option may be to use a wildcard and the LIKE keyword in the WHERE clause. Two popular examples include the underscore (_) and percent sign (%).

The underscore wildcard accounts for a single character. For example, the WHERE clause WHERE columnname LIKE '_at'; will return bat, cat, hat, mat, rat, pat, and vat, but not mate, rate, scat, or spat because of the number of characters.

While the underscore allows for any character in one space, a percent sign allows for any number of characters or no characters. For example, a query including the WHERE clause of WHERE columnname LIKE %smith% will return Smith, Smithsonian, Smithfield, Blacksmith, and Wordsmith.

DELETE: Used to delete rows from a database. Should always be used with a WHERE clause, as in DELETE FROM tablename WHERE parameter=parameter;. If the WHERE clause is not included, all rows will be deleted from the table.

If you want to delete all rows from the table, TRUNCATE TABLE tablename; should be used. It is a much faster method and has other features such as restarting any auto_increment counts.

UPDATE: Used to modify data within a record. As with DELETE, a WHERE clause should be used, or there can be disastrous results. The format of the command is UPDATE *tablename* SET *column=value* WHERE *columnname=value*;. If there will be more than one column changed, they should be separated by commas after the SET keyword, as in SET *column1=value1,column2=value2*.

USING PHPMYADMIN

While it is very important to understand the principles of the Data Definition Language, sometimes a visual tool can be helpful—which is where phpMyAdmin can come in. This is a powerful Web-based application that serves as a front-end to a MySQL database.

ON THE CD

It can be downloaded for free from Sourceforge.net, or off the companion CD-ROM in software/ phpmyadmin. The following steps use the software on the CD-ROM:

1. Copy the phpmyadmin folder into the C:\Apache2\htdocs directory.
2. Open a browser and type *http://localhost/phpmyadmin/* in the address bar. This should open the page shown in Figure 8.29.

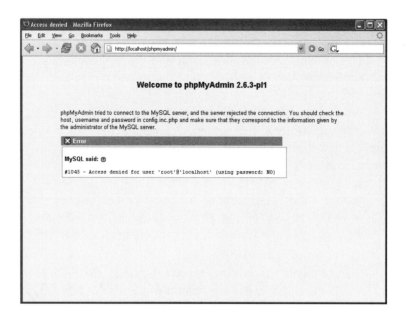

FIGURE 8.29   Testing phpMyAdmin in a browser.

3. As shown in Figure 8.29, an error has occurred. This is to be expected because the MySQL user, root, has a password. Open the file `config.inc.php` with a text editor and modify the line `$cfg['Servers'][$i]['password']` `= '';` to `$cfg['Servers'][$i]['password']    = 'password';`. Save the file and refresh the browser window. Figure 8.30 should appear.

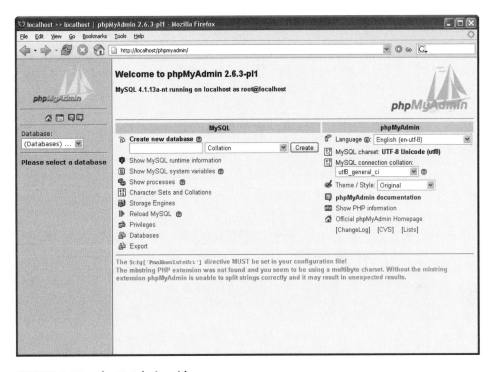

FIGURE 8.30   phpMyAdmin with errors.

4. Notice the text at the bottom— "The `$cfg['PmaAbsoluteUri']` directive MUST be set in your configuration file! The mbstring PHP extension was not found and you seem to be using a multibyte charset. Without the mbstring extension phpMyAdmin is unable to split strings correctly and it may result in unexpected results." These warnings are appearing due to modifications still needed in the `config.inc.php` and `php.ini` files.
5. Open phpmyadmin/config.inc.php with a text editor, find the line `$cfg['PmaAbsoluteUri_DisableWarning']  =  FALSE;`, and change it to `$cfg['PmaAbsoluteUri_DisableWarning'] = TRUE;`.

This is a departure from an earlier procedure. Previously, it was recommended that the $cfg['PmaAbsoluteUri'] = ''; line be modified to include the full path to the phpMyAdmin directory, as in $cfg['PmaAbsoluteUri'] = 'http://localhost/phpmyadmin/';. This is no longer the recommended method as of version 2.3.0 according to the documentation.

6. Open `php.ini` in `C:\php\`. Find the line `extension_dir = "./"` and change it to `extension_dir = "./extensions/"` for PHP 4 or `extension_dir = "./ext/"` for PHP5 if it has not already been modified. Next, find the line `;extension=php_mbstring.dll`, remove the semicolon, save, and then close `php.ini`.
7. Restart the Apache HTTP Server if PHP was installed as a module.
8. Refresh *http://localhost/phpmyadmin/*. The result should resemble Figure 8.31.

Now that phpMyAdmin is up and running, it is time to take a quick tour. Figure 8.31 shows the Welcome screen. In the parent frame to the left are four links for Home (current page), Query window (for a quick and dirty SQL query), the phpMyAdmin documentation, and MySQL documentation. Below these links is a jump menu where all databases currently attached to the server are listed.

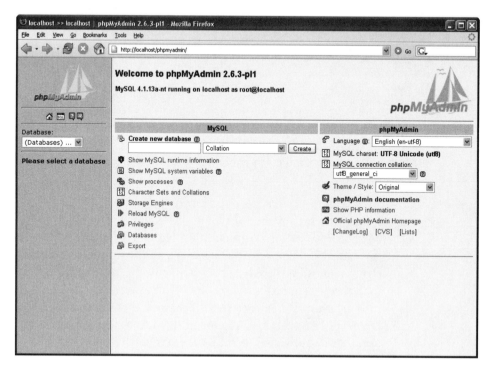

FIGURE 8.31 phpMyAdmin.

In the main frame, front and center is "Create new database with collation options" in a drop-down to the right. Collations are rules determining how symbols in different character sets are compared with one another and are interpreted. For example, the letter "ê" may be mapped to "e." In general, this drop-down can be left alone with the database becoming the MySQL default of *latin1_swedish_ci* (Latin 1, Swedish, case-insensitive).

Underneath Create new database are the following links:

Show MySQL runtime information: Shows current statistics related to the MySQL server, such as when it was started, how long it has been running, and other environmental information.

Show MySQL system variables: Shows values of MySQL system variables, which are used to configure the MySQL server. To the right is a link to the MySQL documentation explaining these variables further at *http://dev.mysql.com/doc/mysql/en/show-variables.html*.

Show processes: Shows any and all processes currently on the server. Can be used to view what is currently accessing the server. Gives the option to kill any processes.

Character Sets and Collations: Defines all Character Sets and Collations available.

Storage Engines: Lists all of the different storage engines available with the current server. All that are in use are listed in blue. Those not in use are grayed out.

Reload MySQL: Restarts MySQL.

Privileges: Accesses the user table in the MySQL database. This is a convenient place to add new users and modify rights.

Databases: Leads to a page that lists all current databases attached to the server. Gives options to select, drop, or add databases.

Export: Used to export databases into other formats.

Creating a New Database in phpMyAdmin

Creating a new database in phpMyAdmin is as easy as typing in the database name in Create a new database and clicking the Create button. This will lead to the screen in Figure 8.32.

When a database is created, phpMyAdmin will offer to create a new table. This can be done in the second half of the screen. Here, just type the name of the table, fill in the number of required fields, and click Go. This will load the screen in Figure 8.33.

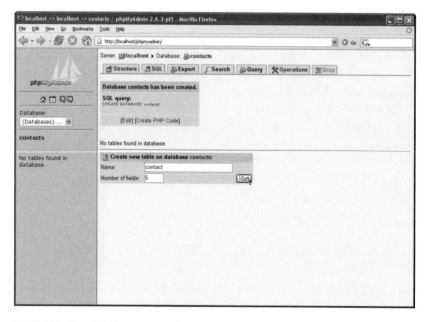

FIGURE 8.32 Database created screen.

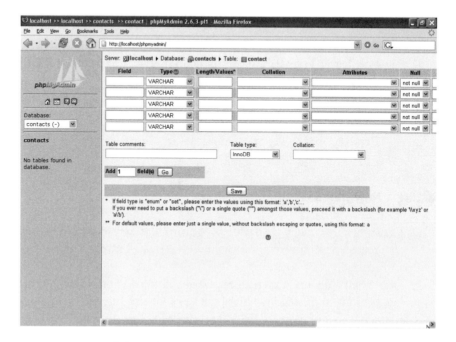

FIGURE 8.33 Defining columns in the `contact` table.

Within this screen, it is easy to complete all of the required information needed for the fields in the database. The first option is the Field name, followed by the Type, Length/Values (for enumeration), Collation, Attributes, and whether the field can be NULL. To see the rest of the fields, the window has to be scrolled to the right by using the scroll bar on the bottom. The last options uncovered are Default, Extra, Primary Key, Index, Unique, and Full text.

Data types and other options will be explored in the next chapter. For now, the fields will be marked as show in Figures 8.34 and 8.35.

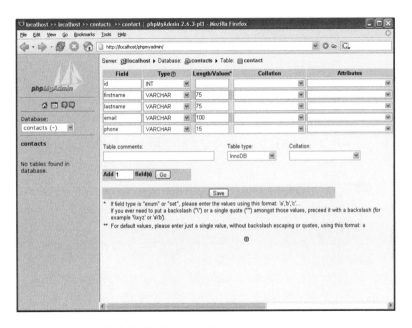

FIGURE 8.34   Left half of table creation screen.

Once Save is pressed, the table is created. The results will be displayed along with other options to interact with the table as shown in Figures 8.36 and 8.37. Notice how the SQL query that was used to make the table is displayed in Figure 8.36? That feature helps users learn SQL queries even while using the phpMyAdmin.

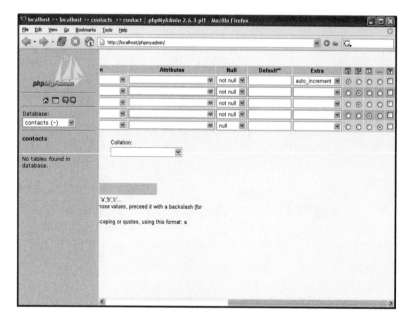

FIGURE 8.35 Right half of table creation screen.

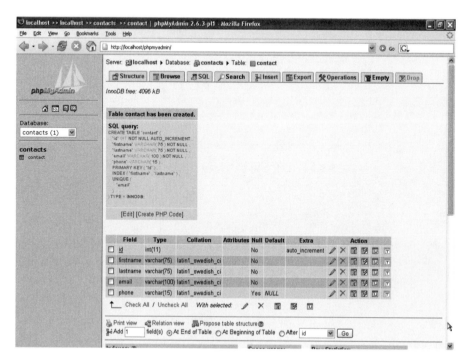

FIGURE 8.36 Results of table creation upper half.

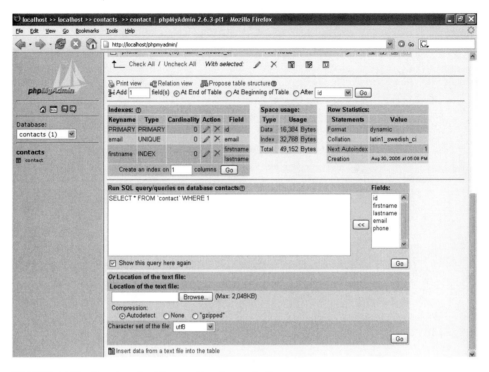

FIGURE 8.37   Results of table creation lower half.

SUMMARY

This concludes the installation and a basic introduction to MySQL with additional coverage of the MySQL monitor and phpMyAdmin. As can be seen, there is a lot to the programs. Coverage continues in Chapter 9, "Communicating with MySQL."

9

Communicating with MySQL

In This Chapter

- Creating the Database
- The Perl DBI Module
- Using PHP Extensions
- Summary

In this chapter, we'll explore communication with MySQL. The communication will be achieved using the Perl DBI module and PHP with the `mysqli` extension.

CREATING THE DATABASE

The first database used in this chapter is called videos. It is a handy database that can be used to catalog a home collection for insurance purposes, or to share information with friends. This database will contain the following information:

Medium: VHS or DVD

Title: Title of the movie

Edition: Theatrical Release, Director's Cut, Special Edition, etc.

Format: Widescreen or Standard

Year: Original release year

Director: Director name

Starring: Actor name

Length: Movie runtime

Rating: MPAA rating

Genre: Action, Animated, Biography, Comedy, Documentary, Drama, Foreign, Historical, Horror, Musical, Romance, or Science Fiction

Description: Basic plot of movie

Notes: Additional information such as "Signed Copy"

Now, all of these fields can be placed into one table, but that may cause some problems. For example, how may people directed the project? There is usually one director, but not always. This means that there has to be more than one field for directors in the table, one director field (making multi-director projects suffer), or directors should be another table altogether. The last approach is preferred and is known as *normalization*.

Normalization

Anytime a database is created, decisions of data placement have to be made. One of the most important of these is how tables relate to one another. That is the backbone of a relational database management system like MySQL.

Normalization is the process of removing redundant data from a database to improve its efficiency and scalability. There are several levels of normalization called *forms*, but most databases stop at the second or third form.

1st Normal Form: Any column repeated within a database should be in a separate table. For example, in the videos database, if more than one director field existed (e.g., director_1, director_2, and so on), that would violate the first normal form.

2nd Normal Form: While 1st Normal Form focuses on repeats on a horizontal axis (column names), 2nd Normal Form shifts focus to any vertical repeats. Consider the following:

VideoID	Medium	Title	Edition	Format
1	VHS	Monsters Inc.	Collector's	Widescreen
2	VHS	Toy Story	10th Anniversary	Widescreen
3	DVD	Shrek	Two-Disc Special	Widescreen

Both medium and format have repeats in the table. According to the rules of 2nd Normal Form, they should be in separate tables.

3rd Normal Form: In 3rd Normal Form, there should be no data that is not directly defined by the primary key. This can be thought of as a number of degrees of separation. For example, a table called employee may have the following fields: employeeID, firstname, lastname, address, city, state, zip, hiredate, supervisor, and supervisorphone. This table is not in 3rd Normal Form. The supervisorphone field is not directly related to the primary key, it is dependant on supervisor. This means that unlike firstname or lastname, it is two degrees off and there should be a supervisor table.

Normalization is a very powerful tool to be used when designing databases, but it should not be taken too far. For example, with the 2nd Normal Form, vertical re- dundancies should be prevented. In the case of the Videos database, that could be taken to mean that the release year field should be in a separate table because it is certain to be repeated. In addition, while parsing out every possible redundancy may save space, there may still be a performance hit because it becomes increasingly complex when retrieving data from and posting data to a database. The database in this chapter will be normalized to 1st Normal Form for simplicity's sake.

Designing the Database

Now that we've looked at normalization, it is time to create the tables. These should be as follows:

```
video           director        star
videoID         directorID      starID
medium          firstname       firstname
title           lastname        lastname
edition
format
year
length
rating
genre
description
notes
```

Now that the basic tables have been created, it is time to look at them again, be- cause there is an issue. While the tables are conforming to the 1st Normal Form, there are many-to-many relationships between the tables. For example, a video can have many stars, and a star can act in many movies. This is a problem in that it can cause issues with normalization, and is difficult to maintain. The ideal relationships are either one-to-one, or one-to-many.

In the videos database, two more tables should be created to correct the situa- tion. These are video_director, and video_star and can be seen as bridging tables. That will create one-to-many relationships going in both directions, and the data- base should now contain the following structure:

video	video_director	director	video_star	star
videoID	videoID	directorID	videoID	starID
medium	directorID	firstname	starID	firstname
title		lastname		lastname
edition				
format				
year				
length				
rating				
genre				
description				
notes				

MySQL Data Types

Now that the tables have been determined, the type of data contained in each field needs to be explored. The type of data defined directly affects the overall size of the database. The following is a list of some of the most common data types and storage requirements used with MySQL as listed on *mysql.com*.

Numeric Data Types:

Column Type	Storage Required
TINYINT	1 byte
SMALLINT	2 bytes
MEDIUMINT	3 bytes
INT, INTEGER	4 bytes
BIGINT	8 bytes
FLOAT	4 bytes

Date Data Types:

Column Type	Storage Required
DATE	3 bytes
DATETIME	8 bytes
TIMESTAMP	4 bytes
TIME	3 bytes
YEAR	1 byte

String Data Types:

Column Type	Storage Required
CHAR(M)	M bytes, $0 <= M <= 255$
VARCHAR(M)	$L+1$ bytes, where $L <= M$ and $0 <= M <= 255$ before MySQL 5.0.3 ($0 <= M <= 65535$ in MySQL 5.0.3 and later
BINARY(M)	M bytes, $0 <= M <= 255$
VARBINARY(M)	$L+1$ bytes, where $L <= M$ and $0 <= M <= 255$
TINYBLOB, TINYTEXT	$L+1$ bytes, where $L < 2^8$
BLOB, TEXT	$L+2$ bytes, where $L < 2^{16}$
MEDIUMBLOB, MEDIUMTEXT	$L+3$ bytes, where $L < 2^{24}$
LONGBLOB, LONGTEXT	$L+4$ bytes, where $L < 2^{32}$
ENUM('$value1$','$value2$',...)	1 or 2 bytes, depending on the number of enumeration values (65,535 values maximum)
SET('$value1$','$value2$',...)	1, 2, 3, 4, or 8 bytes, depending on the number of set members (64 members maximum)

In addition to the different data types are additional column modifiers that can affect what is placed within fields. The list of these and what column types use them is next. They are then defined specifically.

Additional Column Modifiers:

Modifier Name	Applicable Types
AUTO_INCREMENT	All INT Types
BINARY	CHAR, VARCHAR
DEFAULT	All, except BLOB, TEXT
NOT NULL	All Types
NULL	All Types
PRIMARY KEY	All Types
UNIQUE	All Types
UNSIGNED	Numeric Types
ZEROFILL	Numeric Types

PRIMARY KEY: Can be used with any type of input, but is usually associated with INT types. It is an index used to make sure that all values are unique in a column.

NULL: Allows a field to be blank when a new row is entered.

NOT NULL: Will not allow a new row to be added to the database if the field is empty.

AUTO_INCREMENT: Used often on numeric fields that are primary keys. Adds one to the value found in the same field from the previous row, and assigns the result to the current column. It can be used on any integer type TINYINT, SMALLINT, MEDIUMINT, INT or INTEGER, and BIGINT.

BINARY: Used with CHAR and VARCHAR fields. Its purpose is to make the field case sensitive. When any comparison operation takes place like WHERE name="Eric", if the column is specified as BINARY, neither "ERIC" nor "eric" will match—they would without the modifier.

DEFAULT: Allows a default value to be added if nothing is entered.

UNIQUE: Only allows unique values to be added to a column.

UNSIGNED: Treats all numbers positive. This is valuable when the maximum range of digits is needed on a numeric field that will always be positive. For example, SMALLINT allows for numbers ranging from -32768 to 32767. If the column is assigned the UNSIGNED modifier, SMALLINT will allow 0-65525.

ZEROFILL: Fills all blank spaces to the left with zeroes (much like checks). For example, if the field has the modifier MEDIUMINT, and the value going in is 124, it will enter 00000124.

Creating the Videos Database

Here is the SQL script that will create the videos database:

```
CREATE DATABASE videos;
USE videos;
CREATE TABLE video (videoID SMALLINT UNSIGNED NOT NULL PRIMARY KEY
AUTO_INCREMENT,
media VARCHAR (10) NOT NULL,
title VARCHAR(100) NOT NULL,
edition VARCHAR(100) NULL,
format VARCHAR(50) NOT NULL,
year YEAR NOT NULL,
length TIME NOT NULL,
rating VARCHAR(10) NOT NULL,
genre VARCHAR(100) NOT NULL,
description TEXT NULL,
notes TEXT NULL,
INDEX (title,genre)
);

CREATE TABLE video_director (
videoID SMALLINT UNSIGNED NOT NULL,
directorID SMALLINT UNSIGNED NOT NULL,
INDEX (videoID,directorID)
);
```

```
CREATE TABLE  director (
directorID SMALLINT UNSIGNED NOT NULL PRIMARY KEY AUTO_INCREMENT,
firstname VARCHAR(100) NOT  NULL,
lastname VARCHAR(100) NOT NULL,
INDEX (firstname,lastname)
);

CREATE TABLE video_star(
videoID SMALLINT UNSIGNED NOT NULL,
starID SMALLINT UNSIGNED NOT NULL,
INDEX (videoID,starID)
);

CREATE TABLE star(
starID SMALLINT UNSIGNED NOT NULL PRIMARY KEY AUTO_INCREMENT,
firstname VARCHAR(100) NOT NULL,
lastname VARCHAR(100) NOT NULL,
INDEX (firstname,lastname)
);
```

ON THE CD   This SQL script has been saved on the companion CD-ROM as `videos.sql` under `examples/chapter09/`. To import it into MySQL:

1. Copy videos.sql into the C:\Program Files\MySQL\MySQL Server 4.1\bin\ directory.
2. Choose Start | Run and type `cmd` if on Windows 2000/XP/Server 2003, or `command` if using Windows 9X/ME. Click OK.
3. This will load the command prompt. Now, type `CD \Program Files\MySQL\MySQL Server 4.1\bin`.
4. Once in the bin directory, type `mysql -u root -p < videos.sql`. This will create the videos database and all tables.

THE PERL DBI MODULE

DBI stands for *database independent interface*, and allows the use a single set of Perl functions to access many different databases including MySQL, Microsoft SQL Server, Oracle, and more.

DBI has two parts—the module and a driver for the specific database. Programmers rarely have to deal directly with the driver, only with the DBI module. This layer of abstraction enables scripts to be more portable. There are three built-in objects used with DBI: `dbd`, `$dbh`, and `$sth`.

dbd: dbd literally stands for the Database Driver. This is connecting to the database in the background, so programmers have little interaction with it.

$dbh: When DBI connects with a database, the information about the connection is stored in a *database handle* object often called $dbh. This object represents the database connection. Scripts can be connected to many databases at once and have many such database connection objects. A typical connection is created as follows:

```
my $dbh = DBI->connect('DBI:mysql:dbname', 'username', 'password') or
die "Failed to connect. Error returned is: " . DBI->errstr;
```

$sth: The prepare call prepares an SQL query to be executed by the database. If it is successful, it returns a *statement handle* object. Otherwise, it returns an undefined value and fails. The typical usage of the statement handle object is as follows:

```
my $sth = $dbh->prepare('SELECT * FROM tablename WHERE columnname =
value') or die "Couldn't prepare statement: " . $dbh->errstr;
$sth->execute();
```

The prepare portion of an $sth statement prepares the SQL query to be executed. The statement is not actually executed until the third line $sth->execute(); is given. The results of $sth will be stored in one of these possible variables:

```
@row_ary = $sth->fetchrow_array;
$ary_ref = $sth->fetchrow_arrayref;
$hash_ref = $sth->fetchrow_hashref;
```

A common approach is with the use of a while loop:

```
while($sth->fetchrow_array){
        actions;
}
```

Another powerful feature when using a while loop and $sth->fetchrow_array is the ability to assign values to variables as the loop is occurring. There have to be the same number of variables as columns requested in the SELECT statement. The following shows this principle:

```
while($item1,$item2,$item3)=$sth->fetchrow_array){
        actions;
}
```

While all SQL queries can make use of $sth->prepare, it is associated primarily with SELECT queries.

Installing Perl DBI

ActiveState Perl does not install DBI by default, so follow these steps to add it to the current distribution:

1. Click Start | Run, type cmd, and click OK.
2. Type cd \usr\bin to change to the Perl directory.
3. Type ppm and press the Enter key to start the Programmer's Package Manager shown in Figure 9.1. This application is used to download and install packages to enhance Perl. DBI is one such package.

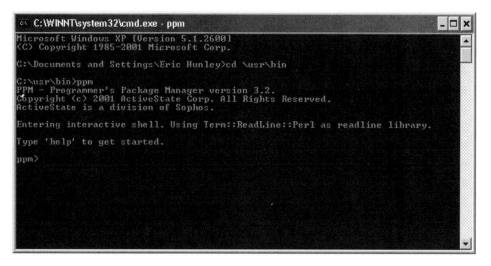

FIGURE 9.1 Starting the Programmer's Package Manager.

4. Within the Programmer's Package Manager, type install DBI. If the operating system is Windows XP with Service Pack 2 installed, Figure 9.2 may appear. If it does, just click Unblock.
5. A slew of lines will cascade in the command prompt window until the ppm> prompt appears again as shown in Figure 9.3.
6. Now that DBI is installed, the driver for MySQL has to be installed as shown in Figure 9.4. This is done by typing install DBD-MySQL and pressing Enter.

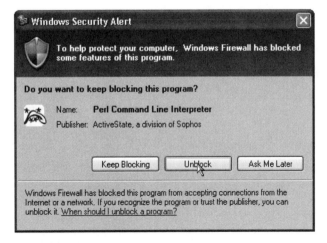

FIGURE 9.2 Windows XP Security Alert.

```
C:\WINNT\system32\cmd.exe - ppm
Installing C:\usr\site\lib\DBD\Sponge.pm
Installing C:\usr\site\lib\DBI\Changes.pm
Installing C:\usr\site\lib\DBI\DBD.pm
Installing C:\usr\site\lib\DBI\FAQ.pm
Installing C:\usr\site\lib\DBI\Profile.pm
Installing C:\usr\site\lib\DBI\ProfileData.pm
Installing C:\usr\site\lib\DBI\ProfileDumper.pm
Installing C:\usr\site\lib\DBI\ProxyServer.pm
Installing C:\usr\site\lib\DBI\PurePerl.pm
Installing C:\usr\site\lib\DBI\Roadmap.pm
Installing C:\usr\site\lib\DBI\W32ODBC.pm
Installing C:\usr\site\lib\DBI\Const\GetInfoReturn.pm
Installing C:\usr\site\lib\DBI\Const\GetInfoType.pm
Installing C:\usr\site\lib\DBI\Const\GetInfo\ANSI.pm
Installing C:\usr\site\lib\DBI\Const\GetInfo\ODBC.pm
Installing C:\usr\site\lib\DBI\DBD\Metadata.pm
Installing C:\usr\site\lib\DBI\ProfileDumper\Apache.pm
Installing C:\usr\site\lib\DBI\SQL\Nano.pm
Installing C:\usr\site\lib\Win32\DBIODBC.pm
Installing C:\usr\bin\dbiprof
Installing C:\usr\bin\dbiprof.bat
Installing C:\usr\bin\dbiproxy
Installing C:\usr\bin\dbiproxy.bat
Successfully installed DBI version 1.48 in ActivePerl 5.8.7.813.
ppm>
```

FIGURE 9.3 Installing DBI.

7. Once everything is installed, it is time to exit PPM, which you can do by using one of three commands: exit, quit, or q shown in Figure 9.5. DBI can now be used successfully. Type exit to leave the command prompt.

```
C:\WINNT\system32\cmd.exe - ppm                                         _ □ ×
Successfully installed DBI version 1.48 in ActivePerl 5.8.7.813.
ppm> install DBD-MySQL
=====================
Install 'DBD-MySQL' version 3.0002 in ActivePerl 5.8.7.813.
=====================
Downloaded 610245 bytes.
Extracting 17/17: blib/arch/auto/DBD/mysql/mysql.lib
Installing C:\usr\site\lib\auto\DBD\mysql\mysql.bs
Installing C:\usr\site\lib\auto\DBD\mysql\mysql.dll
Installing C:\usr\site\lib\auto\DBD\mysql\mysql.exp
Installing C:\usr\site\lib\auto\DBD\mysql\mysql.lib
Installing C:\usr\html\site\lib\Mysql.html
Installing C:\usr\html\site\lib\Bundle\DBD\mysql.html
Installing C:\usr\html\site\lib\DBD\mysql.html
Installing C:\usr\html\site\lib\DBD\mysql\INSTALL.html
Files found in blib\arch: installing files in blib\lib into architecture depende
nt library tree
Installing C:\usr\site\lib\Mysql.pm
Installing C:\usr\site\lib\Bundle\DBD\mysql.pm
Installing C:\usr\site\lib\DBD\mysql.pm
Installing C:\usr\site\lib\DBD\mysql\GetInfo.pm
Installing C:\usr\site\lib\DBD\mysql\INSTALL.pod
Installing C:\usr\site\lib\Mysql\Statement.pm
Successfully installed DBD-MySQL version 3.0002 in ActivePerl 5.8.7.813.
ppm>
```

FIGURE 9.4   Installing MySQL DBI driver.

```
C:\WINNT\system32\cmd.exe                                              _ □ ×
=====================
Install 'DBD-MySQL' version 3.0002 in ActivePerl 5.8.7.813.
=====================
Downloaded 610245 bytes.
Extracting 17/17: blib/arch/auto/DBD/mysql/mysql.lib
Installing C:\usr\site\lib\auto\DBD\mysql\mysql.bs
Installing C:\usr\site\lib\auto\DBD\mysql\mysql.dll
Installing C:\usr\site\lib\auto\DBD\mysql\mysql.exp
Installing C:\usr\site\lib\auto\DBD\mysql\mysql.lib
Installing C:\usr\html\site\lib\Mysql.html
Installing C:\usr\html\site\lib\Bundle\DBD\mysql.html
Installing C:\usr\html\site\lib\DBD\mysql.html
Installing C:\usr\html\site\lib\DBD\mysql\INSTALL.html
Files found in blib\arch: installing files in blib\lib into architecture depende
nt library tree
Installing C:\usr\site\lib\Mysql.pm
Installing C:\usr\site\lib\Bundle\DBD\mysql.pm
Installing C:\usr\site\lib\DBD\mysql.pm
Installing C:\usr\site\lib\DBD\mysql\GetInfo.pm
Installing C:\usr\site\lib\DBD\mysql\INSTALL.pod
Installing C:\usr\site\lib\Mysql\Statement.pm
Successfully installed DBD-MySQL version 3.0002 in ActivePerl 5.8.7.813.
ppm> q

C:\usr\bin>
```

FIGURE 9.5   Exiting PPM.

Adding Records

The first activity that needs to take place in the videos database is the addition of records. This is accomplished with a combination of an HTML and Perl document working together. The HTML document shown next collects all of the video information. It is also displayed in Figure 9.6 and is on the companion CD-ROM as

ON THE CD   examples\chapter09\addvideo.html.

FIGURE 9.6 The form used to collect new video information `addvideo.html`.

```
<html>
<head>
<title>Add a Video</title>
</head>
<body>
<h2>Add a new video</h2>
<form action="cgi-bin/addvideo.pl" method="post">
<table>
<tr><td>Media:</td><td><input type="radio" name="media" value="DVD"
checked="checked" />DVD <input type="radio" name="media" value="VHS"
/>VHS</td></tr>
<tr><td>Title:</td><td><input type="text" name="title" /></td></tr>
<tr><td>Edition:</td><td><input type="text" name="edition" /></td></tr>
<tr><td>Format:</td><td><input type="radio" name="format"
value="Widescreen" checked="checked" />Widescreen <input type="radio"
```

```
name="format" value="Standard" />Standard <input type="radio"
name="format" value="both" />Both</td></tr>
<tr><td>Year:</td><td><input type="text" name="year" size="4"
/></td></tr>
<tr><td>Length:</td><td><input type="text" name="length" value="hh:mm"
size="4" /></td></tr>
<tr><td>Rating:</td><td><input type="radio" name="rating" value="R" />R
<input type="radio" name="rating" value="PG-13" />PG-13 <input
type="radio" name="rating" value="PG" />PG <input type="radio"
name="rating" value="G" />G <input type="radio" name="rating"
value="Unrated" checked="checked" />Unrated </td></tr>
<tr valign="top"><td>Genre:<br />(ctrl-click to<br />multi-select)</td>
    <td><select name="genre" multiple="multiple" size="4">
                    <option value="Action">Action</option>
                    <option value="Adventure">Adventure</option>
                    <option value="Animated">Animated</option>
                    <option value="Biography">Biography</option>
                    <option value="Comedy">Comedy</option>
                    <option value="Documentary">Documentary</option>
                    <option value="Drama">Drama</option>
                    <option value="Foreign">Foreign</option>
                    <option value="Historical">Historical</option>
                    <option value="Horror">Horror</option>
                    <option value="Musical">Musical</option>
                    <option value="Other">Other</option>
                    <option value="Romance">Romance</option>
                    <option value="Sci-fi">Science Fiction</option>
            </select></td></tr>
<tr valign="top"><td>Description:</td><td><textarea name="description"
rows="5" cols="50"></textarea></td></tr>
<tr valign="top"><td>Notes:</td><td><textarea name="notes" rows="2"
cols="50"></textarea></td></tr>
<tr><td></td><td><input type="submit" value="Add Movie" /> <input
type="reset" value="Clear Form" /></td></tr>
</table>
</form>
```

In addition to the addvideo.html document, there is the Perl script that processes the data—addvideo.pl. This script is shown next, in Figure 9.7, and can be found on the companion CD-ROM as examples\chapter09\addvideo.pl.

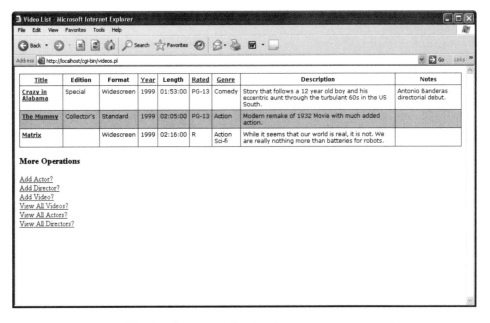

FIGURE 9.7 A new video has been added using the `addvideo.html` and `addvideo.pl` combination.

```perl
#!/usr/bin/perl -w
use strict;
use DBI;
use CGI ':standard';

print "Content-type: text/html\n\n";

my $media = param("media");
my $title = param("title");
my $edition = param("edition");
my $format = param("format");
my $year = param("year");
my $length = param("length");
my $rating = param("rating");
my @genre = param("genre");
my $description = param("description");
my $notes = param("notes");
my $genre = join("<br />",@genre);
```

```
my $dbh = DBI->connect('DBI:mysql:videos', 'root', 'password') or die
"Failed to connect. Error returned is: " . DBI->errstr;


$dbh -> do(qq(INSERT INTO
video(media,title,edition,format,year,length,rating,genre,description,n
otes)
VALUES("$media","$title","$edition","$format","$year","$length","$rat-
ing","$genre","$description","$notes")));
$dbh -> disconnect;
print "<p>The following information has been added to the database:
</p>";
print "<ul>";
print "<li>Media: $media</li>";
print "<li>Title: $title</li>";
print "<li>Edition: $edition</li>";
print "<li>Format: $format</li>";
print "<li>Year: $year</li>";
print "<li>Length: $length</li>";
print "<li>Rating: $rating</li>";
print "<li>Genre: $genre</li>";
print "<li>Description: $description</li>";
print "<li>Notes: $notes</li>";
print "</ul>";

print "<h3>More Operations</h3>";
print "<a href=\"addactor.pl\">Add Actor?</a><br />";
print "<a href=\"adddirector.pl\">Add Director?</a><br />";
print "<a href=\"../addvideo.html\">Add Video?</a><br />";
print "<a href=\"videos.pl\">View All Videos?</a><br />";
print "<a href=\"actors.pl\">View All Actors?</a><br />";
print "<a href=\"directors.pl\">View All Directors?</a><br />";
```

There are two more scripts that add records to the database on the accompanying CD-ROM: examples\chapter09\addactor.pl *and* examples\chapter09\adddirector.pl.

NOTE

ON THE CD

The first part of the script is the typical overhead seen on most Perl scripts ear-lier in this book: the shebang, content-type line, use strict, and use CGI ':stan-dard'. There is a new addition here of use dbi. That is all that is required to put database support into action.

The next set of lines collects data from the form and assigns it to variables in the script. The following code then establishes a connection to the database or returns an error if it fails:

```
my $dbh = DBI->connect('DBI:mysql:videos', 'root', 'password') or die
"Failed to connect. Error returned is: " . DBI->errstr;
```

The next two lines are:

```
$dbh -> do(qq(INSERT INTO
video(media,title,edition,format,year,length,rating,genre,description,n
otes)
VALUES("$media","$title","$edition","$format","$year","$length","$rat-
ing","$genre","$description","$notes")));
$dbh -> disconnect;
```

These lines consist of the query and disconnect from the database. Notice the use of the `$dbh -> do()`. This is the alternative to a `$sth->prepare()` and is available for INSERT, DELETE, and UPDATE queries. It literally immediately performs the assigned task. Here it is inserting a new record into the `video` table. Once the record is inserted, the script is disconnected, and all lines that follow provide feedback to the end user.

Displaying Records

The next SQL query to be covered is the SELECT, which is used to display records. This is accomplished with `videos.pl` written next, shown in Figure 9.8, and stored on the companion CD-ROM in the `examples\chapter09\` folder.

```
#!/usr/bin/perl -w
use strict;
use DBI;
use CGI ':standard';
print "Content-type: text/html\n\n";
print qq(<html><head><title>Video List</title><style
type="text/css">table{ border-bottom: 1px solid #555555; border-right:
1px solid #555555;}td,th {border-left: 1px solid #555555; border-top:
1px solid #555555; font-family: Verdana, Arial, Helvetica, sans-serif;
font-size: 12px}</style></head><body>);
my
```

```perl
($videoID,$media,$title,$edition,$format,$year,$length,$rating,$genre,$
description,$notes,$sort);

if(param("sort")){
    $sort = param("sort");
}else{
    $sort="videoID";
}
my $dbh = DBI->connect('DBI:mysql:videos', 'root', 'password') or die
"Failed to connect. Error returned is: " . DBI->errstr;
my $sth = $dbh->prepare("SELECT * FROM video ORDER BY $sort");
$sth->execute();

print qq(<table cellpadding="5" cellspacing="0">);
print qq(<tr><th><a href="videos.pl?sort=title">Title</a></th><th>Edi-
tion</th><th>Format</th><th><a
href="videos.pl?sort=year">Year</a></th><th>Length</th><th><a
href="videos.pl?sort=rating">Rated</a></th><th><a
href="videos.pl?sort=genre">Genre</a></th><th>Description</th><th>Notes
</th></tr>);
my $count=1;
while(($videoID,$media,$title,$edition,$format,$year,$length,$rating,$g
enre,$description,$notes) = $sth->fetchrow_array()){
    print "<tr ";
    if($count%2 == 0){
            print qq(style="background-color: #DDDDDD" );
    }
    print qq(valign="top"><td><strong><a
href="details.pl?videoID=$videoID">$title</a></strong> </td><td>$edi-
tion </td><td>$format </td><td>$year </td><td>$length
</td><td>$rating </td><td>$genre </td><td>$description
</td><td>$notes </td></tr>);
    $count++;
}
print "</table>";

print "<h3>More Operations</h3>";
print "<a href=\"addactor.pl\">Add Actor?</a><br />";
print "<a href=\"adddirector.pl\">Add Director?</a><br />";
print "<a href=\"../addvideo.html\">Add Video?</a><br />";
print "<a href=\"videos.pl\">View All Videos?</a><br />";
print "<a href=\"actors.pl\">View All Actors?</a><br />";
print "<a href=\"directors.pl\">View All Directors?</a><br />";
print "</body></html>";
```

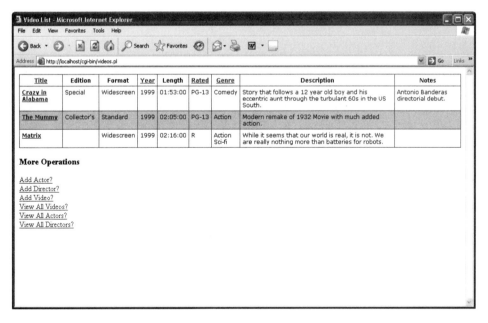

FIGURE 9.8 videos.pl.

This script starts the same as the previous script with the addition of a print(qq()); statement adding more HTML, because there is no accompanying HTML document. The rest of the Perl scripts in this chapter are the same way.

Before the database connection is established, or the $sth->prepare is given, the following code is placed on the page:

```
if(param("sort")){
    $sort = param("sort");
}else{
    $sort="videoID";
}
```

This code enhances the utility of the script. The actual SQL query is SELECT * FROM video ORDER BY $sort. Notice the use of $sort. This means that the results of the query will be organized according to the value sent in $sort. When looking at the if/else conditional, it can be seen that this one of two things: a value sent from external variables received via a GET or POST, or videoID.

Where is the external value coming from? Look further down the script. Notice in the HTML that there are links added to some of the headings, specifically Title, Year, Rated, and Genre. These links are sending a value for $sort that is being used by the if/else conditional and ultimately the SQL statement. If nothing has been sent, or it is the first time the page is loaded, videoID acts as the default.

This gives the end user flexibility in organizing the results. He simply has to click on a column head, and the page will reload with the results sorted in the order requested. This is a common feature of search results on large e-commerce sites.

Removing Records

To demonstrate removing records, or the DELETE SQL query sent from Perl, actordelete.pl will be used. This is displayed here, in Figure 9.9, and is on the companion CD-ROM (along with its counterpart directordelete.pl) in examples\ chapter09\.

ON THE CD

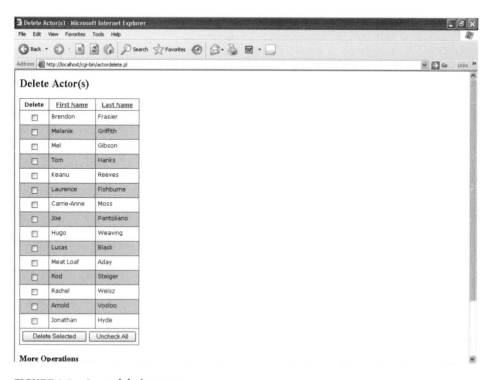

FIGURE 9.9 Actor deletion page.

```perl
#!/usr/bin/perl -w
use strict;
use DBI;
use CGI ':standard';
print "Content-type: text/html\n\n";
print qq(<html><head><title>Delete Actor(s)</title><style
type="text/css">table{ border-bottom: 1px solid #555555; border-right:
1px solid #555555;}td,th {border-left: 1px solid #555555; border-top:
1px solid #555555; font-family: Verdana, Arial, Helvetica, sans-serif;
font-size: 12px}</style></head><body>);
my ($starID,$firstname,$lastname,$sort,@delete);

if(param("sort")){
    $sort = param("sort");
}else{
    $sort="starID";
}
print "<h2>Delete Actor(s)</h2>";
if(param("process")){
    @delete = param("delete");
    my $dbh = DBI->connect('DBI:mysql:videos', 'root', 'password') or
    die "Failed to connect. Error returned is: " . DBI->errstr;
    foreach(@delete){
        $dbh -> do(qq(DELETE FROM star WHERE starID=$_));
    }
    $dbh -> disconnect;
    print "<p>" . scalar @delete . " actors have been deleted from the
    database.</p>";
    print qq(<p><a href="actordelete.pl">Delete More?</a><br />);
    print qq(<a href="actors.pl">View All?</a></p>);
}else{
my $dbh = DBI->connect('DBI:mysql:videos', 'root', 'password') or die
"Failed to connect. Error returned is: " . DBI->errstr;
my $sth = $dbh->prepare("SELECT * FROM star ORDER BY $sort");
$sth->execute();

print qq(<form action="actordelete.pl" method="post"><table
cellpadding="5" cellspacing="0">);
print qq(<tr><th>Delete</th><th><a
href="actordelete.pl?sort=firstname">First Name</a></th><th><a
```

```
href="actordelete.pl?sort=lastname">Last Name</a></th></tr>);
my $count=1;
while(($starID,$firstname,$lastname) = $sth->fetchrow_array()){
    print "<tr ";
    if($count%2 == 0){
        print qq(style="background-color: #DDDDDD" );
    }
    print qq(valign="top"><td align="center"><input type="checkbox"
    name="delete" value="$starID" /></td><td>$firstname </td><td>$last
    name</td></tr>);
    $count++;
}
print qq(<tr><td colspan="3"><input type="submit" value="Delete
Selected" /> <input type="reset" value="Uncheck All" /><input
type="hidden" name="process" value="1" /></table>);
}
print "<h3>More Operations</h3>";
print "<a href=\"addactor.pl\">Add Actor?</a><br />";
print "<a href=\"adddirector.pl\">Add Director?</a><br />";
print "<a href=\"../addvideo.html\">Add Video?</a><br />";
print "<a href=\"videos.pl\">View All Videos?</a><br />";
print "<a href=\"actors.pl\">View All Actors?</a><br />";
print "<a href=\"directors.pl\">View All Directors?</a><br />";
print "</body></html>";
```

In this script, two SQL queries are being used. The first is the SELECT query, which is used to populate the form, and the second is the DELETE query. The conditional if(param("process")) determines which of the two statements will be performed. It is looking for the hidden form field process. If it exists, the @delete array will be created from param("delete"), and a foreach loop will be used to delete each record with the starID matching the current value in the array.

Updating Records

ON THE CD

The last of the four primary SQL queries we'll cover is UPDATE. This is demonstrated with actorupdate.pl found here, in Figure 9.10, and on the companion CD-ROM (along with the similar directorupdate.pl) under examples\chapter09.

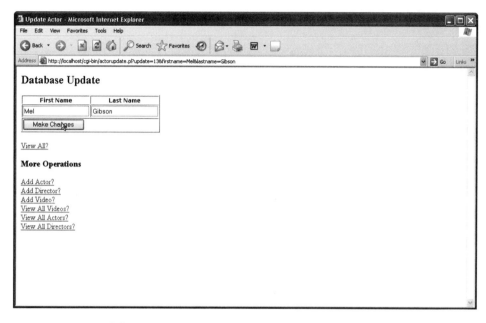

FIGURE 9.10   Updating records.

```perl
#!/usr/bin/perl -w
use strict;
use DBI;
use CGI ':standard';
print "Content-type: text/html\n\n";
print qq(<html><head><title>Update Actor</title><style
type="text/css">table{ border-bottom: 1px solid #555555; border-right:
1px solid #555555;}td,th {border-left: 1px solid #555555; border-top:
1px solid #555555; font-family: Verdana, Arial, Helvetica, sans-serif;
font-size: 12px}</style></head><body>);
my ($starID,$firstname,$lastname,$update,$process);

$starID=param("update");
$firstname=param("firstname");
$lastname=param("lastname");
$process = param("process");
print "<h2>Database Update</h2>";
```

```perl
if($process){
    print "<p>The record has been updated.</p>";
    my $dbh = DBI->connect('DBI:mysql:videos', 'root', 'password') or
die "Failed to connect. Error returned is: " . DBI->errstr;
    $dbh -> do(qq(UPDATE star SET
firstname="$firstname",lastname="$lastname" WHERE starID=$starID));

    my $sth = $dbh->prepare("SELECT * FROM star WHERE starID =
$starID");
    $sth->execute();
    ($starID,$firstname,$lastname) = $sth ->fetchrow_array();
    $dbh -> disconnect;

    print qq(<form action="actorupdate.pl" method="post"><table>);
    print qq(<tr><th>First Name</th><th>Last Name</th></tr>);
    print qq(<tr><td><input type="text" name="firstname" value="$first
name" /></td><td><input type="text" name="lastname" value="$last
name" /></td></tr>);
    print qq(<tr><td colspan="2"><input type="submit" value="Make
Changes" /><input type="hidden" name="process" value="1" /><input
type="hidden" name="update" value="$starID"
/></td></tr></table></form>);
}else{
    print qq(<form action="actorupdate.pl" method="post"><table>);
    print qq(<tr><th>First Name</th><th>Last Name</th></tr>);
    print qq(<tr><td><input type="text" name="firstname" value="$first
name" /></td><td><input type="text" name="lastname" value="$last
name" /></td></tr>);
    print qq(<tr><td colspan="2"><input type="submit" value="Make
    Changes" /><input type="hidden" name="process" value="1" /><input
type="hidden" name="update" value="$starID"
/></td></tr></table></form>);
}

print qq(<a href="actors.pl">View All?</a></p>);
print "<h3>More Operations</h3>";
print "<a href=\"addactor.pl\">Add Actor?</a><br />";
print "<a href=\"adddirector.pl\">Add Director?</a><br />";
print "<a href=\"../addvideo.html\">Add Video?</a><br />";
print "<a href=\"videos.pl\">View All Videos?</a><br />";
print "<a href=\"actors.pl\">View All Actors?</a><br />";
print "<a href=\"directors.pl\">View All Directors?</a><br />";
print "</body></html>";
```

This script works in conjunction with `actors.pl` (also on the companion CD-ROM in `examples\chapter09\`). The end user will click the `Update?` link next to a listed actor, which will take him to this script. The URL in the link click points to `actorupdate.pl`, and sends the variables `starID`, `firstname`, and `lastname` via GET.

This information in turn is used to populate form fields the user can change. Once these are changed and the user clicks Make Changes, the page is reloaded with the hidden `process` field being sent.

When the page is reloaded, it sees the process field and sends a query with new information to update the database and reloads. It also prepares and sends a SELECT query to repopulate the form. This way, the user can see the changes that were made, and make more if necessary.

USING PHP EXTENSIONS

PHP has long been known for its strong support of MySQL, and is probably more associated with that RDBMS than any other. This makes programming for MySQL communication a breeze.

One of the most popular forms of communication with MySQL has been through the usage of the `mysql` extension. This extension offers numerous built-in functions that can be found at *http://www.php.net/mysql*. It is effective for communication with MySQL versions prior to 4.1. For versions later than 4.1, `mysqli` is recommended. This update will be used throughout this chapter for all examples since MySQL 4.1 is included on the companion CD-ROM.

Enabling `mysqli`

PHP5 now offers improved support for MySQL 4.1.3 and later with the `mysqli` extension. The "i" literally stands for improved. It operates much like the original `mysql` extension, which works with lower versions of MySQL. In fact, in most cases, the functions are identical with the exception of just one letter, such as `mysql_fetch_array` is now `mysqli_fetch_array` in the new extension.

If an earlier version of MySQL is installed on the server, modify all `mysqli_` commands to `mysql_`.

Using `mysqli`

In this section, the following six functions will be used from the `mysqli` extension:

`mysqli_connect(server,user,password)`: Establishes a connection or link to the MySQL server. This is assigned to a variable for use throughout the script, as in `$link = mysqli_connect(server,user,password)`.

`mysqli_select_db(link,database)`: Selects the database to use on the server, and is the equivalent to the use *dbname* command. This must be used before any SELECT, INSERT, UPDATE, or DELETE queries are sent in a script.

`mysqli_error(link)`: Returns the error given from the MySQL server when a command is unsuccessful. It is not required, but is a good idea.

`mysqli_query(link,query)`: Submits a string query to the database connection (link) established by `mysqli_connect()`. Usually, the query is assigned to a variable as shown in all the examples in this section.

`mysqli_fetch_array(result,type)`: Reads a row from `mysqli_query()` results. The second argument allows the type of result to be changed. Three result types can be used: MYSQLI_ASSOC, MYSQLI_NUM, or MYSQLI_BOTH. The first type, MYSQLI_ASSOC, will return the row as an associative array with column names as keys and the row contents as values. The second, MYSQLI_NUM, returns a standard numeric indexed array. The last option, MYSQLI_BOTH, returns both types of arrays, and is the default. Other functions retrieve results, such as `mysqli_fetch_assoc()` and `mysqli_fetch_row()`, but `mysqli_fetch_array()` has its functionality built in and will be used for all the examples here.

`mysqli_close(link)`: Closes the connection to MySQL.

These functions will accomplish most general database tasks required with MySQL, and some are dependant on others. For example, all of the `mysqli` functions are dependant on `mysqli_connect()` because database functions cannot be performed without a connection. The following is a list of the four most commonly used SQL queries, and the functions that are required:

SELECT: `mysqli_connect()`, `mysqli_select_db()`, `mysqli_query()`, `mysqli_fetch_array()` or a variation, and `mysqli_close()`.

INSERT: `mysqli_connect()`, `mysqli_select_db()`, `mysqli_query()`, and `mysqli_close()`.

UPDATE: `mysqli_connect()`, `mysqli_select_db()`, `mysqli_query()`, and `mysqli_close()`.

DELETE: `mysqli_connect()`, `mysqli_select_db()`, `mysqli_query()`, and `mysqli_close()`.

Creating the Database

The first thing we need to do here is create a new database. SQL queries sent by server-side languages are not limited to the data manipulation language commands SELECT, INSERT, UPDATE, and DELETE. They can also be used for the Data Definition Language. A server-side language can send any acceptable SQL command to a database server, which you saw in the previous chapter with phpMyAdmin.

Based on this principle, instead of importing some SQL code, the script createdatabase.php will be used to create the database for this section. It is shown here and can be found on the companion CD-ROM in examples\chapter09\.

```
<html>
<head>
    <title>Create Database</title>
</head>
<body>
<h1>Database Creation Page</h1>
<?php

//Connect to MySQL
$db="audiobooks";
$link = mysqli_connect("localhost","root","password");
$sql = "CREATE DATABASE $db";

//Create Database
if(mysqli_query($link,$sql)){
    echo "<p>The database <strong>audiobooks</strong> has been
created.</p>";
}else{
    echo "<p>Failed to create database: <strong>" . mysqli_error($link)
. "</strong></p>";
}

mysqli_select_db($link,$db);

//Create audiobook Table
$sql = "CREATE TABLE audiobook(
audiobookID MEDIUMINT UNSIGNED NOT NULL AUTO_INCREMENT,
title VARCHAR(200) NOT NULL,
author VARCHAR(200),
narrator VARCHAR(200),
year YEAR NOT NULL,
edition VARCHAR(10) NOT NULL,
format VARCHAR(20) NOT NULL,
```

```
series VARCHAR(50),
seriesnum TINYINT UNSIGNED NOT NULL,
genre VARCHAR(100) NOT NULL,
description MEDIUMTEXT NOT NULL,
notes TINYTEXT NOT NULL,
PRIMARY KEY (audiobookID),
INDEX (title, series, author, narrator)
)";

if(mysqli_query($link,$sql)){
    echo "<p>The table <strong>audiobook</strong> has been
created.</p>";
}else{
    echo "<p>Failed to create table: <strong>" . mysqli_error($link) .
"</strong></p>";
}

mysqli_close($link);
?>
</body>
</html>
```

As you can see, this is not a complicated database; it is, in fact, a flat database. Unlike the database used in the Perl section of this chapter, this database is not scalable due to the lack of normalization.

The most obvious examples of it not being normalized are the inclusion of the author and narrator fields. If this were to be a large database, they would need to be removed to their own tables. However, for the purposes of this section, only one table is being used to simplify the examples. It is assuming a personal collection and should work fine.

Within the script are two queries being sent to the database. The first of these creates the database audiobooks, and the second the table audiobook. In between this two queries is the command mysqli_select_db($link,$db);. As stated before, this command acts as use *dbname* and is necessary to create the table.

Adding New Records

As we saw in the Perl section, the first SQL data manipulation statement will involve be INSERT. However, unlike the Perl section, it will take place on one page – addbook.php. This script is shown here, in Figure 9.11, and is on the companion CD-ROM in examples\chapter09\.

ON THE CD

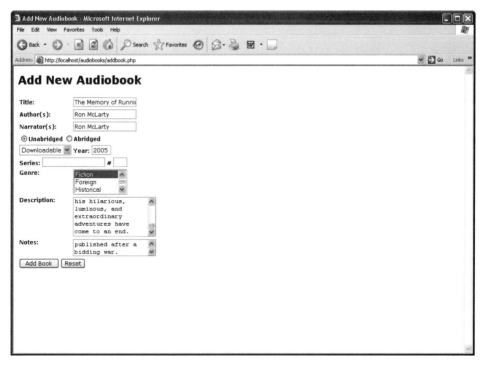

FIGURE 9.11 Adding an audiobook.

```html
<html>
<head>
    <title>Add New Audiobook</title>
    <style type="text/css">
        h1,h2,h3,p,input{
            font-family: Verdana, Helvetica, Arial, sans-serif;
        }
        p,input{
            font-size: 12px;
        }
        p{
            font-weight: bold;
        }
    </style>
</head>
<body>
<h2>Add New Audiobook</h2>
<?php
```

```php
if($_POST['process']){
    $db = "audiobooks";
    $link = mysqli_connect("localhost","root","password");

    $title = $_POST['title'];
    $author = $_POST['author'];
    $narrator = $_POST['narrator'];
    $edition = $_POST['edition'];
    $format = $_POST['format'];
    $year = $_POST['year'];
    $series = $_POST['series'];
    $seriesnum = $_POST['seriesnum'];
    $genre = join($_POST['genre'], ", ");
    $description = htmlentities($_POST['description']);
    $notes = htmlentities($_POST['notes']);

    $sql = "INSERT INTO audiobook(title,author,narrator,edition,
    format,year,series,seriesnum,genre,description,notes) VALUES
    ('$title','$author','$narrator','$edition','$format','$year',
    '$series','$seriesnum','$genre','$description','$notes')";

    mysqli_select_db($link,$db);
    if(mysqli_query($link,$sql)){
        echo "<p>The audiobook <strong>$title</strong> has been
        added.</p>";
    }else{
        echo "<p>Failed to add $title: <strong>" . mysqli_error($link)
        . "</strong></p>";
    }
    echo "<p><a href=\"" . $_SERVER['PHP_SELF'] . "\">Add Another?</a></p>";
    echo "<p><a href=\"audiobooks.php\">View All Books</a></p>";
}else{
?>
<form action="<?=$_SERVER['PHP_SELF'];?>" method="post">
<table>
<tr><td><p>Title: </p></td><td><input type="text" name="title"
/></td></tr>
<tr><td><p>Author(s): </p></td><td><input type="text" name="author"
/></td></tr>
<tr><td><p>Narrator(s): </p></td><td><input type="text" name="narrator"
/></td></tr>
<tr><td colspan="2"><p><input type="radio" name="edition"
value="Unabridged" checked="checked" />Unabridged <input type="radio"
name="edition" value="Abridged" />Abridged</p></td></tr>
<tr><td><select name="format"><option value="Downloadable">Download-
able</option><option value="CD">CD Audio</option><option value="Cas-
```

```
sette">Cassette</option></select></td><td><p>Year: <input type="text"
name="year" size="4" /></p></td></tr>
<tr><td colspan="2"><p>Series: <input type="text" name="series" /> #
<input type="text" name="seriesnum" size="2" /></p></td></tr>
<tr valign="top"><td><p>Genre: </p></td><td>
        name="genre[]" size="3" multiple="multiple">
            <option value="Action">Action</option>
            <option value="Adventure">Adventure</option>
            <option value="Biography">Biography</option>
            <option value="Humor">Humor</option>
            <option value="Fantasy">Fantasy</option>
            <option value="Fiction" selected="selected">Fiction</
            option>
            <option value="Foreign">Foreign</option>
            <option value="Historical">Historical</option>
            <option value="Horror">Horror</option>
            <option value="Mystery">Mystery</option>
            <option value="Non-Fiction">Non-Fiction</option>
            <option value="Other">Other</option>
            <option value="Romance">Romance</option>
            <option value="Sci-fi">Science Fiction</option>
            <option value="Suspense">Suspense</option>
            <option value="Thriller">Thriller</option>
        </select></td></tr>
<tr valign="top"><td><p>Description: </p></td><td><textarea
name="description" rows="5" /></textarea></td>
<tr valign="top"><td><p>Notes: </p></td><td><textarea name="notes"
rows="2" /></textarea><input type="hidden" name="process" value="1"
/></td>
<tr> <td colspan="2"><input type="submit" value="Add Book" /> <input
type="reset" value="Reset" /></td></tr>
</table>
<?php
}
?>
</form>
</body>
</html>
```

Like many of the previous Perl scripts, this is broken into two parts: the form collecting information, and the code receiving information. It is controlled by an if/else conditional. It first checks for $_POST['process']. If this form variable exists, database connectivity will be established, and incoming $_POST variables will be processed. Once the variables have been processed, the following lines add the information to the database:

```
$sql = "INSERT INTO
audiobook(title,author,narrator,edition,format,year,series,seriesnum,ge
nre,description,notes)
VALUES('$title','$author','$narrator','$edition','$format','$year','$se
ries','$seriesnum','$genre','$description','$notes')";

    mysqli_select_db($link,$db);
    if(mysqli_query($link,$sql)){
        echo "<p>The audiobook <strong>$title</strong> has been
        added.</p>";
    }else{
        echo "<p>Failed to add $title: <strong>" . mysqli_error($link)
. "</strong></p>";
    }
```

The first of these establishes which database is being used, and the if/else conditional tests for a successful data entry. The mysqli_query() function could be used by itself, but there would be no useful feedback if it failed. This version adds feedback by checking for success, and then supplying the error received from MySQL with the mysqli_error() function. This function only requires the connection information as an argument.

Viewing Records

ON THE CD

The script audiobooks.php will be used to view records from the database. It is written here, shown in Figure 9.12, and included on the companion CD-ROM in examples\chapter09\.

```
<html>
<head>
    <title>All Audiobooks</title>
    <style type="text/css">
        h1,h2,h3,p,input,td{
            font-family: Verdana, Helvetica, Arial, sans-serif;
        }
        p,input,textarea,td{
            font-size: 12px;
        }
        p{
            font-weight: bold;
```

```
            }
        </style>
    </head>
    <body>
    <div style="float: right">
    <form action="<?=$_SERVER['PHP_SELF'];?>" method="post">
    Search for: <input type="text" name="search" /><br />
    <input type="radio" name="kind" value="title" checked="checked" />Title
    <input type="radio" name="kind" value="author" />Author <input
    type="radio" name="kind" value="narrator" />Narrator <input
    type="radio" name="kind" value="series" />Series<br />
    <input type="submit" value="Search" />
    </form>
    </div>
    <h2>All Audiobooks</h2>
    <p><a href="addbook.php">Add A New Book</a></p>
    <?php
    if(!isset($_GET['sort'])){
        $sort="audiobookID";
    }else{
        $sort=$_GET['sort'];
    }
        $db = "audiobooks";
        $link = mysqli_connect("localhost","root","password");
        mysqli_select_db($link,$db);
        $sql = "SELECT * FROM audiobook ORDER BY $sort";
    if(isset($_POST['search'])){
        $search = $_POST['search'];
        $kind = $_POST['kind'];
        $sql = "SELECT * FROM audiobook WHERE $kind LIKE '%$search%'";
    }
        $result = mysqli_query($link,$sql);
        echo "<table style=\"width: 100%; border: solid 1px #000000\">";
        echo "<tr style=\"background-color: #DDDDDD\"><th style=\"width:
        25%\">Audiobook Info:</th><th>Book Description:</th>";
        $count = 1;
        while($row = mysqli_fetch_array($result)){
            $title = $row['title'];
            $author = $row['author'];
            $narrator = $row['narrator'];
            $edition = $row['edition'];
            $format = $row['format'];
            $year = $row['year'];
```

```
        $series = $row['series'];
        $seriesnum = $row['seriesnum'];
        $genre = $row['genre'];
        $description = $row['description'];
        $notes = $row['notes'];
        echo "<tr valign=\"top\"";
        if($count%2==0){echo " style=\"background-color: #DDDDDD\"";}
        echo "><td><h3><a href=\"" . $_SERVER['PHP_SELF'] .
        "?sort=title\">Title:</a> $title</h3><a href=\"" .
        $_SERVER['PHP_SELF'] . "?sort=author\">Author:</a>
        <strong>$author</strong><br /><br /><a href=\"" .
        $_SERVER['PHP_SELF'] . "?sort=narrator\">Narrator:</a>
        <strong>$narrator</strong><p>$edition</p><p>&copy;$year</p><p>
        $genre</p>";
        if($series){
            echo "<a href=\"" . $_SERVER['PHP_SELF'] .
            "?sort=series,seriesnum\">Series:</a> $series
            #$seriesnum<br />";
        }
        echo "";
        echo "</td><td>$description";
        if($notes){
            echo "<p>Notes:</p>$notes";
        }
        echo "<p><a href=\"updatebook.php?audiobookID=". $row['audio
        bookID']. "\">Update Record?</a>      
        <a href=\"deletebook.php?audiobookID=" . $row['audiobookID'] .
        "\">Delete Record?</a></p></td></tr>";
        $count++;
    }
    echo "</table>";
?>
<p><a href="addbook.php">Add A New Book</a></p>
</body>
</html>
```

The basic formula of the script is an SQL SELECT Query that is output into a table. There is also a sorting mechanism built in. Notice the following lines of code:

```
if(!isset($_GET['sort'])){
    $sort="audiobookID";
}else{
    $sort=$_GET['sort'];
}
```

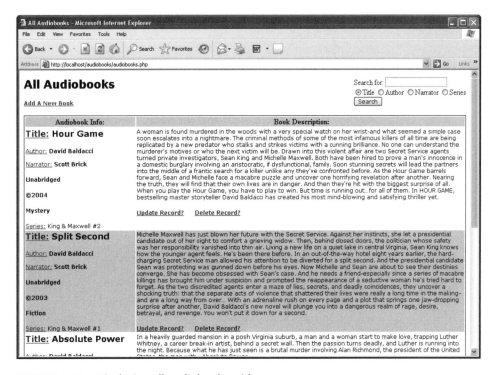

FIGURE 9.12   Displaying all audiobooks with `audiobooks.php`.

This is like the Perl script shown earlier. The labels Title, Author, Narrator, and Series have a link attached, which sends `sort` via GET. The `if/else` checks for the existence of the variable and assigns it to `$sort`. If nothing has been sent, or the page is loading for the first time, `$sort` is given the value of `audiobookID`. The SELECT query will then be placed in order of the value within `$sort`.

This script also has the links `Delete Record?` and `Update Record?`, which are anchor tags that add the `audiobookID` value to the end of the URL.

Exploring the Search Form

One thing different about this script is the addition of a search form. It is shown in action in Figures 9.13 and 9.14.

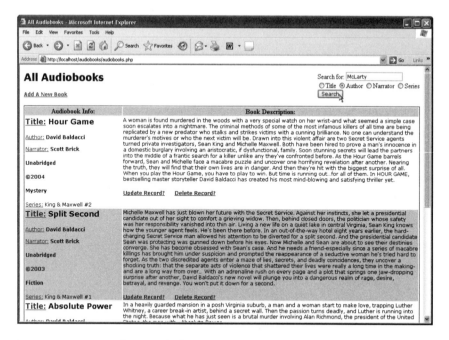

FIGURE 9.13 Entering search data.

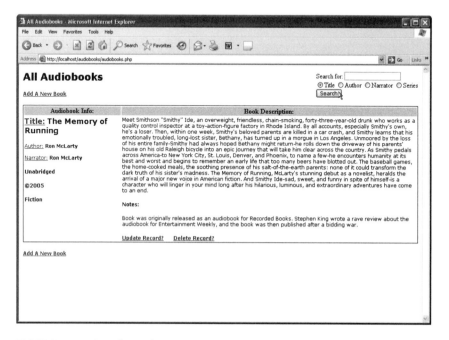

FIGURE 9.14 Search results.

This is a handy little utility, and is created with the following `if` conditional:

```
if(isset($_POST['search'])){
    $search = $_POST['search'];
    $kind = $_POST['kind'];
    $sql = "SELECT * FROM audiobook WHERE $kind LIKE '%$search%'";
}
```

The top right of the page shows a small search form made up of two fields: `search` and `kind`. The `search` field is populated with user input, and `kind` is a radio set. These variables are used to create a new SQL query that replaces the normal query on the page. This is due to the order of the statements on the page.

The new SQL statement uses the `WHERE` clause with `LIKE %$search%`. The user's request will be put in between the percent signs, which allow for any number of characters before and after, thereby maximizing results. This allows users to search for first names, last names, or partial titles as an example.

Deleting Records

ON THE CD

The next SQL query statement to explore with PHP is `DELETE`. This is accomplished with the `deletebook.php`. It is shown here, in Figure 9.15, and on the accompanying CD-ROM in `examples\chapter09\`.

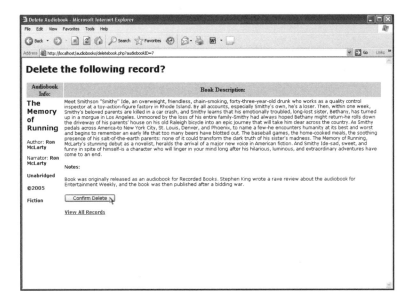

FIGURE 9.15 Record deletion form with `deletebook.php`.

```html
<html>
<head>
    <title>Delete Audiobook</title>
    <style type="text/css">
        h1,h2,h3,p,input,td{
            font-family: Verdana, Helvetica, Arial, sans-serif;
        }
        p,input,textarea,td{
            font-size: 12px;
        }
        p{
            font-weight: bold;
        }
    </style>
</head>
<body>
<?php
    $db = "audiobooks";
    $link = mysqli_connect("localhost","root","password");
    mysqli_select_db($link,$db);
    $audiobookID = $_GET['audiobookID'];
    if($_POST['confirm']){
        $audiobookID = $_POST['audiobookID'];
        $sql = "DELETE FROM audiobook WHERE audiobookID=$audiobookID";
        if($result = mysqli_query($link,$sql)){
            echo "<h2>Record successfully deleted from Audiobooks</h2>";
        }else{
            echo "<h2>Record was not deleted from Audiobooks:</h2>";
            echo "<p>" . mysqli_error($link) . "</p>";
        }
        echo "<p><a href=\"audiobooks.php\">View All Records</a></p>";
    }else{
        $sql = "SELECT * FROM audiobook WHERE audiobookID= \$audiobookID";
        $result = mysqli_query($link,$sql);
        $row = mysqli_fetch_array($result);
        echo "<h2>Delete the following record?</h2>";
        $title = $row['title'];
        $author = $row['author'];
        $narrator = $row['narrator'];
        $edition = $row['edition'];
        $format = $row['format'];
        $year = $row['year'];
        $series = $row['series'];
        $seriesnum = $row['seriesnum'];
```

```
$genre = $row['genre'];
$description = $row['description'];
$notes = $row['notes'];
echo "<table>";
echo "<tr style=\"background-color: #DDDDDD\"><th
width=\"200\">Audiobook Info:</th><th>Book Description:
</th></tr>";
echo "<tr valign=\"top\">";
echo "<td><h3>$title</h3>Author: <strong>$author</strong><br
/><br />Narrator: <strong>$narrator</strong><p>$edition</p><p>&
copy;$year</p><p>$genre</p>";
if($series){
    echo "Series:<strong> $series #$seriesnum</strong><br />";
}
echo "</td><td>$description";
if($notes){
    echo "<p>Notes:</p>$notes";
}
echo "<form action=\"" . $_SERVER['PHP_SELF'] . "\" method=\
"post\"><input type=\"Submit\" value=\"Confirm Delete\"
/><input type=\"hidden\" name=\"confirm\" value=\"1\" /><input
type=\"hidden\" name=\"audiobookID\" value=\"$audiobookID\"
/></form><p><a href=\"audiobooks.php\">View All Records</a></p>
</td></tr>";
echo "</table>";
    }
?>
</body>
</html>
```

This page is dependant on the audiobooks.php page. As mentioned earlier, that page feeds the audiobookID value to this page. When the page is loaded for the first time, it passes the audiobookID into a SELECT query and builds a table that displays the record in question. A tiny form is also created with a single button and the hidden field confirm. This allows the user to confirm whether the record in question should be deleted. There is a second option that will return the user to audiobooks.php. This will also appear after the record is deleted.

Updating Records

The last query type UPDATE is accomplished with updatebook.php. This is shown next, in Figure 9.16, and can be found on the companion CD-ROM in examples chapter09\.

ON THE CD

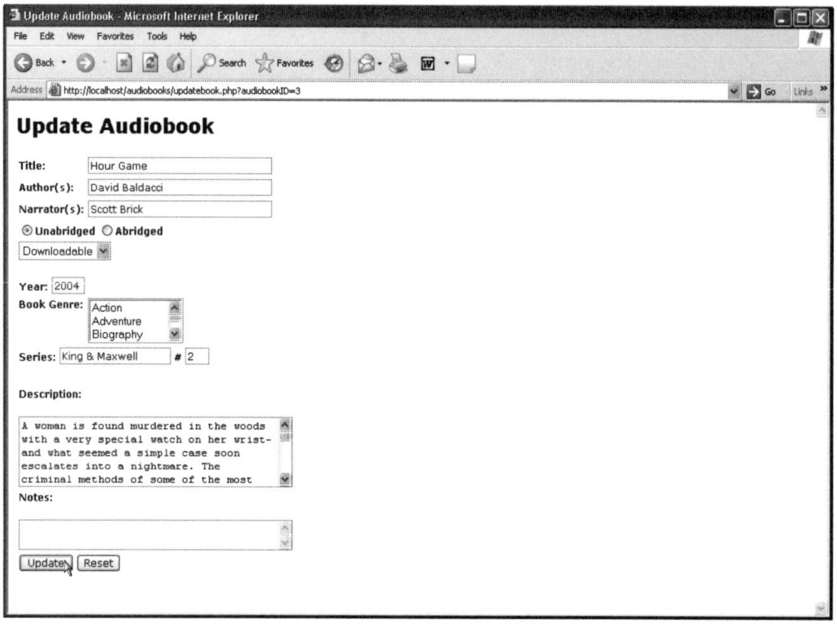

FIGURE 9.16   Record Update form `updatebook.php`.

```html
<html>
<head>
    <title>Update Audiobook</title>
    <style type="text/css">
        h1,h2,h3,p,input{
            font-family: Verdana, Helvetica, Arial, sans-serif;
        }
        p,input{
            font-size: 12px;
        }
        p{
            font-weight: bold;
        }
    </style>
</head>
<body>
<h2>Update Audiobook</h2>
<?php
    $db = "audiobooks";
    $link = mysqli_connect("localhost","root","password");
    mysqli_select_db($link,$db);
```

```php
if($_POST['process']){
    $audiobookID = $_POST['audiobookID'];
    $title = $_POST['title'];
    $author = $_POST['author'];
    $narrator = $_POST['narrator'];
    $edition = $_POST['edition'];
    $format = $_POST['format'];
    $year = $_POST['year'];
    $series = $_POST['series'];
    $seriesnum = $_POST['seriesnum'];
    $genre = join($_POST['genre'], ", ");
    $description = $_POST['description'];
    $notes = $_POST['notes'];

    $sql = "UPDATE audiobook SET title='$title',author='$author',narrator=
    '$narrator',edition='$edition',format='$format',year=$year,
    series='$series',seriesnum='$seriesnum',genre='$genre', description=
    '$description',notes='$notes' WHERE audiobookID='$audiobookID'";

    if(mysqli_query($link,$sql)){
        echo "<p>The audiobook <strong>$title</strong> has been
        updated.</p>";
    }else{
        echo "<p>Failed to update $title: <strong>" . mysqli_error
        ($link) . "</strong></p>";
    }
        echo "<p><a href=\"audiobooks.php\">View All Records</a></p>";
}else{
    $audiobookID = $_GET['audiobookID'];
    $sql = "SELECT * FROM audiobook WHERE audiobookID=$audiobookID";
    $result = mysqli_query($link,$sql);
    $row = mysqli_fetch_array($result);
?>
<form action="<?=$_SERVER['PHP_SELF'];?>" method="post">
<table>
<tr><td><p>Title: </p></td><td><input type="text" name="title"
value="<?=$row['title'];?>" size="35" /></td></tr>
<tr><td><p>Author(s): </p></td><td><input type="text" name="author"
value="<?=$row['author'];?>" size="35" /></td></tr>
<tr><td><p>Narrator(s): </p></td><td><input type="text" name="narrator"
value="<?=$row['narrator'];?>" size="35" /></td></tr>
<tr><td colspan="2"><p><input type="radio" name="edition"
value="Unabridged"<?php if($row['edition'] == "Unabridged"){echo "
checked=\"checked\"";} ?> />Unabridged <input type="radio" name="edi-
tion" value="Abridged"<?php if($row['edition'] == "Abridged"){echo "
checked=\"checked\""; } ?> />Abridged</p></td></tr>
```

```
<tr><td colspan="2"><select name="format"><option
value="Downloadable"><?php if($row['format'] == "Downloadable") echo "
selected=\"selected\"";?>>Downloadable</option><option value="CD"<?php
if($row['format'] == "CD") echo " selected=\"selected\"";?>>CD
Audio</option><option value="Cassette"<?php if($row['format'] == "Cas-
sette") echo "
selected=\"selected\"";?>>Cassette</option></select><p>Year: <input
type="text" name="year" size="4" value="<?=$row['year'];?>"
/></p></td></tr>
<tr valign="top"><td><p>Book Genre:</p></td><td>
        <select name="genre[]" size="3" multiple="multiple">
            <option value="Action"<?php if(strstr($row['genre'],
            "Action")){echo " selected=\"selected\"";}?>>Action
            </option>
            <option value="Adventure"<?php if(strstr($row['genre'],
            "Adventure")){echo " selected=\"selected\"";}
            ?>>Adventure</option>
            <option value="Biography"<?php if(strstr($row['genre'],
            "Biography")){echo " selected=\"selected\"";} ?>>Biography
            </option>
            <option value="Humor"<?php if(strstr($row['genre'],
            "Humor")){echo " selected=\"selected\"";}?>>Humor</option>
            <option value="Fantasy"<?php if(strstr($row['genre'],
            "Fantasy")){echo " selected=\"selected\"";}?>>Fantasy
            </option>
            <option value="Fiction"<?php if(strstr($row['genre'],
            "Fiction")){echo " selected=\"selected\"";}?>>Fiction
            </option>
            <option value="Foreign"<?php if(strstr($row['genre'],
            "Foreign")){echo " selected=\"selected\"";}?>>Foreign
            </option>
            <option value="Historical"<?php
if(strstr($row['genre'],"Historical"))
            {echo " selected=\"selected\"";}?>>Historical</option>
            <option value="Horror"<?php if(strstr($row['genre'],
            "Horror")){echo " selected=\"selected\"";}?>>Horror
            </option>
            <option value="Mystery"<?php if(strstr($row['genre'],
            "Mystery")){echo " selected=\"selected\"";}?>>Mystery
            </option>
            <option value="Non-Fiction"<?php if(strstr($row['genre'],
            "Non-Fiction")){echo " selected=\"selected\"";}
            ?>>Non-Fiction</option>
            <option value="Other"<?php if(strstr($row['genre'],
            "Other")){echo " selected=\"selected\"";}?>>Other</option>
            <option value="Romance"<?php if(strstr($row['genre'],
```

```
               "Romance")){echo " selected=\"selected\"";}?>>Romance
               </option>
               <option value="Sci-fi"><?php if(strstr($row['genre'],
               "Sci-fi")){echo " selected=\"selected\"";}?>>Science
               Fiction</option>
               <option value="Suspense"><?php if(strstr($row['genre'],
               "Suspense")){echo " selected=\"selected\"";}?>>Suspense
               </option>
               <option value="Thriller"><?php if(strstr($row['genre'],
               "Thriller")){echo " selected=\"selected\"";}?>>Thriller
               </option>
          </select></td></tr>
<tr><td colspan="2"><p>Series: <input type="text" name="series"
value="<?=$row['series'];?>" /> # <input type="text" name="seriesnum"
size="2" value="<?=$row['seriesnum'];?>" /></p></td></tr><tr><td
colspan="2"> </td></tr>
<tr valign="top"><td colspan="2"><p>Description: </p><textarea
name="description" rows="5" cols="40"
/><?=$row['description'];?></textarea></td>
<tr valign="top"><td colspan="2"><p>Notes: </p><textarea name="notes"
rows="2" cols="40"><?=$row['notes'];?></textarea><input type="hidden"
name="process" value="1" /><input type="hidden" name="audiobookID"
value="<?=$audiobookID;?>" /></td>
<tr> <td colspan="2"><input type="submit" value="Update" /> <input
type="reset" value="Reset" /></td></tr>
</table>
<?php
}
?>
</form>
</body>
</html>
```

Like deletebook.php, this page is dependant on an audiobooks.php link. When this page loads, a form is populated with all of the information in the record from the SELECT query performed when the page loads.

This page uses a couple of techniques to populate the form. Some of the fields are easy, such as author, narrator, year, and so forth. The tricky fields to address are the format and genre select fields.

To handle the format field, a series of if conditionals is used. The basic conditional is <?php if($row['format'] == "*choice*") echo " selected=\"selected\"";?> and is placed inside the option tag. If there is a match, selected="selected" will populate the tag, and Downloadable, CD, or Cassette will be chosen.

The `genre select` field is a little trickier, because there can be more than one genre chosen, and the values are joined into a single string. The `strstr()` function is used to overcome this issue. Each option has a `strstr()` function searching for the relevant term. If the term is found, `selected="selected"` is added to the option field, which will allow the user to select multiple options.

It is a courtesy to have all fields pre-populated for a user. This will enable him to only change what fields are necessary.

SUMMARY

This chapter concludes the book. As can be seen in all the chapters, a WAMPP server can be a very powerful tool. The book started with an exploration of the overall Web and Internet process flow and then moved on to installing and configuring the Apache HTTP server.

Next came the installation and basic exploration of both PHP and Perl, followed by an installation and introduction to MySQL.

With this final chapter, all components of the WAMPP server are working in conjunction with one another. With the knowledge gained from the book, it is possible to establish a Web presence with an extra Windows computer.

Appendix
A An HTML Primer

In This Appendix

- History of HTML
- HTML Structure
- The Future with XML and XHTML
- Summary

HISTORY OF HTML

HTML is the primary language used for the Web today. While there are many technologies available, HTML is the glue that ties all these components together. It took many years before HTML was created, with several steps along the way.

GML and SGML—The Origin

It all started with SGML, or the Standardized General Markup Language. SGML is what is known as a meta markup language; in other words, its job is not to format data but to describe it.

In the late 1960s, it was common practice among large publishers to format every piece of data as a specific format name. This system worked, but was dependant on having specific programming and equipment that understood the instructions. Stanley Rice, a New York book designer, suggested that a universal catalog of editorial structure tags be created. Instead of a specific instruction, a term such as *heading* could be used. The specialized equipment, in turn, could translate the universal terms into the formatting available.

Another individual who was influential to the concept of separating information from format was William Tunnicliffe, chairman of the Graphic Communications Association (GCA) Composition Committee. He brought up this topic in a meeting at the Canadian Government Printing Office in 1967. The committee adopted this principle and developed GenCode.

Charles Goldfarb, leading an IBM research project, created the Generalized Markup Language (GML) with the assistance of Edward Mosher and Raymond Lorie.

By 1980, the first working draft of SGML, based on GML, was published, and by 1983, it began to be adopted by the United States Internal Revenue Service and Department of Defense.

On to HTML and the WWW

The development of SGML was running almost parallel with the growth of the Internet. While the Internet had unlimited potential because of its ability to connect millions of computers into a giant worldwide network, it was essentially incomplete. No Web browsers existed at this point, and there was no way for documents to be posted and viewed. If you wanted a document, you had to download it to your hard drive and use the proper application to open it.

The World Wide Web and HTML were created to overcome this major limitation. Tim Berners-Lee, a scientist at CERN (l'Organisation Européenne pour la Recherche Nucléaire [European Organization for Nuclear Research]) invented the World Wide Web in 1990. He also created HTML as a language to work with the Web. A copy of the original HTML draft can be found on the World Wide Web Consortium Web site at *www.w3.org/History/1991-WWW-NeXT/Implementation/HyperText.m*.

The driving principle behind the Web is hypertext and the all-important link. Hypertext is the principle of combining pieces of text and images to complete whole documents with relationships. It is very similar to how people think—starting with one thread of thought and then drifting to a related thought as conclusions are formulated. Using the principle of hypertext turns the Web into an almost living entity.

Hypertext uses standard referencing mechanisms as its model, like dictionaries and footnotes in scientific notation. The truly revolutionary principle within is having the ability to have a footnote on the bottom of a page forcing the user to seek out a referenced document, and actually *linking* to the document with a simple click.

HTML STRUCTURE

As a language, HTML uses a system of programming called *tags*. Tags are contained within angle brackets; for example, <tag>. Two elements are available within the angle brackets: the tag name and attributes, which further define the tag. (Not all tags have attributes, and they are not always required.) Values are used to define attributes as follows:

```
<tagname attributename="value">
```

Two basic types of tag are used: *closing* and *empty*. Tags that close have both an opening and closing tag with a slash before the tag name in the closing tag (<tag>Content</tag>) and content in between. Empty tags have only a single opening tag.

Core Tags

The highest level of structure in HTML contains the core tags, which are required to have an HTML document. Starting at the top, you have what is often referred to as the *root* tag: <html>Page Content</html>. All information within the Web page must be contained within the opening and closing <html>.

Usually placed directly after the opening <html> is the opening <head> tag. The head of the document is for all information not displayed on the page. The most well-known item within is the <title> tag, which displays the title of the document at the top of the browser window. The <title> tag is not mandatory but should always be used, because the title is the most basic information used by search engines to describe your page. Without it, you see your page listed as Untitled Document, which is considered unprofessional, so treat the title as an essential tag.

Other uses for the head section of the document are for <meta> tag, which gives further information about the page in addition to instructions for the browser, such as redirection and the language in which the document should be read. <meta> tags can be seen as information about the document itself rather than the content within.

Over time, Dynamic HTML (DHTML) was created. It is not a specification itself, but rather a term describing the use of multiple technologies to extend Web pages. The most notable components of DHTML are JavaScript and Cascading Style Sheets (CSS). JavaScript is a client-side scripting technology (it runs in the user's browser) that helps pages be more interactive with effects such as images that swap when the user's mouse hovers over them. CSS were developed to give more formatting options to HTML and to separate the formatting from the content. Both of these references are often found in the <head> of the document so they load first and are always available during the life of the page.

Following the closing <head> tag is the opening <body> tag. The body of the document is where you find all information that is displayed on the Web page. If you want information to be seen by the user, it must be inside the opening and closing <body> tags. The basic structure of an HTML document follows:

```
<html>
    <head>
        <title></title>
    </head>
    <body>
    </body>
</html>
```

With the basic tags, you have a Web page. It won't be much to look at because it is blank, but you always have these tags on your page as a basic template.

White Space, Comments, and Case

In HTML, white space is generally ignored. What this means is that the code listed previously could just as easily been written as <html><head><title></title></head> <body></body></html> with no ill effects.

There are two camps on this issue, both of which have sound arguments. The first set of designers and developers feels that putting some degree of space between elements makes the code far easier to read and thus more approachable. If an error occurs on a line and only so much content is on the line, it is easier to track the error, unlike in a file where the entire page is one giant line. Pages can be quite long as more and more elements are added.

The second set feels that although white space is generally ignored, it must be parsed. This theory is correct because the browser must go through the code to determine what to do with it—even white space. This parsing does cause a slight penalty in performance on the page, but it is usually negligible.

You can compromise between the two thoughts by breaking up the code into line breaks, but use no more than one line break between tags. This way, you can read the code more easily but still be able to see more of it at once without scrolling. If you want, you could delete all white space after the page is proven functional, but not before.

HTML comments must also be addressed. Comments are used to add notes to code and can be referenced later. They are available in the source but are invisible to the users.

Comments are an invaluable tool and should be used in any form of programming. By using them, you can note what you are trying to accomplish in a certain area of a document or script. It may seem silly because developers are so possessed with the creation of the page at the time that it seems they will never forget what was intended—but who would remember all the programming a year or two later?

One comment is available in HTML and works for both single and multiple lines. An HTML comment starts with a left-angle bracket, an exclamation point (commonly referred to as a "bang" in programmingese), and followed with two dashes. The text of the comment follows and is closed with two dashes and a right-angle bracket, as shown in the following code:

```
<!-- I'm an HTML comment,so you can't see me on the page -->
```

The last thing to discuss is case. Throughout all HTML standards (1–4.01), using uppercase or lowercase text did not matter. It was common practice for developers to use all uppercase for their HTML tags and lowercase for scripts so they could more easily differentiate between them. Times have changed, and with the use of XHTML coming into practice (XHTML is covered later in this appendix), lowercase should always be used.

Block-Level Tags

Let's jump into the body of the document by looking at block-level tags. Block-level tags are larger-level tags that contain major content like headings, paragraphs, and lists, to name a few. Let's look at a basic HTML document:

```
<html>
    <head>
```

```
        <title>A Basic Web Page</title>
    </head>
    <body>
        A Basic Web Page
    </body>
</html>
```

Open your favorite text editor and type the preceding code. If you are using Notepad, you must select All Files in the drop-down menu in the Save As dialog box and type *sample.html* in the File Name text box. If you are using a Macintosh, use TextEdit. The issues in a Macintosh are a bit more complicated. First, make sure you choose Format > Make Plain Text. When you are prompted to Convert Document to Plain Text?, click OK. When you save the document, click File > Save As. Then, in the drop-down menu that reads Western (Mac OS Roman), select Unicode (UTF-16). Make sure you uncheck Hide extension and save the file as *sample.html*. When the dialog box prompting you to Save Plain Text opens, click Don't Append. This option causes the document to be saved as an HTML page.

Make certain you use an actual text editor. A word processing program like Microsoft Word should never be used because it adds extra information that can cause issues with the HTML file when it is displayed.

The point of all of this is to show how any text editor can be used to write HTML. That flexibility is one of the great benefits of HTML—it was designed to be written with any basic text editor. The code you typed results in the page shown in Figure A.1.

This page is a great start, but notice that you have nothing more than plain text reading "A Basic Web Page." The Web page is displaying exactly what you told it. The title of the page is "A Basic Web Page," as seen in the top of the window. The text on the page reads the same thing, but it doesn't stand out. This brings you to the first block-level tag, the heading. Six levels of headings are displayed with the tags <h1> through <h6>. The results of these tags are shown in Figure A.2.

Notice that after the <h4> tag, the headings are smaller than the normal text of "A Basic Web Page." This decrease in size is by design. Although the headings may be smaller, they still stand out. Also notice how each heading (no matter how small or large) is on its own line. This is because headings are block-level elements, meaning they literally take up an imaginary block running across the page. By default, nothing coexists on the same line. (Exceptions, like images, are covered later.)

The next block-level tag is the paragraph tag, denoted by <p>, which, according to original HTML standards, has an optional closing tag. When a paragraph is used, the block of text has an empty space, one line deep, separating it from the previous paragraph or text, similar to double-spaced text in a word processor.

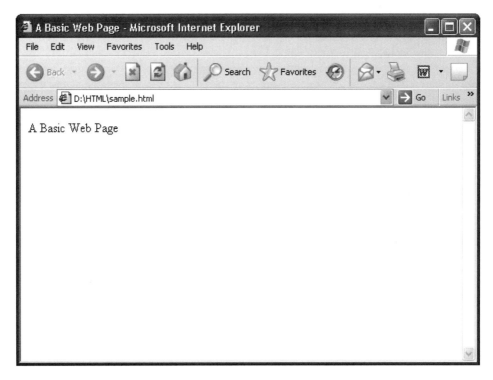

FIGURE A.1   A basic Web page.

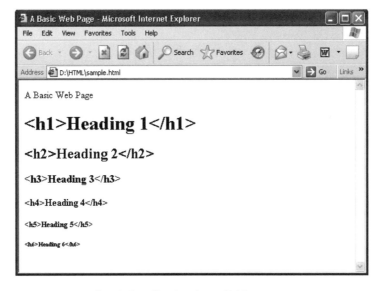

FIGURE A.2   The six heading levels available.

An alternative to a paragraph is the <blockquote> tag. A block quote causes a block of text to be indented on both sides with space above and below. Figure A.3 shows the results of <p> and a <blockquote> on a page.

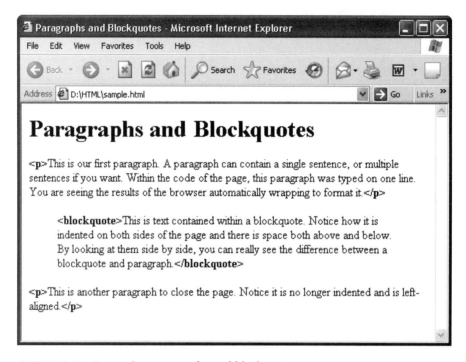

FIGURE A.3   Comparing paragraphs and block quotes.

A common block-level element used to visually separate content on a page is the <hr> (horizontal rule) tag. This tag simply creates a visible line across the page with space above and below.

The last block-level element discussed is the <pre> tag. The <pre> tag stands for preformatted text and is unique in that it is the one tag that uses spaces put in by the designer. Although the typical behavior of HTML is to strip all white space and line returns, save one space, <pre> makes use of these. When you place content within an opening and closing <pre> tag, the browser renders it using a monospace font by default, and all your spaces, tabs, and line returns are preserved.

Introducing Attributes

Within HTML, tags are further defined with attributes. If no attributes are defined, you are leaving the formatting up to the browser, which will act in its default manner. This is why all of the formatting tags you have created so far are left aligned, which is the default browser behavior for these block-level tags.

Attributes are declared after the tag name as shown:

```
<tag attribute="value">
```

Let's begin by looking at the tags you have been working with—the block-level tags. When dealing with block-level tags, your main attribute is alignment. You have three choices: left, right, and center. Left is the usual default when dealing with block-level tags and is often consider the easiest to read with long blocks of text.

Figure A.4 is your sample page with different values applied to the align attribute.

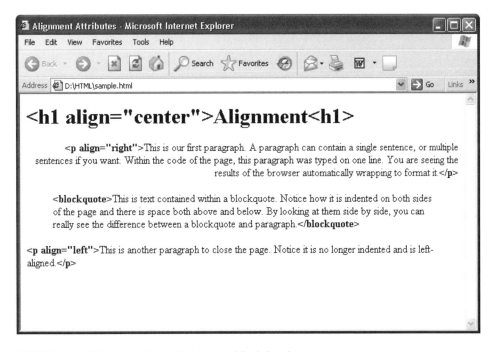

FIGURE A.4 Using the align attribute on block-level tags.

The `<div>` Tag

When you must align multiple elements on a page that share the same value, it can be rather tedious to state the attribute inside of each. This is where the `<div>` tag can be handy. Surrounding all of the block-level elements with one `<div>` tag affects all of them at once. You can override the `<div>` tag on a single element if you want to have it aligned differently. The following code taken from your sample Web page demonstrates the principle:

```
<html>
    <head>
        <title>Alignment Attributes</title>
    </head>
    <body>

        <div align="center">

        <h1>Alignment Principles</h1>
        <h2>Looking at the Div tag</h2>
        <p align="left">This is our first paragraph. A
        paragraph can contain a single sentence, or multiple
        sentences if you want. Within the code of the page,
        this paragraph was typed on one line. You are seeing
        the results of the browser automatically wrapping to
        format it.</p>

        </div>

    </body>
</html>
```

Notice in the example how the paragraph has an `align="left"` attribute? By explicitly stating that the paragraph is left aligned, the attribute overrides the `<div>` tag. You can think of this as a rule of specificity, or that which is closest to the text wins. Because the `align` attribute is within the `<p>` tag surrounding the text, it is closer to the content reflected in the paragraph and wins.

Line-Level Elements

The next level of element examined is the line-level element. Line-level elements are used to manipulate words within a block-level element. Whereas block-level tags affect larger areas, such as an entire element, line-level tags are more finite. They can be used to change a single word or several words.

The key thing to remember about line-level elements is that they can never be placed around a block-level element—this breaks the nesting rules within HTML. The browser may display the content correctly (browsers are made to be forgiving), but the pages are invalid. If you want an entire block-level element to be modified with a line-level tag, place the opening line-level tag just after the opening block-level tag, and then close it immediately before the closing block-level element.

Two of the most popular line-level elements are bold and italic, which are represented as `<b>content</b>` and `<i>content</i>`, respectively. However, they really are not the proper choice for HTML. The proper tag to use for bolding a section of text is `<strong>`; use `<em>` (emphasize) for italic. These tags are compatible with screen readers. Screen readers often ignore `<b>` and `<i>` tags but will stress the content between `<strong>` and `<em>` appropriately for vision-impaired visitors to your Web site.

Another popular line-level tag is the `<font>` tag. The `<font>` tag is interesting because it has no effect on text. It requires attributes to further define how it affects your content. The two most popular attributes are `size` and `color`. Seven sizes are available within HTML, appropriately named 1 through 7, representing 20-percent increments. They are referred to in either a relative or an absolute manner.

Relative uses +/– the number that is relative to the current font size. For example, if you want to have a font appear one size larger than the default, type `<font size="+1">`. This attribute causes the selected content to be 20-percent larger than the current size. Figure A.5 displays the results of font sizing.

It is important to avoid using too small of a font because it is difficult for users to read. The users' platform can also cause issues. Fonts appear smaller on Macintosh computers because they use 72 dpi (dots per inch) as the default resolution versus the 96 dpi on Windows machines.

Font color can be determined by using one of two methods: name or RGB value. When declaring a color by name, you must declare one of the 16 known colors that can be displayed in any browser on any platform. These colors are Aqua, Black, Blue, Fuchsia, Gray, Green, Lime, Maroon, Navy, Olive, Purple, Red, Silver, Teal, White, and Yellow. A known color is declared as `<font color="black">`, for example. Other nonstandard names may work in some browsers, but they are not displayed in all browsers on all platforms.

The second method of declaring a font color value is by defining its RGB attributes. RGB stands for Red, Green, Blue, and the hexadecimal number represents how much of each is used to display the color. The color is declared with a preceding # (hashmark) followed by the RGB value, as in `<font color="#000000">` (the

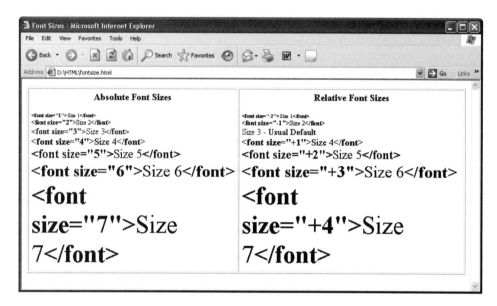

FIGURE A.5   Absolute and relative font sizing.

RGB value for black). The # is a flag denoting that the upcoming information is in a hexadecimal format.

The <font> tag has been officially deprecated by the W3C (World Wide Web Consortium) and will be removed from a future version of XHTML. The preferred method of coloring and sizing text is with CSS. This appendix discusses the <font> tag only for familiarity when exploring and revising current Web sites.

The last line-level tag discussed is the line-break tag, <br>. This tag is used at line level on any block-level element to cause a line of text to be broken to the next line. It differs from a <p> tag in that it is at the line level and breaks only to the next line, whereas a <p> tag adds an empty line of space between elements. It is a useful tag when you want to have items displayed without extra space between them, such as for a contact information block.

The <img> Tag

The <img>, or image tag, has enough importance that it is explored separately. Like the <font> tag, without attributes, <img> has no functionality on its own. Common attributes used with <img> are src (source), align, width, height, and alt (alternate text).

The src attribute is arguably the most important attribute because it is used to give the browser the path to the actual image. Because the image is not text, it cannot be embedded directly on the page. When you give the browser the source information, it retrieves the image separately, and then places it on the page where you have declared it with the `<img>` tag. The source of the image can be local (on the same server as the page) or remote (another Web site or location). When you choose a remote image, you must include the protocol (usually *http://*) in the path, or the image will not load correctly. For example, you would use the syntax `<img src="http://www.domainname.com/imagefilename.ext"  >`.The *http://* flags the browser, letting it know that the image is not stored in the Web server file system and that it must go back out to the Internet and retrieve it.

The `align` attribute, when used with an image, is different from what you saw with block-level tags like `<h1>`–`<h6>` and `<p>`. First, only two values are available— left and right—because where the other block-level elements align to the actual page, images align to the text that follows them.

The default behavior of an image is to be placed on the page as a block-level element with no text around it. The first window in Figure A.6 demonstrates this. If you want the image to have the text after it wrap to it, use the `align` attribute. The second window in Figure A.6 shows the result of `<img src="images/mtgoat.jpg" align="left">`. Notice how the image is placed to the left of the text.

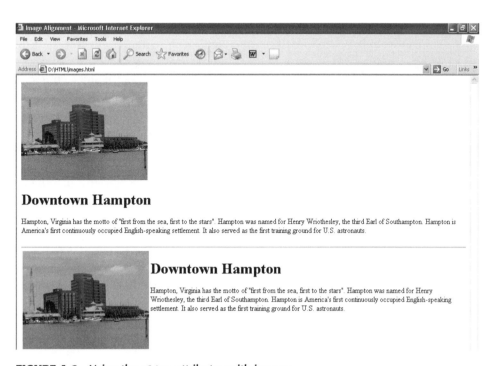

FIGURE A.6 Using the `align` attributes with images.

Now, let's look at the width and height attributes of the <img> tag. It is sometimes thought that width and height can be used to resize images on the page to make them larger or smaller. This is untrue. Although width and height can cause an image to appear as a different size on the page, they do not change the physical file size of the image.

When width and height are used in an attempt to make an image appear larger, pixelation occurs, which does not look good. On the opposite note, if width and height are used to shrink an image, the image will appear clear, but the physical size still does not change. Therefore, a large image displayed at a small size makes the page load just as slowly as if it were displayed at its full size. If you want to resize an image, use a graphics application to modify it, not the browser.

Image width and height attributes should be considered as placeholders for the browser. This practice gives the user a better experience. If width and height are not used, the browser loads all of the text in a tight block, and then retrieves the image and moves the text down the page while it loads the image. This practice can be distracting to the user, who may begin to read the content on the page only to have it suddenly jump down the page when the image appears.

When width and height are used for the image, the space for the image is reserved, and the text is placed around the reserved area. Then, the user can read the text without having it suddenly moved.

The last <img> tag attribute covered is alt. Often called an alt tag (it's actually an attribute), it is frequently overlooked. You use the alt attribute to display text in place of a picture, in case the user is not displaying images. This text is especially important for visually impaired users who cannot see the image but should know what the content is (through the use of a screen reader). It is also important for users who may be viewing the page on other devices or have a poor bandwidth connection. These users often turn off images to load the pages more quickly.

In either case, the text you put in the alt attribute is displayed instead of the image. This text is also displayed when a user mouses over the image in most browsers. The syntax of the tag including alt is something like <img src="images/filename.ext" width="100" height="100" alt="Another description of the picture.">.

Another attribute commonly used with images is name, *or its modern equivalent* id. *This attribute is used if the image is going to have a script, such as JavaScript, referring to it, commonly seen with rollover images. The* name *attribute has been deprecated in HTML in favor of the new* id *attribute, but both can be used for forward and backward compatibility. Many designers give the* name *and* id *attributes the same value. Remember, however, that they must be unique on the page.*

Anchor Tags and Hyperlinks

Possibly the most important tag in HTML is the anchor tag, `<a>`. It is how hyperlinks are created. Without hyperlinks, the Web would be nothing more than a giant hard disk with no real connectivity between files. Three primary attributes are available for the anchor tag: `href`, `name`, and `id`.

The `href` attribute is used to create a link. The syntax used for hyperlinks is formatted as `<a href="filepath.html">Linked text or image</a>`. As with a path to an image, you can refer to a local or remote file. Three types of reference are available: remote or absolute path, local-document relative, and local-root relative.

A remote link must have the entire path, including the *http://*. As with images, these characters flag the browser to go out to the Internet.

A local path relative to the document can be as simple as the filename of the page you want to load if both files live in the same directory. It can also involve climbing up and down directories to find the file. The format is to use `../` for every parent directory (directory above the current) and then the path back down if there is any. For example, if the current file lives in `siteroot/products/product1/support/page.html`, but the image is located at `siteroot/images/imagename.ext`, you could call it from the document using the path `../../../images/imagename.ext`. This code tells the browser to go up three directories, then into *images*, and select the file. The process using this type of relative path is commonly known as *bottom-up*.

The alternative is to path off the root with a method known as *top-down*. This method involves using a preceding / (slash) in the path. A preceding slash tells the browser to go all the way to the root of the site. Using the previous example, the path would be `/images/imagename.ext`. This method is useful if you use the same image or link in multiple locations throughout the site because the path is location independent.

When you are pointing to a page outside of your current Web site, it is often popular to use the `target` attribute. The `target` attribute comes from frames and has four values: `_self`, `_blank`, `_parent`, and `_top`. The first attribute, `_self`, is the default. It simply tells the browser to load the new page into the current browser window. Next is `_blank`, which tells the browser to load the new page into a new browser window. Your current page is still open in the current window.

Then is _parent, which is used with frames. In frames, your window may be split into multiple panes, with one controlling the others. This pane is known as the *parent* frame. When you select the value of _parent, the new page loads into the parent frame.

The last value is _top. This target breaks the frameset and loads the new page in the current window, with all panes disappearing.

With standard Web pages, you would only consider using _blank, which loads the content into a new window. This target is popular if you want to link to an external Web site. This way, if the users close the window with the external site, your site is still there.

The syntax for adding the target attribute is `<a href="http://www.external-site.com/" target="_blank">Linked text or Image</a>`.

When you decide to use an image instead of text to place your link, simply drop in an image tag where you would place your clickable text like this: `<a href="new-page.html"><img src="imagename.ext"></a>`. An issue you may encounter is that a blue border surrounds an image by default when using a link (much the same as text is underlined). You can stop this by adding a `border` attribute to the `<img>` tag as follows:

```
<a href="newpage.html"><img src="imagename.ext" border="0"></a>.
```

The other main attribute used with an anchor tag is the `name` or `id`. Whereas `href` can be thought of as a pointer to another location, `name` or `id` can be thought of as a target. This method is especially popular for navigating long Web pages, such as FAQs (Frequently Asked Questions). It is used in combination with an `<a href="">` to be fully functional.

The process works when you surround content lower on the page with `<a name="chosenname" id="chosenname">Content</a>`. The `name` or `id` you give the tag must be a single word or multiple words with a dash or underscore tying them together.

On the upper part of the page, create a pointer to your target in the following manner: `<a href="#chosenname">Linked Text or Image</a>`. Notice the #. This is a flag to the browser stating that the link is internal to the page. It can also be pointed to an internal link on another page by using the syntax `<a href="otherpage. html#chosen-name">Linked Text or Image</a>`. Figure A.7 shows the use of hyperlink types.

NOTE

Some confusion exists over the use of name *or* id *as an attribute. The* name *attribute has been deprecated and will be removed in the future. The main issue, however, is that* id *is a new attribute and is not supported by many older browsers. The recommendation is to use both in the same tag for maximum compatibility.*

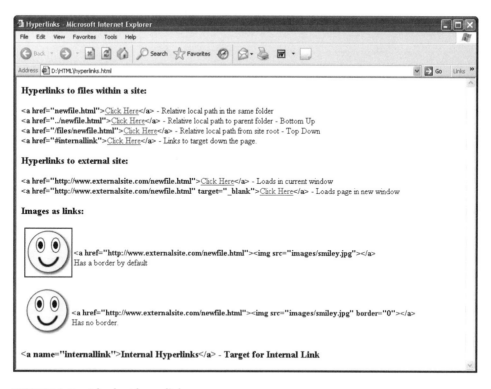

FIGURE A.7 A look at hyperlinks.

A Look at Lists

In the modern world, pithiness has become a standard. Rather than writing long passages in these days of sound bites, short, concise comments are popular. Bullet statements have entered into nearly every environment, and HTML allows their creation in the format of lists. Three list types are available in HTML: unordered (bulleted), ordered (numbers and letters), and definition lists (term and definitions).

Let's first look at unordered lists. Unordered lists come in three character types: bullets (now called discs), open circles, and squares. The default is the bullet character. Unlike the tags we looked at previously, lists involve more than one tag. You first use the overall list tag. In the case of an unordered list, it is `<ul>`. Then, you need to tag the items in the list. For both unordered and ordered lists, that is `<li>`. The overall code required to make an unordered list is

```
<ul>
    <li>Item 1</li>
    <li>Item 2</li>
    <li>Item 3</li>
</ul>
```

This code makes a three-item bulleted list. To make an ordered list with the default values of numbers 1, 2, 3, use the `<ol>` tag as shown:

```
<ol>
    <li>Item 1</li>
    <li>Item 2</li>
    <li>Item 3</li>
</ol>
```

If you want to change your list type, use the `type` attribute. The different `type` attributes follow:

`<ul type="disc">` (previously was `bullet`, but the term has been deprecated): Available for unordered lists. It creates a solid circle. This is the default unordered list type.

`<ul type="circle">`: Available for unordered lists. Creates a hollow circle.

`<ul type="square">`: Available for unordered lists. Creates a solid square.

`<ol type="1">`: Available for ordered lists. Creates numbers next to each item. This is the default ordered list type.

`<ol type="A">`: Available for ordered lists. Creates an uppercase letter sequence.

`<ol type="a">`: Available for ordered lists. Creates a lowercase letter sequence.

`<ol type="I">`: Available for ordered lists. Creates an uppercase roman numeral sequence.

`<ol type="i">`: Available for ordered lists. Creates a lowercase roman numeral sequence.

As you can see, multiple options are available with ordered and unordered lists. Let's look at another important attribute, `start`. When you have a large ordered list and must interrupt it with other content, how do you get the list to resume where you left off? That is where the `start` attribute comes in.

To use this attribute, populate your list with items until you come to the point where new content is added to the page. Close your list. Add your content, and then create a new ordered list with the start attribute reflecting what number with which to resume counting. This attribute works with all types of lists. For example, if you leave off on the letter *D*, set your start attribute to equal 5, and the new list will begin on the letter *E*. An example follows:

```
<ol type="A">
    <li>Item A</li>
    <li>Item B</li>
    <li>Item C</li>
    <li>Item D</li>
</ol>
<p> New content needed on the page.</p>
<ol type="A" start="5">
    <li>Item E</li>
    <li>Item F</li>
    <li>Item G</li>
</ol>
```

The unordered/ordered list item discussed next is the nested list, which is a list within a list. Be careful when using these types of lists because it can be confusing to make sure you follow the nesting rules properly. A nested list must be declared within the open and close of a list item. An example of a nested list follows:

```
<ol type="I">
<li>Item I
<ol type="A">
            <li>Item A</li>
            <li>Item B</li>
            <li>Item C</li>
        </ol>
    </li>
<li>Item II</li>
<li>Item III
<ol type="A">
            <li>Item A</li>
            <li>Item B</li>
            <li>Item C</li>
        </ol>
    </li>
</ol>
```

Notice in the example that Item I and Item III each have a list within them, whereas Item II does not. Item I and Item III do not have the `</li>` until after the `</ol>` of the sublist within. This is how you can create an outline format. Figure A.8 shows the results of multiple ordered and unordered lists.

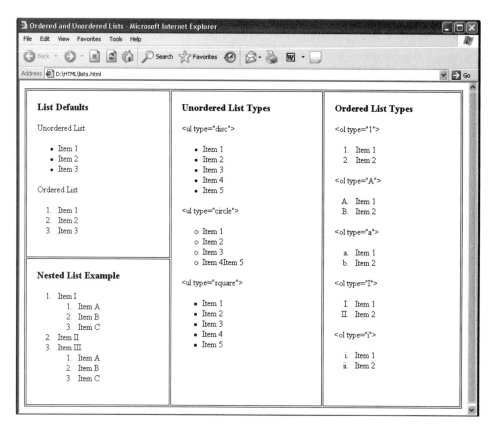

FIGURE A.8 Looking at ordered and unordered lists.

The last list type covered is the definition list, creatively tagged `<dl>`. The definition list differs from the other lists in that it uses three tags. The first tag is the `<dl>`, which starts the list. Next you have the `<dt>` (definition term) tag, which is aligned to the left of the page. Last is the `<dd>` (definition description), which is indented from the `<dt>`. This list type is commonly used with the `<b>`, or preferably the `<strong>` tag around the content in the `<dt>` to bold the definition term.

A Look at Tables

Tables could be considered the designer's best friend. Using everything you have learned up to this point, you may have discovered that you don't have much control over layout on a page. This is where tables come in. Prior to the use of tables, the only layout mechanism available was the `<pre>` tag and `align` attributes in images and block-level elements. Although these attributes may work to a degree, they have nowhere near the power available with tables.

Every table opens with an appropriately named `<table>` tag. Within this tag, you have `<tr>` (table rows) tags, which hold rows of `<td>` (table data cells) tags, which hold the actual content. You can also use `<th>` (table header cells) tags instead of `<td>` tags on the first row in the table if you want the text to be centered and bolded by default.

Other technologies, like layers with CSS, have been written as a replacement for tables, but for forward and backward compatibility, you can't beat tables for formatting. Tables contain both rows (`<tr>`) and cells (`<td>`) for laying out all of your content, with the basic structure being:

```
<table>
    <tr>
        <td>Actual Content</td>
        <td>More Content</td>
    </tr>
</table>
```

Tables contain rows, which in turn contain cells or headers. Cells contain all of the content. They can contain any element on a page you have seen so far, and even other tables, using a method called *nested tables*. Figure A.9 shows basic and nested tables.

As you can see from Figure A.9, a nested table is nothing more than a table within a cell of another table. Let's now look at some `<table>` attributes:

align: Determines how the table is aligned on the page. Values are left, right, and center. This attribute has been deprecated in preference to CSS.

bgcolor: Specifies the background color of the table.

cellpadding: Specifies how much space surrounds the content within a cell.

cellspacing: Specifies the amount of space between cells.

border: Specifies if a border appears around all the cells in a table and how thick it is.

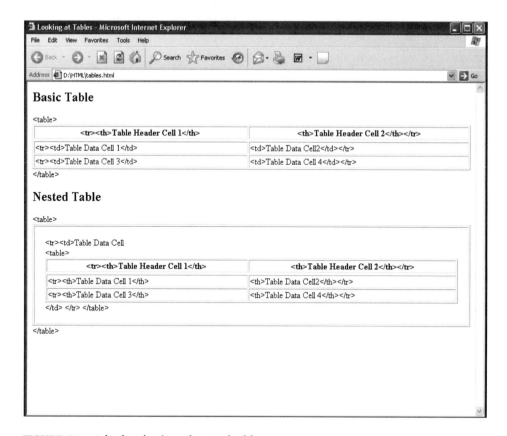

FIGURE A.9 A look at basic and nested tables.

Attributes of <tr>:

align: Aligns data within all cells in a row unless overwritten by <td align="">. Values are left, right, and center.

bgcolor: Adds a background color to all cells within a row.

valign: Affects the vertical alignment of data in cells within a row. Possible values include top, bottom, middle, and baseline. The default is middle. This attribute is one of the most valuable available in table rows and cells. With the default being middle, sometimes when you place content on a Web page with an image in one cell and text in an adjoining cell, you may encounter some problems. You may want the top of the image to align with the top of the text in the next cell, but when you add text that is longer than the height of the image, the image floats down the page. By setting the `valign` attribute to `top` in either the `<tr>` or `<td>` tag, all of the data stays aligned at the top of the cells, effectively stopping the drift.

Attributes of <td>:

`align`: Aligns data within cells. Values are left, right, and center.

`bgcolor`: Adds a background color to cells.

`colspan`: Allows a cell to extend beyond its normal width to encompass however many cells are declared.

`height`: Provides the browser with a recommended height. This attribute has been deprecated.

`rowspan`: Acts in the same manner as `colspan`, only for rows.

`valign`: Affects the vertical alignment of data in cells. Possible values include top, bottom, middle, and baseline. The default is middle.

`width`: Provides the browser with a recommended width. This attribute has been deprecated.

With the availability of multiple attributes within the three primary tags making up tables, you have a great deal of control over content. Tables with attributes are shown in Figure A.10.

Exploring Forms

The last HTML element covered is the form. Forms are the only way to collect input from a user in standard HTML and are extremely important for any type of e-commerce site.

Like many other tags, forms open with the self-explanatory `<form>` tag. The form is a major element that can contain multiple elements, including tables, but they cannot contain other forms. Tables often are used to format the form fields with the text in a neat manner. The form has several attributes. Among the most important are the `name/id`, `action`, and `method` attributes. The `name` attribute is important because the form is not an independent entity; it works in conjunction with another script or program, which is often expecting data from a form of a particular `name` or `id`. The `name` attribute has been left in for backward compatibility.

The `action` attribute identifies the path to the script that will handle the contents of the form. It is initiated when the Submit button is pressed.

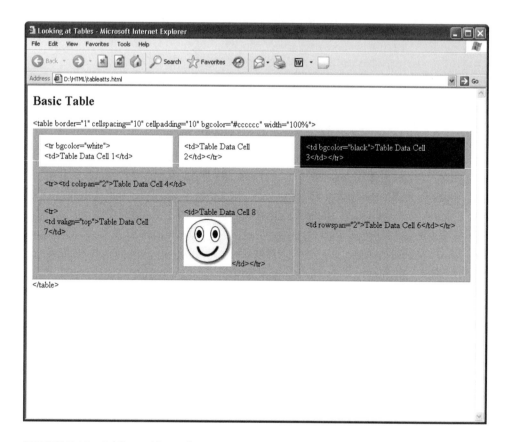

FIGURE A.10   Adding table attributes.

The method attribute dictates what method is used when the form is submitted to a script. Two methods are available: get and post. The get method appends the contents of the form to the end of the URL when the form is submitted. This method is not secure. URLs requested are added to server log files, which are often available over the Internet. The get method must never be used when collecting personal or financial information from users. This is the default method, so if you don't explicitly state post, get is used.

The alternative is the post method. The post method is more secure than get because it sends the information in the body of the document and not the URL. It can also send more information than the get method can.

Although the get *method is less secure, it is not always a bad method to use. Most search engines use the* get *method for searches. This method allows them to parse the server log files to find out what search terms are more popular so they can optimize their service. The key thing to remember is to never use* get *if security is involved.*

Within the form, your main element is the `<input>` tag. The input is defined by the `type` attribute. Several `type` attributes follow:

`<input type="text" name="fieldname">`: Creates a basic text field for collecting user input. This is the default input type and is created if `type` is not specified. Other attributes available with this type are `width`, which is the visible character width of the field, and `maxlength` that sets a limit on the amount of characters the user can input.

`<input type="password" name="fieldname">`: Acts in the same manner as a text field, but the input is displayed as asterisks to prevent someone from reading over the user's shoulder.

`<input type="checkbox" name="fieldname" value="assignedvalue">`: Collects multiple predefined options. The `name` attribute is critical for this input type because related checkboxes share the same name. The `value` is determined by the developer to represent what each checkbox will return. If you want to have one of the checkboxes preselected, you can use the `checked="checked"` attribute on the desired checkbox.

`<input type="radio name="fieldname" value="assignedvalue">`: Similar to the checkbox, but restricts the user's choice to only one. To have one radio button preselected, use the `checked="checked"` attribute.

`<input type="submit value="label">`: Creates the specialized Submit button. This type works in conjunction with the form `action` and `method`. When it is pressed, all data in the form is collected into a list and sent to the script URL listed in the action. The `name` attribute is not as critical on this element because its primary function is just to submit rather than pass any data on its own. You can use the `value` attribute to change what the label on the button reads. Otherwise, it reads whatever the browser default is, usually Submit or Submit Form.

`<input type="image" name="fieldname" src="imagename.ext" alt="Alternate Text">`: Makes an image act as a Submit button. It can take normal image attributes; and the `alt` attribute should be used.

`<input type="reset value="label">`: Clears all user input on the form when clicked. Again, you can use the `value` attribute to relabel the button.

`<input type="button value="label"`: Creates a basic push button. The `value` attribute is used to give it a label. Another script is usually tied to it.

`<input type="hidden name="fieldname">`: Passes information that you don't want to be seen on the form. This can prove valuable for controlling form input.

Let's now look at another tag available within forms, `<textarea>`. The `<textarea>` tag is handy for when you want to have a greater amount of user input in a field. It can also be used to display text in a smaller area on a page because it creates scrollbars when the text extends beyond the height of the box. The format for the text area is a bit different in that it requires a separate closing tag, even if you do not have text in it. Its basic format is `<textarea></textarea>`.

The text area has the following attributes to define how it is displayed and what can be entered:

`name`: Assigns a name to the element for association with the data.

`rows`: Specifies how many visible lines are in the box.

`cols`: Specifies the width of the box in characters.

`readonly`: Makes the text area read-only. This attribute is useful if you don't want the user to be able to enter data, such as when you want the text area to only display content.

The last tag discussed in forms is `<select>`, which is used in different tasks. This first is to create a menu in which the user can select either one or multiple items, depending on whether you choose the `multiple="multiple"` attribute. This field is useful for when you have a long list of selections from which to choose, such as a list of U.S. state postal abbreviations. You can have all 50 entries in a field that takes up only one line. A portion of the code to accomplish this follows:

```
<select name="state">
    <option>AL</option>
    <option>AK</option>
    <option>AZ</option>
    <option>AR</option>
</select>
```

Notice the overall tag is <select>, and each item to select is an <option>. This format is similar to a list. If you want the form to display more than one item at once, you specify how many rows you want displayed by using the size="number" attribute. If you want to have an option to be preselected, use the selected="se-lected" attribute within the option tag.

You also can give the user the ability to choose more than one option by using the multiple="multiple" attribute as follows:

```
<select name="items" size="4" multiple="multiple">
    <option selected="selected">Item 1</option>
    <option>Item 2</option>
    <option>Item 3</option>
    <option>Item 4</option>
</select>
```

Another option available with the select tag is the ability to have submenus by using the <optgroup> tag. Note that support for this tag is a bit spotty with browsers. Older browsers do not display the content. The basic syntax for using <optgroup> to create submenus follows as follows:

```
<form name="myform" action="somescript.cgi" method="post">
    <select name="menu">
<option selected="selected">Choose One</option>
        <optgroup label="Menu 1">
            <option>Item 1</option>
            <option>Item 2</option>
            <option>Item 3</option>
        <optgroup label="Menu 2">
        <option>Item 1</option>
            <option>Item 2</option>
            <option>Item 3</option>
        <optgroup label="Menu 2">
</select>
<input type="submit" value="Send">
</form>
```

Figure A.11 shows various options available on forms.

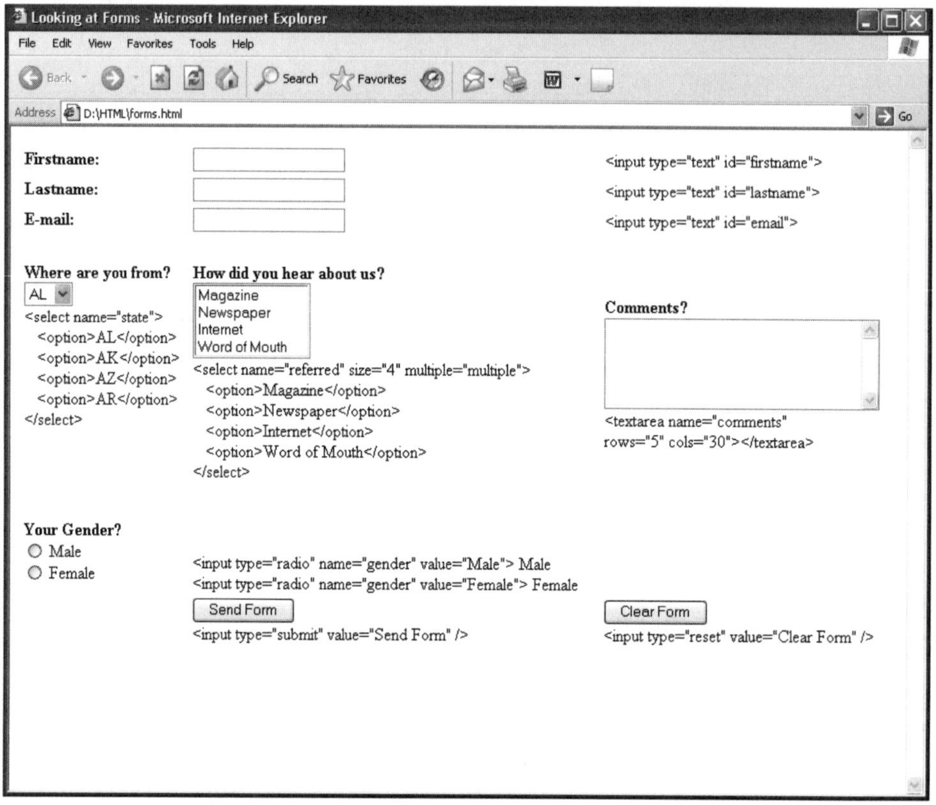

FIGURE A.11 Looking at form elements.

HTML Special Characters

Within HTML, you sometimes need to use a character that is either not available or is already a part of the language but would cause conflicts. This is where special characters come in.

All special characters in HTML start with the ampersand (&) character, then the name or code for the character, and then end with a semicolon. An example is &, which is the special character for the &, which requires a special character because it is part of the language. A short list of some common special characters follows:

  (non-breaking space): Provides a blank space on the page. Use this character if you want more spaces than the single space allowed in HTML.

`&quot;` (**straight quote**): Creates a quotation mark inside of your text. Quotation marks can cause issues because they are used around values.

`&lt;` (**left-angle bracket**): Creates a less-than sign. Because this character is part of a tag, it can cause issues on the page.

`&gt;` (**right-angle bracket**): Creates a greater-than sign. Like the less-than sign, it is part of an HTML tag.

`&amp;` (**ampersand**): Creates an ampersand. This character is used to start special characters in HTML, so using it in text causes a conflict.

`&copy;`: Creates a copyright symbol.

`&trade;`: Creates a trademark symbol.

`&reg;`: Creates a registered trademark symbol.

`&deg;` (**degree symbol**): Creates a degree (for temperatures) symbol.

`&cent;`: Creates a cent symbol.

`&pound;`: Creates a pound sterling symbol.

This list is by no means complete. A good place to look at character entity references is on the W3C Web site at *www.w3.org/MarkUp/html3/latin1.html*. This page has a listing of special characters that were available as of HTML 3 for maximum compatibility with older browsers.

Within the `<head>` Tag

As mentioned previously, the head of the HTML document is for hidden information. The content within is usually more about the page itself than the formatting of the document. This is where you find information for search engines to help the page be listed.

Outside of the `<title>`, the most prominent tag seen in the head is `<meta>`. It is defined by its attributes and has many functions. Two main defining `<meta>` attributes are `http-equiv` and `name`.

The first attribute you will look at is `http-equiv`. This is used to act as an HTML header, or instructions to the browser on how to handle the page. Some of its popular values are:

Content-type `<meta http-equiv="Content-Type" content="text/html; charset=iso-8859-1">`: Gives information on the page type.

Refresh `<meta http-equiv="refresh" content="http://www.sitename.com/">`: Used to redirect the browser to another page.

Expires `<meta http-equiv="expires" content="Mon, 25 Aug 2003 12:00:00 GMT">`: Informs the browser when the contents of the page expire.

Pragma `<meta http-equiv="pragma" content=""no-cache">`: Prevents browsers from caching (storing a copy) of the page.

Window-target `<meta http-equiv="Window-target" content="_top">`: Prevents a browser from displaying the page within a frame.

The second attribute is the name attribute. It is supposed to be for content that is not related to HTTP headers. However, more and more blurring occurs in the distinction over time and with different browsers. At any rate, some of the most popular meta name tags follow:

Author `<meta name="author" content="Eric Hunley">`: Identifies the author of the Web page. Many HTML editors fill in this tag or use the alternative `<meta name="generator" content="toolname">`.

Description `<meta name="description" content="A sentence or two">`: Provides a description of either the company or content on the page for search engines.

Keywords `<meta name="keywords" content="word1, word2, etc.">`: Creates a comma-separated list of keywords related to the content on the page. Be careful to not use too many because some search engines interpret that as search spamming. Twenty or fewer is a fairly safe bet.

Robots `<meta name="robots" content="all">`: Instruct robots or spiders (programs used by search engines to build their databases) how the site should be handled. Several values are available:

all: Page is indexed and all links followed with subsequent pages indexed.

none: Page is not indexed and no links are to be followed.

index: Page is indexed.

noindex: Page is not indexed, but links are followed.

follow: Links are followed.

nofollow: Page is indexed, but links are not followed.

noimageindex: Images on the page are not indexed, but text may be.

noimageclick: Images are not linked directly.

Combinations: Robot values can also be combined to achieve a more granular effect, for example: `<meta name="robots" content="index, no-follow">`. This code states that the page should be indexed, but links should not be followed.

`Rating <meta name="rating" content="general">`: Adds a rating to the content on your page. Some values include "general," "14 years," "mature," and "restricted."

One of the unfortunate issues with `<meta>` tags and their attributes is that they are not consistently followed by browsers and search engines. You must be certain that you understand your audience's capability and should research up-to-date information on search engines that you want to interact (or not) with your site.

Other tags you frequently see in the head of an HTML document are script tags and links to stylesheets. The head is an ideal location for these tags because often the content of the programming must be available when the content on the page loads. The head ensures that the scripts and styles are loaded and available throughout the life of the document.

The DOCTYPE Declaration

At the top of an HTML document, you often see what is known as the `doctype` declaration. This item states what standard was used to write the page. It is used to validate the pages using an HTML validator and as an assistant for browsers to render the elements properly. By following the exact standards and declaring the `doctype`, your odds are greatly increased at having your content displayed correctly.

The `doctype` declaration is the first thing listed on the page before the opening `<html>` tag. An example `doctype` declaration follows:

```
<dis>     <!DOCTYPE HTML PUBLIC "-//W3C//DTD HTML 4.01 Transitional//EN"
<dis>     "http://www.w3.org/TR/html4/loose.dtd">
```

Note that the `doctype` declaration is case sensitive.

THE FUTURE WITH XML AND XHTML

While HTML and SGML have served well over time, they are becoming dated. New languages have been created to help overcome this effect.

XML

SGML is a powerful but complex language that has grown over the years. Due to its age, much of it seemed a bit cryptic, so the W3C put together a committee to create a subset of SGML that would have the power of SGML but more of the simplicity of HTML. This was the birth of XML.

The basic principle of XML is to separate content from formatting, or to create self-describing data. You can create your own tags to label the data in a meaningful manner. For instance, if you are making a page with contact information, you may have the following code in HTML:

```
<html>
    <head><title>Contacts</title></head>
<body>
<p><strong>Sally Smith</strong><br >
<em>Customer Service Rep</em><br>
<em><strong>Acme International</strong></em><br>
123 Main Street<br>
Anywhere, Arizona, 85733<br>
(602) 555-5252<br>
sally@acme.com</p>
</body>
</html>
```

Although this code would display adequately in a browser, you really have no picture of what the data means. The same information written in XML follows:

```
<?xml version="1.0"?>
<contacts>
    <contact>
        <lastname>Smith</lastname>
        <firstname>Sally</firstname>
        <position>Customer Service Rep</position>
        <company>Acme International</company>
        <address>123 Main Street</address>
        <city>Anywhere</city>
        <state>AZ</state>
        <phone>(602) 555-5252</phone>
        <email>sally@acme.com</email>
    </contact>
</contacts>
```

Notice how the code now has some meaning. You don't know how it will display or what will display it, but you can look at the raw data and derive meaning. This is the power of XML. Whereas HTML is all about formatting of data for display, XML is about describing the data.

By pulling out the formatting elements, the data can now be moved around to any number of applications. The data is used on the Web and on desktop software, which opens up sharing of data with many applications and developers. Now, developers can create the data with any application they want and send it out as XML. It doesn't matter if you don't have the same program; your program just needs to know how to read the XML.

XHTML

One of the first challenges with XML was how to bridge the gap to HTML. The answer was to write an XML application based on HTML 4.01. This led to the creation of XHTML.

XHTML is based on HTML 4.01, but follows XML syntax rules. To make the language clearer and ultimately easier to work with, XML contains very strict syntax rules.

The primary rules are that it doesn't allow tags that don't close, it is case sensitive, and all attributes must have values within quotes. The way it affects tags from HTML follows:

Case-sensitive: All tags must be written in lowercase text.

All tags must close: This requirement is handled in two ways.

If a tag is surrounding content, such as a `<p>`, `<li>`, or `<tr>` tag, you must put a closing tag on the end, such as `</p>`, `</li>`, or `</tr>`.

If the tag is an empty tag, or a tag with no content on the page, you must make it self-closing. For example, a `<br>` (break) tag must now be written as `<br />`. (There must be a space between the tag name and closing slash). Some other tags affected are `<hr />`, `<img src="imagename.ext" alt="My Image" />`, and `<input type="text" name="firstname" />`.

All attributes must have values in quotes: This requirement is handled in two ways.

For some boolean selections, HTML 4 allowed for short tags, as in `<input type="checkbox" name="item1" checked>`. This shortcut method is not allowed in XHTML because `checked` has no value. To properly write this tag to be XHTML compliant, you must type `<input type="checkbox" name="item1" checked="checked" />`. While the `checked="checked"` may feel redundant, it is correct because it is the only possible value available for the attribute. This attribute was already defined in HTML 4, but the language allowed the shortcut.

In HTML 4.01, not all values required quotation marks. For example, `<td align=right width=100>` would be interpreted by a browser. In XHTML, however, all values must be within quotation marks. The preceding tag must read `<td align="right" width=100>`.

Although these rules may seem fussy and tedious to follow, they actually make the language easier to work with and offer greater consistency in the pages created. For example, you could get away with not having quotation marks in some but not all values. Who wants to try to remember when it is allowed? XHTML forces consistent and clear rules that cause less headaches in the long run. A good reference point for XHTML rules is located on the W3C Web site at *www.w3.org/TR/xhtml1/*.

Another important rule with XHTML is that, in an effort to enforce accessibility standards, all images must have the `alt` *attribute.*

SUMMARY

Your quick tour through HTML and related technologies is now complete. All output in this book needs to be read in a Web browser. This is accomplished through HTML.

Appendix

B

About the CD-ROM

The companion CD-ROM contains support files for exercises in the book, trial versions of all the software included in Macromedia Studio MX 2004 for both PC and Macintosh, a copy of all figures used in the book, and an Open Source Web server bundle for Windows including Apache, MySQL, PHP, and PERL. The following is a description of the directory structure and what is contained within:

Examples: Contains scripts that are used in the book, organized by chapters.

Figures: Contains full color copies of all images used in the book.

Software: Includes all of the open source software used in the book—Apache HTTP Server version 2.0, Crimson Editor, MySQL, Perl, PHP, and phpMyAdmin.

SYSTEM REQUIREMENTS

Apache HTTP Server Version 2.0

Apache 2.0 is recommended for Windows NT-based systems only. These include Windows NT, Windows 2000 Professional and Server (All types), Windows XP Home and Professional, and Windows 2003 Server. It is not fully tested with Windows 9X/Me and should not be used on this platform as a production server.

Crimson Editor

The system requirements for this software are as follows:

- Win95 or higher, WinNT 4.0 or higher
- 4 MB free disk space.
- Updated Windows Installer if Windows 95 or NT is being used

MySQL 4.1

MySQL 4.1 can only be installed as a service on Windows NT-based operating systems

ActiveState ActivePerl

The system requirements from ActiveState for this software are as follows:

- Recommended 75 MB hard disk space for typical install
- Web browser for online help
- All Windows platforms: IE 5.5+
- Windows 95: DCOM for Windows 95
- Windows NT: Service Pack 5+
- Windows Installer requirements
- If you are using an older version of Windows, you will need to download a system update to install ActivePerl:
  - For Win95/98/Me
  - For WinNT/2000
  - Windows XP does not need to be updated
  - Windows Server 2003 does not need to be updated

PHP 4 and 5

If PHP is to be installed as an Apache module, Apache HTTP Server must be already installed.

phpMyAdmin

The requirements for this program from *phpmyadmin.com* are as follows:

- PHP 4.1.0 or newer
- If you want to display inline thumbnails of JPEGs with the original aspect ratio, you also need GD2 support in PHP
- Starting with phpMyAdmin 2.6.1, MIME-based transformations that use an external program need PHP 4.3.0 or newer
- MySQL 3.23.32 or newer
- If PHP 5 is used, enable either the mysql or the improved mysqli extension. Directions for the mysql extension are shown in Chapter 5, and in Chapter 9 for mysqli

The companion CD-ROM contains support files for exercises in the book, trial versions of all the software included in Macromedia Studio MX 2004 for both PC and Macintosh, a copy of all figures used in the book, and an Open Source Web server bundle for Windows including Apache, MySQL, PHP, and PERL. The following is a description of the directory structure and what is contained within:

examples: Contains scripts that are used in the book, organized by chapters.

figures: Contains full color copies of all images used in the book.

software: Includes all of the open source software used in the book—Apache HTTP Server version 2.0, Crimson Editor, MySQL, Perl, PHP, and phpMyAdmin.

Index